Understanding Trade Secret Law

Carolina Academic Press Understanding Series

Understanding Administrative Law, Sixth Edition
William Fox, Jr.

Understanding Alternative Dispute Resolution
Kristen M. Blankley and Maureen A. Weston

Understanding Animal Law
Adam Karp

Understanding Antitrust and Its Economic Implications, Seventh Edition
E. Thomas Sullivan and Jeffrey L. Harrison

Understanding Bankruptcy, Fourth Edition
Jeffrey Ferriell and Edward J. Janger

Understanding California Community Property Law
Jo Carrillo

Understanding Capital Punishment Law, Fourth Edition
Linda E. Carter, Ellen S. Kreitzberg, and Scott W. Howe

Understanding Civil Procedure, Sixth Edition
Gene R. Shreve, Peter Raven-Hansen, and Charles Gardner Geyh

Understanding Civil Procedure: The California Edition
Walter W. Heiser, Gene R. Shreve, Peter Raven-Hansen, and Charles Gardner Geyh

Understanding Civil Rights Litigation, Second Edition
Howard M. Wasserman

Understanding Conflict of Laws, Fourth Edition
William M. Richman, William L. Reynolds, and Chris A. Whytock

Understanding Constitutional Law, Fourth Edition
John B. Attanasio and Joel K. Goldstein

Understanding Contracts, Fourth Edition
Jeffrey Ferriell

Understanding Copyright Law, Seventh Edition
Marshall A. Leaffer

Understanding Corporate Law, Fifth Edition
Arthur R. Pinto and Douglas M. Branson

Understanding Corporate Taxation, Third Edition
Leandra Lederman and Michelle Kwon

Understanding Criminal Law, Eighth Edition
Joshua Dressler

Understanding Criminal Procedure: Vol. 1: Investigation, Seventh Edition
Joshua Dressler, Alan C. Michaels, and Ric Simmons

Understanding Criminal Procedure: Vol. 2: Adjudication, Fourth Edition
Joshua Dressler and Alan C. Michaels

Understanding Disability Law, Third Edition
Mark C. Weber

Understanding Election Law and Voting Rights
Michael R. Dimino, Sr., Bradley A. Smith, and Michael E. Solimine

Understanding Employee Benefits Law
Kathryn L. Moore

Understanding Employment Discrimination Law, Second Edition
Thomas R. Haggard

Understanding Employment Law, Third Edition
Paul M. Secunda, Richard A. Bales, and Jeffrey M. Hirsch

Understanding Environmental Law, Third Edition
Philip Weinberg and Kevin A. Reilly

Understanding Estate and Gift Taxation, Second Edition
Brant J. Hellwig and Robert T. Danforth

Understanding Evidence, Fifth Edition
Paul C. Giannelli

Understanding Family Law, Fourth Edition
John Gregory, Peter N. Swisher, and Robin Wilson

Understanding Federal and California Evidence
Paul C. Giannelli

Understanding Federal Courts and Jurisdiction, Second Edition
Linda Mullenix, Martin H. Redish, and Georgene Vairo

Understanding Federal Income Taxation, Sixth Edition
J. Martin Burke and Michael K. Friel

Understanding the First Amendment, Seventh Edition Russell L. Weaver

Understanding Immigration Law, Third Edition
Kevin R. Johnson, Raquel Aldana, Bill Ong Hing, Leticia M. Saucedo, and Enid Trucios-Haynes

Understanding Insurance Law, Sixth Edition
Robert H. Jerry, II and Douglas Richmond

Understanding Intellectual Property Law, Fourth Edition
Tyler T. Ochoa, Shubha Ghosh, and Mary LaFrance

Understanding International Business and Financial Transactions, Fourth Edition
Jerold A. Friedland

Understanding International Criminal Law, Third Edition
Ellen S. Podgor and Roger S. Clark

Understanding International Law, Second Edition
Stephen C. McCaffrey

Understanding Jewish Law, Second Edition
Steven H. Resnicoff

Understanding Juvenile Law, Fifth Edition
Martin Gardner

Understanding Labor Law, Fifth Edition
Douglas E. Ray, Calvin William Sharpe, and Robert N. Strassfeld

Understanding the Law of Terrorism, Second Edition
Erik Luna and Wayne McCormack

Understanding the Law of Zoning and Land Use Controls, Third Edition
Barlow Burke

Understanding Lawyers' Ethics, Fifth Edition
Monroe H. Freedman and Abbe Smith

Understanding Local Government, Second Edition
Sandra Stevenson

Understanding Modern Real Estate Transactions, Fourth Edition
Alex M. Johnson, Jr.

Understanding Negotiable Instruments and Payment Systems, Second Edition
William H. Lawrence

Understanding Nonprofit and Tax Exempt Organizations, Second Edition
Nicholas P. Cafardi and Jaclyn Fabean Cherry

Understanding Partnership and LLC Taxation, Fourth Edition
Jerold A. Friedland

Understanding Patent Law, Third Edition
Amy L. Landers

Understanding Products Liability Law, Second Edition
Bruce L. Ottley, Rogelio A. Lasso, and Terrence F. Kiely

Understanding Property Law, Fourth Edition
John G. Sprankling

Understanding Remedies, Third Edition
James M. Fischer

Understanding Sales and Leases of Goods, Third Edition
William H. Henning, William H. Lawrence, and Henry Deeb Gabriel

Understanding Secured Transactions, Fifth Edition
William H. Lawrence, William H. Henning, and R. Wilson Freyermuth

Understanding Securities Law, Seventh Edition
Marc I. Steinberg

Understanding Taxation of Business Entities
Walter D. Schwidetzky and Fred B. Brown

Understanding Torts, Sixth Edition
John L. Diamond, Lawrence C. Levine, and Anita Bernstein

Understanding Trade Secret Law
John G. Sprankling and Thomas G. Sprankling

Understanding Trademark Law, Fourth Edition
Mary LaFrance

Understanding Trusts and Estates, Sixth Edition Roger W. Andersen and Susan Gary

Understanding White Collar Crime, Fourth Edition
J. Kelly Strader

Understanding Trade Secret Law

John G. Sprankling
PROFESSOR OF LAW
UNIVERSITY OF THE PACIFIC
MCGEORGE SCHOOL OF LAW

Thomas G. Sprankling
COUNSEL
WILMER CUTLER PICKERING HALE & DORR LLP

CAROLINA ACADEMIC PRESS
Durham, North Carolina

Library of Congress Cataloging-in-Publication Data

Names: Sprankling, John G., 1950- author. | Sprankling, Thomas G., author.
Title: Understanding trade secret law / by John G. Sprankling, Thomas G. Sprankling.
Description: Durham, North Carolina : Carolina Academic Press, LLC, 2020. | Series: Understanding series
Identifiers: LCCN 2020000833 | ISBN 9781531011956 (paperback) | ISBN 9781531011963 (ebook)
Subjects: LCSH: Trade secrets--Law and legislation--United States.
Classification: LCC KF3197 .S67 2020 | DDC 346.7304/8--dc23
LC record available at https://lccn.loc.gov/2020000833

Carolina Academic Press
700 Kent Street
Durham, North Carolina 27701
Telephone (919) 489-7486
Fax (919) 493-5668
www.cap-press.com

Printed in the United States of America

To Gail and Doug

J.G.S.

To my two best gals (but especially Alexis)

T.G.S.

Contents

Preface

As the American economy continues its transition to the information age, property rights in information are becoming more important. Terms like "patent," "copyright," and "trademark" have become part of public discourse. But one type of intellectual property—which protects everything from a proprietary recipe for fried chicken to the algorithm governing the world's largest search engine—has remained relatively unknown until recently.

Trade secret law—which protects confidential information that is not readily ascertainable or generally known—has expanded to meet the needs of an era when raw information divorced from any physical form has significant value. This subject has evolved from a state common law doctrine into a field dominated by state and federal statutes. Almost all states have adopted statutes based on the Uniform Trade Secrets Act. And, more recently, the enactment of the Defend Trade Secrets Act has created a federal remedy for trade secret misappropriation.

Today trade secrets are more valuable than ever. Virtually every business relies on trade secrets, ranging from the largest tech company to the smallest florist. As the Congressional Research Service has noted, "the strength and competitiveness of domestic firms increasingly depends upon their know-how and intangible assets," information protected as trade secrets.[1] As a result, trade secret litigation has increased exponentially.

The goal of this book is to explain trade secret law clearly and succinctly to students, attorneys, and judges, while being mindful of the ever-evolving policies and tensions that underlie the field. Trade secret doctrine seeks to promote commercial morality and incentivize innovation, while not unduly interfering with free competition and labor mobility. As a result, it reflects a balance of conflicting interests.

Many people helped us with this book. We are grateful to Gail Heckemeyer, Clark Kelso, Gregory Lantier, and Michael Vitiello who read parts of the book and provided useful suggestions. We also thank the National Conference of Commissioners on Uniform State Laws for permission to include the Uniform Trade Secrets Act (as amended in 1985) and its accompanying commentary as an appendix to the book.

This book contains our personal views on trade secret law. It does not necessarily reflect the views of the University of the Pacific or Wilmer Cutler Pickering Hale &

1. Cong. Research Service, The Role of Trade Secrets in Innovation Policy 2 (2010).

Dorr LLP. And because the audience for this book is students, attorneys, and judges, it should not be used as a substitute for the advice of an attorney about a specific problem involving trade secret law.

John G. Sprankling
Thomas G. Sprankling

January 2020

Understanding Trade Secret Law

Chapter 1

Introduction to Trade Secrets

§ 1.01 Protecting Information

We live in the information age. Today the acquisition, control, and use of information drive both our economy and society in general. As a result, information is rapidly becoming more valuable than any other type of asset.

Trade secret law is the main tool for protecting information. It covers virtually every type of valuable information, even information not used in a "trade" or business. The Google search algorithm, the formula for Coca-Cola, the system used by the

New York Times to rank best-selling books, and the ingredients of WD-40 are all examples of trade secrets.

A trade secret is information that has actual or potential economic value from not being known or readily ascertainable by others, which the owner makes reasonable efforts to keep secret. State and federal law both impose liability for the wrongful acquisition, disclosure, or use of a trade secret.

Trade secret law and patent law are close cousins, since both safeguard information. But trade secret law provides four key advantages:[1]

- *Much broader scope of protection*: Almost any information with economic value can qualify for trade secret protection. In contrast, the criteria for issuance of a patent are quite rigorous. As a result, trade secret law encompasses far more information than patent law does.
- *No government approval needed*: A trade secret arises automatically, without any government approval, when the legal elements are met. But a patent can only be issued by the U.S. Patent and Trademark Office after a long and expensive process.
- *No public notice:* A trade secret owner can—and is required—to keep the information secret. In contrast, a core policy underlying patent law is public disclosure; the applicant must reveal the product or process to the public in exchange for a limited property right.
- *Potential infinite duration*: Trade secret protection can potentially last forever—until the secret is either lost through public disclosure or ascertained by another party who uses proper methods. A patent lasts for only 20 years from the application date.

The field of trade secret law has expanded dramatically since its birth in the nineteenth century. It began as a response to small-scale industrial theft; for example, a dishonest employee at a manufacturing plant might steal a paper diagram of a secret machine and sell it to a competing company. However, in recent decades, trade secret law has evolved in response to new challenges, such as the emergence of the digital age, the shift toward an information-based economy, the expansion of global commerce, and the rising threat of theft. Trade secret theft "exacts a cost on U.S. companies ... of between $160 and $480 million each year."[2] In response to these challenges, the United States has developed the most sophisticated system in the world for protecting trade secrets.

§ 1.02 Trade Secrets and the Economy

Trade secrets play a vital role in the American economy. Large corporations, small businesses, and individual entrepreneurs all rely on trade secrets. As a con-

1. However, patent law provides much stronger protection. *See* § 3.02[B].
2. H.R. Rep. No. 114-529, at 4 (2016).

gressional report summarized: "Comprising all types of financial, scientific, technical, engineering, or other forms of information, trade secrets are an integral part of the operation, competitive advantage, and financial success of many U.S.-based companies."[3]

For example, companies involved in research and development activity reported in a National Science Foundation survey that trade secrets were their most important form of intellectual property.[4] A study of American firms engaged in international commerce conducted by the U.S. International Trade Commission reached the same conclusion.[5] It is estimated that publicly traded American companies own trade secrets worth $5 trillion. To put this figure in context, the total market value of the 500 largest American corporations is about $21 trillion. Experts agree that trade secrets will be even more important—and thus more valuable—in the future.

Trade secrets are also crucial for small businesses and entrepreneurs. The established family-owned restaurant, the new high-tech startup, and the inventor working at home all rely on trade secret law to protect their intangible assets, such as business methods, customer lists, financial strategies, innovative products, marketing plans, new inventions, and novel processes.

Today companies struggle to protect their trade secrets against theft. Secrets are most commonly misappropriated by employees, though an increasing number are stolen by strangers through cyber-espionage and other methods. The rate of trade secret theft is accelerating for several reasons: (1) employees are more likely to change jobs than in the past; (2) data is increasingly digitized, so it is easier to steal; (3) foreign espionage is a growing problem; and (4) trade secrets are more valuable than ever.

§ 1.03 Why Protect Trade Secrets?

[A] Competing Policies

Why should valuable information that is deliberately hidden from the public receive special protection? Two core policies justify this law: preserving commercial morality and encouraging innovation. Courts traditionally emphasized the commercial morality rationale, while modern courts increasingly focus on the innovation goal. However, the scope of trade secret law is constricted by other policies, including ensuring free competition and protecting employee mobility. The resulting doctrine reflects a careful balance of conflicting policies.

3. Sen. Rep. No. 114-220, at 1 (2016).

4. National Science Foundation, Business Use of Intellectual Property Protection Documented in NSF Survey (2012).

5. U.S. International Trade Commission, Trade, Investment, and Industrial Policies in India (2014).

[B] Policy Justifications

[1] Preserving Commercial Morality

In *Kewanee Oil Co. v. Bicron Corp.*, the Supreme Court explained that one of the core policies underpinning trade secret law was the "maintenance of standards of commercial ethics."[6] Under this approach, the law safeguards commercial morality by penalizing the disclosure or use of a trade secret that is obtained by improper methods, such as a crime, tort, or breach of confidence. By outlawing such unethical behavior, the law helps to ensure that businesses compete on a level playing field.

For example, in *E.I. duPont deNemours & Co. v. Christopher*, the Fifth Circuit imposed liability where the defendants obtained trade secrets by taking aerial photographs of new construction at plaintiff's plant.[7] The court stressed that " 'the undoubted tendency of the law has been to recognize and enforce higher standards of commercial morality in the business world.' "[8] It concluded:

> [W]e realize that industrial espionage of the sort here perpetrated has become a popular sport in some segments of our industrial community. However, our devotion to free wheeling competition must not force us into accepting the law of the jungle as the standard of morality expected in our commercial relations.[9]

[2] Encouraging Innovation

The second core policy identified by the *Kewanee Oil* Court was "the encouragement of invention"—a justification based on utilitarian theory.[10] It explained:

> Trade secret law will encourage invention in areas where patent law does not reach, and will prompt the independent innovator to proceed with the discovery and exploitation of his invention.... Competition is fostered and the public is not deprived of the use of valuable, if not quite patentable, invention.[11]

Information is a "public good." As a practical matter, once information is disclosed, millions of people can use it without payment. Thus, without some form of protection, no one has enough incentive to invest the time and money needed to develop valuable new ideas and knowledge. Trade secret law—like patent law—provides the needed economic inducement by ensuring that the creator will be able to bar others from using the information without her consent. This allows her to disclose the secret to employees and others who are necessary to profit from its use, without danger

---

6. 416 U.S. 470, 481 (1974).

7. 431 F.2d 1012 (5th Cir. 1970).

8. *Id.* at 1015 (quoting Hyde Corp. v. Huffines, 314 S.W.2d 763, 773 (Tex. 1958)).

9. *Id.* at 1016.

10. *Kewanee Oil*, 416 U.S. at 481. The Court also mentioned a third policy—protection of privacy. *Id.* at 487. Later courts have largely ignored this policy.

11. *Id.* at 485. In practice, today inventors of patentable inventions sometimes opt for trade secret protection instead of seeking patents. *See* § 3:02[C].

that the secret will be immediately lost. Accordingly, trade secret law serves the public welfare by incentivizing the creation of new products and services.

As the First Circuit summarized in *Burten v. Milton Bradley Co.*, "[t]he underlying goal of the law which protects trade secrets, like that which protects copyrights and patents, is to encourage the formulation and promulgation of ideas by ensuring that creators of ideas benefit from their creations."[12]

[C] Policy Limitations

[1] Ensuring Free Competition

Free competition is a core value in our market economy. Although patent law provides the inventor with a monopoly, its anti-competitive impact is minimized for several reasons: (a) only a comparatively small number of inventions meet the rigorous standards for patent protection; (b) the patentee must disclose the secret of the invention to the public, which can use the information to develop better products and services; and (c) after 20 years, anyone can freely use the patented invention.

But these restrictions do not readily apply to trade secrets because: (a) the threshold for protection is much lower and, accordingly, trade secret law protects far more information; (b) the holder need not disclose the information to the public; and (c) a trade secret might potentially last forever.

Accordingly, the law imposes significant limits on trade secret protection to ensure that it does not unduly impair free competition.[13] For example, as the *Kewanee Oil* Court observed:

> Trade secret law provides far weaker protection in many respects than the patent law. While trade secret law does not forbid the discovery of the trade secret by fair and honest means, e.g., independent creation or reverse engineering, patent law operates "against the world," forbidding any use of the invention for whatever purpose for a significant length of time.[14]

Thus, any competitor is free to use the trade secret—without the holder's consent—if it can either independently create the secret or reverse engineer the secret product or process.[15]

[2] Protecting Employee Mobility

Another core value that restricts the scope of trade secret law is protection of employee mobility. As the Restatement (Third) of Unfair Competition states: "There is

12. 763 F.2d 461, 467 (1st Cir. 1985).

13. Other examples include: the requirement that the holder make "reasonable" efforts to avoid loss of secrecy (*see* § 2.05); the rule that public disclosure terminates the trade secret (*see* § 6:02); and the use of lead-time injunctions (*see* § 7:03[B][2]).

14. *Kewanee Oil*, 416 U.S. at 489–90.

15. Reverse engineering is the process by which a person "takes an already existing product and works backward to re-create its design and/or manufacturing process." United Tech. Corp. v. FAA, 102 F.3d 688, 690 n. 1 (2d Cir. 1996).

a strong public interest in preserving the freedom of employees to market their talents and experience in order to earn a livelihood."[16] This policy both respects the personal autonomy of individual employees and, more broadly, promotes free competition by allowing widespread dissemination of knowledge and skills.

Because trade secrets are misappropriated most frequently by departing employees, the law must strike an appropriate balance between safeguarding the employer's secrets and protecting the employee's right to choose her employment.[17] Striking the balance too far in favor of the employer might have the unfortunate side effect of barring the employee from changing jobs at will. It is well settled that an employee's general knowledge and skill is not a trade secret. An employee may use that knowledge and skill in a new job, free from any claim of misappropriation. In *CVD, Inc. v. Raytheon Co.*, the First Circuit explained that this principle "effectuates the public interest in labor mobility, promotes the employee's freedom to practice a profession, and [protects] freedom of competition."[18]

§ 1.04 Sources of Trade Secret Law

[A] Evolution of Trade Secret Law

There are two main sources of trade secret law: the Uniform Trade Secrets Act (UTSA)[19] and the federal Defend Trade Secrets Act (DTSA).[20]

Traditionally, trade secrets were governed by state common law. Over time, almost all states adopted the 1985 UTSA, a model law drafted by the Uniform Law Commission with the goal of making trade secret doctrine consistent across the country. Currently the only non-UTSA state is New York.[21] Many states enacted the UTSA without changes, while others deviated from the original text in certain places. As a result, the *state laws* governing trade secrets differ somewhat in their details, but are broadly similar.

In 2016, Congress enacted the DTSA, which created a civil federal remedy for trade secret misappropriation largely modeled on the UTSA. The DTSA is the most important development in intellectual property law in decades. It promises—at least in theory—to create a uniform body of *federal law* governing trade secrets, akin to the well-developed protections for copyrights, patents, and trademarks.

---

16. Restatement (Third) of Unfair Competition § 42 cmt. b.

17. *See* Chapter 8.

18. 769 F.2d 842, 852 (1st Cir. 1985).

19. *See* Appendix A for the text of the UTSA.

20. The Defend Trade Secrets Act of 2016, Pub. L. No. 114-153, 130 Stat. 376, was enacted as an amendment to the Economic Espionage Act of 1996, Pub. L. No. 104-294, 110 Stat. 3488 (EEA). The EEA, which imposed criminal penalties for trade secret theft, was codified as 18 U.S.C. § 1831–1839; the DTSA amended many of these sections. For convenience, we will refer to the combined DTSA/EEA as the DTSA, unless otherwise indicated. *See* Appendix B for the text of the EEA, as amended by the DTSA.

21. Alabama and North Carolina have not officially adopted the UTSA, but their statutes governing trade secrets are similar to the UTSA in many respects.

Three other sources of trade secret law that paved the way for the UTSA and DTSA are still important today in varying degrees: the Restatement of Torts; the Restatement (Third) of Unfair Competition; and the Economic Espionage Act.

[B] Restatement of Torts (1939)

Trade secret protection was traditionally a common law doctrine.[22] This case law evolved gradually in state courts for over a century, until Restatement of Torts § 757 distilled it into a short set of principles in 1939. For the next four decades, courts routinely cited this Restatement as the leading source of trade secret law.[23]

But § 757 was both skeletal and vague. For example, it did not attempt to define the term "trade secret"; a comment to the section insisted that such a definition was "not possible."[24] Instead, it provided six factors for determining whether information qualified for trade secret protection.[25]

Although § 757 helped to clarify the scope of trade secret law, it proved to be inadequate as the field expanded. Its vagueness led to unpredictable results, and its failure to address key issues was problematic. As a result, trade secret law varied widely from state to state, which ultimately led to adoption of the UTSA. However, this section retains some vitality because courts occasionally cite to it when interpreting their state versions of the UTSA.[26]

[C] Uniform Trade Secrets Act (1979 and 1985)

The National Conference of Commissioners on Uniform State Laws adopted the UTSA in 1979 to bring greater uniformity to trade secret law. Today, nearly all states use the slightly revised version of the act approved in 1985. The UTSA is—by far—the most important source of modern trade secret law.

The UTSA drafters explained that despite the growing importance of state trade secret law:

> [T]his law has not developed satisfactorily. In the first place, its development is uneven. Although there typically are a substantial number of reported decisions in states that are commercial centers, this is not the case in less pop-

22. The first trade secret case in the United States was Vickery v. Welsh, 36 Mass. 523 (1837), which concerned a secret method of making chocolate.

23. Two other sections of the Restatement of Torts were also relevant to trade secrets. Section 758 governed the liability of a person who received another person's trade secret without notice that it was secret, while § 759 imposed liability on a competitor who used improper means to obtain "information about another's business" in order to advance "a rival business interest."

24. Restatement of Torts § 757 cmt. b.

25. *Id.*

26. Over the last decade, courts cited § 757 more than 400 times. *See, e.g.*, Optic Graphics, Inc. v. Agee, 591 A.2d 578, 585 (Md. App. 1991) ("Although all of the Restatement's factors no longer are required to find a trade secret, those factors still provide helpful guidance to determine whether the information in a given case constitutes 'trade secrets' within the definition of the statute.").

> ulous and more agricultural jurisdictions. Second, even in states in which there has been significant litigation, there is undue uncertainty concerning the parameters of trade secret protection, and the appropriate remedies for misappropriation of a trade secret.[27]

They also noted that—despite these concerns—§ 757 was among the sections omitted from the 1978 Restatement (Second) of Torts.

The UTSA provides a comprehensive set of statutes to govern trade secret protection. While the drafters noted that it "codifies the basic principles of common law trade secret protection"—thus incorporating principles from § 757—it actually goes well beyond this point. For example, it provides unitary definitions for key terms such as "trade secret" and "misappropriation," clarifies the available defenses, and follows the "better reasoned cases" on remedies.[28]

UTSA § 8 provides that the act shall be applied and construed to "effectuate its general purpose to make uniform the law with respect to the subject of this [Act] among the states enacting it." Accordingly, a court in a UTSA state can generally use the case law developed in any other UTSA state as relevant authority.[29]

In practice, the UTSA has not produced as much uniformity as its drafters hoped. A handful of states—including California—adopted the 1979 version. Although most states enacted the 1985 version, about half did so with significant changes.

[D] Restatement (Third) of Unfair Competition (1995)

The inclusion of trade secret provisions in the 1995 Restatement (Third) of Unfair Competition was somewhat anachronistic. By that time, the vast majority of states had codified their trade secret laws by adopting the UTSA, and it seemed likely that others would do so as well. Accordingly, there was a diminishing need to clarify common law principles, which is the traditional function of a Restatement. Still, the drafters expressed the hope that its provisions would be "applicable both to common law actions and actions under the Uniform Trade Secrets Act or analogous civil legislation."[30]

Surprisingly, the Restatement has proven to be a valuable source of modern trade secret law. It largely follows the UTSA approach, but often provides statements of the law that are more comprehensive. As a result, it serves as a valuable aid for interpreting the UTSA and DTSA.[31]

---

27. UTSA pref. note.

28. *Id.*

29. *See, e.g.,* Amoco Prod. Co. v. Laird, 622 N.E.2d 912, 917–19 (Ind. 1993).

30. Restatement (Third) of Unfair Competition § 39 rep. note.

31. One court commented that this Restatement has already "supplanted" Restatement of Torts § 757 on trade secret law issues. Briefing.com v. Jones, 126 P.3d 928, 931 (Wyo. 2006). However, courts have cited its trade secret provisions only about 200 times in the last decade—much less frequently than the Restatement of Torts section.

[E] Economic Espionage Act (1996)

The enactment of the Economic Espionage Act (EEA) in 1996 was a milestone—the first major federal legislation designed to protect trade secrets.[32] It imposes criminal penalties for economic espionage and other forms of trade secret theft. Congress adopted the EEA to deal with the increasing threat that foreign governments and other actors pose to trade secrets in "the high-technology, information age."[33] As the legislative history reflects, trade secret material "is a prime target for theft precisely because it costs so much to develop independently, because it is so valuable, and because there are virtually no penalties for its theft."[34]

[F] Defend Trade Secrets Act (2016)

The 2016 Defend Trade Secrets Act (DTSA) established a civil remedy for trade secret misappropriation at the federal level. Because it does not preempt state law, trade secret owners have two separate layers of protection. A plaintiff may choose to sue under state law, the DTSA, or both.

Congress enacted the DTSA for two reasons: (1) to make trade secret law more uniform; and (2) to provide effective enforcement. First, the House of Representatives report on the bill explained that state laws were not uniform: "While 48 states have adopted variations of the UTSA, the state laws vary in a number of ways and contain built-in limitations that make them not wholly effective in a national and global economy."[35] It observed that the DTSA would "provide a single, national standard for trade secret misappropriation with clear rules and predictability for everyone involved."[36]

Second, Congress recognized that federal courts were better able to enforce trade secret laws, since they are not confined by state boundaries. The House report stressed that state courts could not "efficiently order discovery and service of process" in cases involving multiple states; nor could they take "swift action ... across state lines to preserve evidence" or "keep a trade secret thief from boarding a plane and taking the secret beyond the reach of American law."[37]

The DTSA is largely based on the 1985 version of the UTSA. The legislative history makes this clear, repeatedly explaining that particular DTSA provisions were "modeled on" or "drawn directly from" UTSA sections. The two laws: (1) use similar definitions of the term "trade secret"; (2) have nearly identical liability standards; and (3) contain very similar remedy provisions. As a result, federal courts can—and, in practice, regularly do—use UTSA decisions to help interpret the DTSA.

---

32. 18 U.S.C. §§ 1831–1839. *See* Chapter 9.
33. H.R. Rep. No. 104-788, at 4 (1996).
34. *Id.* at 5.
35. H.R. Rep. No. 114-529, at 4 (2016).
36. *Id.* at 6.
37. *Id.* at 4.

Yet the DTSA differs from the UTSA in a few respects. In particular, it: (1) establishes a new "whistleblower" immunity when a person confidentially discloses a trade secret under certain circumstances;[38] (2) authorizes an ex parte order for the seizure of property necessary to prevent the dissemination of a misappropriated trade secret;[39] and (3) restricts injunctions that bar employees from taking new jobs.[40] Further, while the DTSA and UTSA share *similar* definitions for most key terms, the definitions are often not *identical*; this may ultimately lead to a divergence in how the two statutes are interpreted.

§ 1.05 Tort Law or Property Law?

[A] Conflicting Theories

Is trade secret protection based on tort law or property law?[41] For over a century, courts and scholars have debated this fundamental question. The tort approach is premised on the policy of preserving commercial morality. Accordingly, it focuses on *wrongful conduct* by the person who misappropriates the trade secret. In contrast, the property approach is based on the policy of promoting innovation and focuses on protecting the *rights* of the trade secret holder, in order to ensure an adequate incentive for invention.

The resolution of this debate is important because it should logically shape the contours of trade secret doctrine. In general, the tort approach predominated until the 1980s, when it was eclipsed by the property approach. As a result, modern trade secret law has been sculpted by both theories.

[B] Tort Theory

Under the tort approach (sometimes called the "confidential relationship" approach), the primary task of trade secret law is to deter and punish wrongful conduct, and thereby safeguard commercial morality. This approach essentially views misappropriation of secret information as an intentional tort. From this perspective, the doctrine is mainly concerned with bad actors, such as the employee who violates the duty of secrecy owed to the employer by disclosing a trade secret to a competitor or the thief who obtains a trade secret through burglary.

The Supreme Court endorsed this approach in the 1917 decision of *E.I. duPont deNemours Powder Co. v. Masland*, where plaintiffs sought an injunction to prevent a former employee from disclosing or using trade secrets.[42] Justice Holmes explained:

---

38. *See* § 6.05[D].

39. *See* § 7.02[B].

40. *See* § 7.02[C][2].

41. Trade secrets and certain other forms of information may also be protected by contract. *See* § 8.03[C].

42. 244 U.S. 100 (1917).

> The word ... "property" as applied to ... trade secrets is an unanalyzed expression of certain secondary consequences of the primary fact that the law makes some rudimentary requirements of good faith. Whether the plaintiffs have any valuable secret or not the defendant knows the facts, whatever they are, through a special confidence that he accepted. The property may be denied, but the confidence cannot be. Therefore the starting point ... is not property ... but that the defendant stood in confidential relations with the plaintiffs.... These have given place to hostility, and the first thing to be made sure of is that the defendant shall not fraudulently abuse the trust reposed in him.[43]

In the wake of *Masland*, American courts emphasized the tort approach. The 1939 Restatement of Torts stated that the goal of trade secret law was to deter improper conduct, not to protect property rights:

> The suggestion that one has a right to exclude others from the use of his trade secret because he has a right of property in the idea has been frequently advanced and rejected. The theory that has prevailed is that the protection is afforded only by a general duty of good faith and that the liability rests upon breach of this duty; that is, breach of contract, abuse of confidence or impropriety in the method of ascertaining the secret.[44]

As a result, the Restatement's trade secret provisions largely reflected the tort approach, which in turn influenced American courts for decades.

[C] Property Theory

Under the property view, the main function of trade secret law is essentially the same as patent law—promoting innovation. By protecting trade secrets as a form of property, the law provides an economic incentive for innovators to develop new and valuable information that will ultimately benefit the public in general.

The Supreme Court's 1984 decision in *Ruckelshaus v. Monsanto Co.* reflected the ascendancy of the property theory.[45] In holding that secret data was "property" under the Takings Clause of the Fifth Amendment, the Court observed that the "general perception of trade secrets as property is consonant with a notion of 'property' that extends beyond land and tangible goods and includes the products of an individual's 'labour and invention.' "[46]

The gradual adoption of the UTSA by state legislatures expanded the influence of the property view. Although in form the act tries to strike a middle ground between

---

43. *Id.* at 102.

44. Restatement of Torts § 757 cmt. a.

45. 467 U.S. 986 (1984). A decade earlier, in Kewanee Oil Co. v. Bicron Corp., 416 U.S. 470 (1974), the Court appeared to assume that trade secrets were property. In deciding whether federal patent law preempted Ohio's trade secret law, it phrased one issue as "whether the States are forbidden to act at all in the area of protection of the kinds of intellectual property which may make up the subject matter of trade secrets." *Id.* at 478.

46. *Ruckelshaus*, 467 U.S. at 1003 (quoting 2 Blackstone, Commentaries *405).

the competing theories,[47] its substantive provisions emphasize the property approach. Employing similar diplomacy, the Restatement (Third) of Unfair Competition delicately avoids labeling a trade secret as "property" and instead refers to it as an "intangible trade value."[48]

Congress was less subtle in enacting the DTSA, which expressly recognizes trade secrets as property. As the Senate Judiciary Committee report acknowledged: "Trade secrets are a form of intellectual property that allow for the legal protection of commercially valuable, proprietary information and make up an increasingly important part of American companies' intellectual property portfolios."[49] Accordingly, the DTSA repeatedly uses the word "owner" to describe the holder of a trade secret, a term it defines as "the person or entity in whom or in which rightful legal or equitable title to ... the trade secret is reposed."[50]

[D] Synthesis

Modern trade secret law is best viewed as an amalgam of the tort and property approaches. Over time, the importance of the tort view has waned, as the property view has expanded. But both approaches remain relevant today. Neither view—standing alone—explains all the doctrines that comprise trade secret law.

Consider these examples of the tension between the approaches, which are discussed in later chapters:

- *Existence of trade secret*: A trade secret cannot exist if the information is "readily ascertainable."[51] This reflects the property focus on incentives, as there is no need to provide an incentive to create ascertainable information. Using the tort approach, however, some cases have held that misappropriation of readily ascertainable information is improper.
- *Misappropriation*: A defendant is liable for misappropriation only if he uses "improper means" to acquire the secret or knowledge of the secret,[52] a rule that reflects the tort focus on wrongful conduct. Under the property approach, it could be argued that any disclosure or use should be a misappropriation, regardless of how the secret was obtained.
- *Injunctions*: A modern court will issue an injunction only for the period necessary for the defendant to reverse engineer the trade secret,[53] which

---

47. However, the UTSA drafters referred to "the owner of the trade secret" in a comment, which reflects the property approach. UTSA § 1 cmt.

48. Restatement (Third) of Unfair Competition § 38.

49. Sen. Rep. No. 114-220, at 1 (2016).

50. 18 U.S.C. § 1839(4).

51. *See* § 2.04[C].

52. *See* §§ 4.02[D], 4.03[E].

53. *See* § 7.03[B][2].

reflects the property view about the extent of the required incentive. In contrast, the tort approach might well support a perpetual injunction as a form of punishing the wrongdoer.

- *Damages*: Damages for misappropriation can be measured by the defendant's unjust enrichment, not merely by the plaintiff's loss;[54] this reflects tort theory, which penalizes a wrongdoer. The property approach would logically measure damages only by the plaintiff's loss, which is usually a sufficient incentive.

Trade secret law will continue to evolve in the future. Based on present trends, it seems likely that the influence of the property view will grow over time. As a result, doctrines reflecting the tort approach may slowly transition toward a more property-based view—at least where the statutory text permits.

§ 1.06 Trade Secrets as Intellectual Property

[A] Property Rights

Today it is generally accepted that trade secrets are a form of intellectual property, even though trade secret law still reflects the tort theory to some extent.

It is traditional to define "property" as a metaphorical bundle of rights.[55] In general, the owner of a trade secret holds three key rights: (1) the right to exclude others from disclosing or using the information; (2) the right to transfer the information; and (3) within limits, the right to use the information. The right to use the secret, of course, may be restricted by other laws. If A develops an idea for a new type of nuclear weapon, for example, he may not be able to build that weapon.

However, the rights of the trade secret owner are not absolute; they must be balanced against the interests of society, consistent with utilitarian theory. As Judge Posner explained in *ConFold Pacific, Inc. v. Polaris Industries, Inc.*:

> ConFold believes mistakenly that a trade secret is a property right in the same sense in which a person has a property right in his mattress. A property right in the latter sense is a right good against the whole world, which a trade secret is not, because it is perfectly lawful to "steal" a firm's trade secret by reverse engineering.[56]

Like other forms of intellectual property, a trade secret may be: assigned or licensed to another party; placed in a trust; devised in a will; mortgaged to secure a debt; taxed; or distributed as an asset upon divorce or partnership dissolution.

---

54. *See* § 7.04[B][4].

55. *See, e.g.*, Kaiser Aetna v. United States, 444 U.S. 164, 176 (1979) (referring to the "bundle of rights that are commonly characterized as property").

56. 433 F.3d 952, 958–59 (7th Cir. 2006).

[B] Obtaining Ownership

Most commonly, a person obtains ownership of a trade secret by creating it. If B creates an idea that qualifies for protection—for example, a concept for a new laser system—B owns that idea. The result may be different, however, if B is an employee. In some situations, the idea belongs to B's employer instead.[57]

A distinctive feature of trade secret law—compared to copyright and patent law—is that the owner does not hold exclusive rights in the information. Two doctrines weaken the rigor of trade secret protection: independent creation and reverse engineering.[58] First, suppose C independently develops the same laser system concept six months after B did; now C also owns the secret. Second, suppose instead that B sells a product that utilizes the secret; D buys the product and after extensive work is able to reverse engineer it to discover the secret. On these facts, B and D each own the secret.

A person who owns a trade secret—such as B, C, or D in the examples above—is entitled to disclose it to others. If B freely discloses the laser system concept to E, E also owns the secret. However, at some point widespread disclosure will terminate trade secret protection.[59] Under modern law, a trade secret does not exist if the information is "generally known to ... other persons who can obtain economic value from its disclosure or use."[60]

The commercial transfer of a trade secret is usually done through an assignment or license. Suppose B wants to sell his entire laser system concept to F. B could accomplish this by assigning his idea to F in return for compensation. When this is completed, F owns the secret and B does not.

Alternatively, a party such as B could retain title to the secret, but transfer a lesser interest to another party through a license. For example, B might give F an exclusive license to use the secret for a period of ten years. In this situation, F is the only party who can use the secret. Or B could transfer a nonexclusive license to F, which would authorize F, B, and anyone else B chose to use the secret.

---

57. *See* § 8.02[B], [C].
58. *See* §§ 6.03, 6.04.
59. *See* § 6.02.
60. UTSA § 1(4)(i). *See also* 18 U.S.C. § 1839(3)(B).

Chapter 2

What Is a Trade Secret?

§ 2.01 Introduction

[A] Overview

Under both the Uniform Trade Secrets Act and Defend Trade Secrets Act, a trade secret is:

- "information" that has
- "independent economic value, actual or potential"
- from "not being generally known to, and not being reasonably ascertainable" by "proper means by," other persons "who can obtain economic value from" its "disclosure or use" and
- is the subject of "reasonable" efforts to maintain its secrecy.[1]

This chapter analyzes these elements in depth.

Consider a classic example of a trade secret: the formula for Coca-Cola. The formula is information; it indicates that certain amounts of particular ingredients are used to make the drink. The formula has economic value to the Coca-Cola Company because it provides a monopoly on making this popular beverage, which annually produces billions of dollars in revenue. The formula is not known by anyone outside of the company and—apparently—no one can discover the formula through experimentation. Finally, the company takes care to keep the information secret: the formula is stored in a safe.

The term "trade secrets" originated in an era when only secrets used by "trades" or other businesses were protected. Today this term is misleading, because the doctrine protects a broader range of secrets. It is no longer necessary that the information be used in a trade or business. Thus, information held by non-profit entities (such as religious secrets) or by individuals who are not engaged in a business (such as an idea for a new television series) could be trade secrets.

The types of information that may qualify for trade secret protection are myriad and include: bids; business methods; compilations; computer passwords; computer software; cost data; customer data; designs; drawings; financial statements; formulas; inventions; market research; marketing strategies; patterns; price data; product specifications; production processes; recipes; religious materials; sales data; and social media contacts.

Whether particular information constitutes a trade secret is a question of fact. Accordingly, a well-pleaded complaint for misappropriation will generally survive a motion to dismiss based on the assertion that no trade secret exists.[2] Similarly, it is no easy task to win a summary judgment motion on the basis that information does not qualify for trade secret protection. As a result, a trial is often necessary to determine if the information is a trade secret.

---

1. UTSA § 1(4); 18 U.S.C. § 1839(3).

2. *See, e.g.*, Del Monte Fresh Produce Co. v. Dole Food Co., Inc., 136 F. Supp. 2d 1271 (S.D. Fla. 2001) (denying motion to dismiss even though it was unclear whether plaintiff was contending that the trade secret was a particular variety of pineapple, the genetic code for that variety, or something else). *See also* § 5.06[D].

[B] UTSA/DTSA Definition

The leading definition of a trade secret is set forth in the UTSA, which has been adopted by almost every state:[3]

> [I]nformation, including a formula, pattern, compilation, program, device, method, technique, or process, that:
>
> (i) derives independent economic value, actual or potential, from not being generally known to, and not being readily ascertainable by proper means by, other persons who can obtain economic value from its disclosure or use, and
>
> (ii) is the subject of efforts that are reasonable under the circumstances to maintain its secrecy.[4]

The federal definition of a trade secret in the DTSA is almost identical to the UTSA definition:

> [A]ll forms and types of financial, business, scientific, technical, economic, or engineering information, including patterns, plans, compilations, program devices,[5] formulas, designs, prototypes, methods, techniques, processes, procedures, programs, or codes, whether tangible or intangible, and whether or how stored, compiled, or memorialized physically, electronically, graphically, photographically, or in writing if—
>
> (A) the owner thereof has taken reasonable measures to keep such information secret; and
>
> (B) the information derives independent economic value, actual or potential, from not being generally known to, and not being readily ascertainable through proper means by, another person who can obtain economic value from the disclosure or use of the information.[6]

There are two differences between the UTSA and DTSA definitions.[7] First, the UTSA encompasses *all* types of information, while the DTSA covers only *six* specific types of information—suggesting, perhaps, that the UTSA may provide broader protection in some instances. It is not clear, however, whether this is a meaningful distinction.

---

3. The principal holdout is New York. Some states have adopted the UTSA with significant changes. Alabama and North Carolina have not officially adopted the act, but their statutes are similar to it in many respects.

4. UTSA § 1(4).

5. This reference to "program devices" is presumably a typographical error in the statute, and should instead read "programs, devices." The DTSA definition was modeled on the parallel UTSA provision, which defines "information" in part to include a "program, device" and other items.

6. 18 U.S.C. § 1839(3).

7. To date, courts have agreed that the UTSA and DTSA definitions are effectively the same. *See, e.g.*, Teva Pharm. USA, Inc. v. Sandhu, 291 F. Supp. 3d 659, 675 (E.D. Pa. 2018) ("[T]hey essentially protect the same information...."); Founder Starcoin, Inc. v. Launch Labs, Inc., 2018 WL 3343790, at *4 (S.D. Cal. July 9, 2018) ("[T]he definitions ... are virtually the same...."). The authors are not aware of a case where this has been a dispositive issue.

Second, because the DTSA is based on the power of Congress to regulate foreign and interstate commerce, a federal trade secret must be linked to a product or service in such commerce.[8] However, the legislative history of the DTSA indicates that its trade secret definition was not intended to be "meaningfully different" from the UTSA definition.[9] Indeed, a committee report explains that the DTSA changes to the EEA definition were "to bring the Federal definition of a trade secret in conformity with the definition used in the Uniform Trade Secrets Act."[10] Moreover, courts have repeatedly held that similar Commerce Clause requirements for other federal statutes are easily satisfied.[11]

[C] Compared to Restatement of Torts

The 1939 Restatement of Torts attempted to harmonize the conflicting state definitions of a trade secret. Its §757 broadly discussed liability for misappropriating a trade secret, without providing a definition of the term. A comment to this section stressed that "[t]he subject matter of a trade secret must be secret," but noted that "[a]n exact definition of a trade secret is not possible."[12] The comment went on to explain that:

> A trade secret may consist of any formula, pattern, device or compilation of information which is used in one's business, and which gives him an opportunity to obtain an advantage over competitors who do not know or use it.... [I]t is not simply information as to single or ephemeral events in the conduct of the business.... A trade secret is a process or device for continuous use in the operation of the business.[13]

The comment to §757 identified six factors for determining whether particular information "is one's trade secret":

> (1) the extent to which the information is known outside of his business;
>
> (2) the extent to which it is known by employees and others involved in his business;
>
> (3) the extent of measures taken by him to guard the secrecy of the information;
>
> (4) the value of the information to him and to his competitors;
>
> (5) the amount of effort or money expended by him in developing the information;

---

8. *See* §4.04.

9. Sen. Rep. No. 114-220, at 10 (2016).

10. *Id.*

11. *See, e.g.*, United States v. Klopf, 423 F.3d 1228, 1238 (11th Cir. 2005) (noting that, in several contexts, courts have held that commerce elements require only a "minimal" connection between the violation of the law and interstate commerce).

12. Restatement of Torts §757 cmt. b.

13. *Id.*

(6) the ease or difficulty with which the information could by properly acquired or duplicated by others.[14]

This six-factor test was widely adopted by American courts and, as a result, became the dominant test for determining whether a trade secret existed.

Yet this approach was problematic. As the Fifth Circuit acknowledged in *Lear Siegler, Inc. v. Ark-Ell Springs, Inc.* when applying the Restatement standard, "[t]he term 'trade secret' is one of the most elusive and difficult concepts in the law to define."[15] There are several reasons for this observation. First, it is often challenging to predict the outcome of any issue that turns on a multi-factor test because reasonable courts could easily disagree about the result. Second, in practice many courts demanded that *all* six parts of the test be satisfied, while most found that a trade secret could exist when only *some* factors were met.[16] Thus, it was difficult for a business to know if its information was protected—and difficult for a competing business to know if it could legally use that information. As the UTSA drafters summarized, this approach produced "undue uncertainty concerning the parameters of trade secret protection."[17]

The UTSA's more concise definition of a trade secret was a response to the inadequacy of the Restatement approach. The drafters explained that one of the UTSA innovations was the "substitution of [a] unitary definition[] of trade secret" in place of the six-factor test.[18] All elements of the unitary definition must be satisfied for a trade secret to exist under the UTSA. Because the act was adopted by almost all states, its test should logically supersede the Restatement approach in those jurisdictions.

In practice, however, courts sometimes still use the Restatement factors in interpreting a particular state's version of the UTSA. For example, in *AirFacts, Inc. v. de Amezaga*, the Fourth Circuit noted that these factors "remain[] useful" in determining when a trade secret exists under Missouri law, even though a state statute adopted the UTSA definition.[19] Similarly, as the Seventh Circuit observed in another case, "[a]lthough the [UTSA] explicitly defines a trade secret ... Illinois courts frequently refer to six common law factors (which are derived from §757 of the Restatement (First) of Torts) in determining whether a trade secret exists...."[20] More surprisingly, courts in UTSA states sometimes blend the Restatement factors with the UTSA definition, creating a hybrid standard.[21] Decisions like these are clearly wrong and best

---

14. *Id.*

15. 569 F.2d 286, 288 (5th Cir. 1978).

16. *See, e.g.*, Learning Curve Toys, Inc. v. PlayWood Toys, Inc., 342 F.3d 714, 722 (7th Cir. 2003) ("Courts from other jurisdictions, as well as legal scholars, have noted that the Restatement factors are not to be applied as a list of requisite elements.").

17. UTSA pref. note.

18. *Id.*

19. 909 F.3d 84, 95 (4th Cir. 2018).

20. *Learning Curve Toys*, 342 F.3d at 722.

21. *See, e.g.*, ScaleFactor, Inc. v. Process Pro Consulting, LLC, 2019 WL 131733, at *5 (W.D. Tex. Mar. 22, 2019) (noting that "[t]o determine whether a trade secret exists under Texas law" courts use the Restatement factors, but then applying the UTSA definition as well).

understood as steps in the transition from the Restatement view to the UTSA approach. It is possible that the adoption of the DTSA will speed this transition, as there is no textual or historical reason to incorporate the Restatement standard when analyzing whether a complaint adequately alleges a trade secret under federal law.

In one sense, the definitions of a trade secret under the UTSA—and, by extension, the DTSA—are narrower than the Restatement approach because all elements of the UTSA definition must be satisfied, while many courts reasoned that only some of the Restatement factors were necessary. For example, in theory a trade secret might be found under the Restatement approach even if feeble measures were taken to guard the secrecy of the information, because the extent of such measures is merely one of six relevant factors. However, the UTSA requires that "reasonable" efforts be taken to maintain secrecy.

On balance, however, the UTSA/DTSA approach substantially expands the definition of a trade secret. For example:

- Virtually any type of information may qualify for protection;
- Information can be a trade secret even if it is not "used" in a "business";
- Information may be known by hundreds or thousands of employees, so long as it is subject to reasonable efforts to keep it secret (e.g., nondisclosure agreements);[22]
- Information need not be in "continuous" use; and
- Information is protected even if it only has "potential" value.

[D] Compared to Restatement (Third) of Unfair Competition

The trade secret definition used by the Restatement (Third) of Unfair Competition is similar to the UTSA/DTSA approach:

> A trade secret is any information that can be used in the operation of a business or other enterprise and that is sufficiently valuable and secret to afford an actual or potential economic advantage over others.[23]

A comment to this section states that the definition "is intended to be consistent with the definition of 'trade secret'" in the UTSA.[24] Perhaps because the Restatement was drafted after the widespread adoption of the UTSA, this section has not been frequently cited.

Unlike the Restatement of Torts, this section does not require that the secret actually be used in operating a business; rather, the standard is met if it *could* be so used in a business or other enterprise, which is close to the UTSA/DTSA approach. But this

22. *See* § 8.03[C].
23. Restatement (Third) of Unfair Competition § 39.
24. *Id.* cmt. b.

section differs from the UTSA/DTSA definitions in an important regard: it does not mandate that the owner undertake reasonable efforts to maintain the secrecy of the information.

§ 2.02 "Information"

[A] Defining "Information"

[1] Overview

Virtually any type of information is eligible for protection as a trade secret under modern law. The UTSA definition, for instance, begins by simply stating that "'trade secret' means information."[25] It then provides non-limiting examples of information that may qualify for protection: "a formula, pattern, compilation, program, device, method, technique, or process."[26] A comment to the definition explains that "method" and "technique" are intended to "include the concept of 'know-how.'"[27] In short, the UTSA covers *all categories* of information.[28]

For example, in *Religious Technology Center v. Netcom On-Line Communication Services, Inc.*, a federal district court interpreted California's version of the UTSA to protect religious writings as trade secrets.[29] It explained that "there is no authority for excluding religious materials from trade secret protection because of their nature. Indeed, there is no authority for excluding any type of information because of its nature."[30]

Does the DTSA protect less information than the UTSA? On its face, the answer appears to be yes. The DTSA covers only *six categories* of information: "financial, business, scientific, technical, economic, or engineering information."[31] It lists "patterns, plans, compilations, program devices, formulas, designs, prototypes, methods, techniques, processes, procedures, programs, or codes" as examples of protected information.[32] Thus, information in a legal opinion letter or a religious secret might not fit into any of the six categories.

---

25. UTSA § 1(4).
26. *Id.*
27. *Id.* cmt.
28. In contrast, many courts have held that the scope of information protected as trade secrets under the Restatement was narrower. *See, e.g.*, Three Dots, Inc. v. Lonny's Wardrobe, Inc., 739 N.Y.S.2d 701, 703 (App. 2002) (identity of suppliers was not a trade secret because it was not a "formula, pattern, device, or compilation of information").
29. 923 F. Supp. 1231 (N.D. Cal. 1995).
30. *Id.* at 1252.
31. 18 U.S.C. § 1839(3).
32. *Id.* The EEA's legislative history provides other examples of information that could qualify as trade secrets: "production processes, bid estimates, production schedules, computer software, and technology schematics." H.R. Rep. No. 104-788, at 4 (1996). The DTSA's legislative history mentions "confidential formulas, manufacturing techniques, and customer lists" as examples of trade secrets. H.R. Rep. No. 114-529, at 2 (2016).

The view that the DTSA definition is narrower is also supported by the policy concerns that led to the enactment of its predecessor statute, the Economic Espionage Act. As the House Judiciary Committee report on the EEA explained, the purpose of the act was to protect American companies from the theft of trade secrets by criminalizing "industrial espionage."[33] The six specified categories seek to encompass the types of information that would be vulnerable to such espionage.[34]

However, the legislative history of the EEA and DTSA also shows that Congress intended the UTSA and federal definitions of a trade secret to be quite similar. The House Judiciary Committee report on the EEA states that the "general categories of information are included in the definition of trade secret for illustrative purposes and should not be read to limit the definition of trade secret. It is the Committee's intent that this definition be read broadly."[35] The subsequent, parallel report for the DTSA similarly explains: "While … minor differences between the UTSA and the Federal definition of a trade secret remain, the Committee does not intend for the definition of a trade secret to be meaningfully different from the scope of that definition as understood by courts in States that have adopted the UTSA."[36]

Accordingly, it is not yet clear whether the DTSA definition is narrower than the UTSA formulation in a significant sense. Future litigation will be necessary to determine the precise parameters of the DTSA categories. Given the DTSA's legislative history and the general similarities between the two statutory schemes, it is possible that courts will interpret the categories broadly. Under this approach, for example, a legal opinion letter might be classified as "business" information that is covered by the DTSA. In practice, many courts appear to assume that the two definitions are essentially the same.

A trade secret is intangible; by definition, it consists of information. Thus, a secret is distinct from any physical object that embodies that secret. For example, in *Del Monte Fresh Produce Co. v. Dole Food Co., Inc.*, the court recognized that a pineapple could not be a trade secret; but it observed that the genetic information for a pineapple variety might qualify for protection.[37] One implication of this principle is that an owner's transfer of an object embodying a trade secret is not a transfer of the secret itself.[38]

The subsections below analyze how the UTSA/DTSA definition of "information" differs from the traditional Restatement of Torts approach.

---

33. H.R. Rep. No. 104-788, at 5 (1996).

34. Additionally, the DTSA only protects a trade secret that is "related to a product or service used in, or intended for use in, interstate or foreign commerce." 18 U.S.C. § 1836(b)(1). *See* § 4.04.

35. H.R. Rep. No. 104-788, at 12 (1996)

36. H.R. Rep. No. 114-529, at 14 (2016).

37. 136 F. Supp. 2d 1271, 1291–93 (S.D. Fla. 2001).

38. However, the public sale of an object that embodies a trade secret will destroy the secret if it is apparent from the object or readily ascertainable from it. *See* § 6.02[C].

[2] Information Not Used in a Business

The Restatement of Torts only protected information that was "used" in the "operation" of a "business."[39] This approach was a logical codification of prior case law, which almost uniformly involved disputes between competing businesses over the use of secret information.

Under the modern view, however, information can be a trade secret even if it is not used in the operation of a business. A comment to the UTSA explains that the change was a "reasonable departure" from the Restatement because it "extends protection to a plaintiff who has not yet had an opportunity or acquired the means to put a trade secret to use."[40] For example, if company A develops an innovative procedure for conducting genetic research, the procedure can be protected even though A has not yet used it. Similarly, if scientist B develops her own novel procedure, it will qualify for trade secret protection even though she is not operating a business.

This change is a major expansion of trade secret law. It extends trade secret protection to a broad spectrum of information *outside* of its use in a business, as long as the information has actual or potential economic value.

Similarly, information need not be used in a business to qualify for protection under the DTSA. However, the DTSA only extends protection to trade secrets that are "related to a product or service used in, or intended for use in, interstate or foreign commerce."[41] This appears to require that the secret be connected to some form of commercial activity that either exists or is planned for the future. Thus, as a practical matter, the universe of information it protects is somewhat smaller than that covered by the UTSA.

Suppose that C, an engineering student, invents a new type of vacuum cleaner that he plans to sell to a large corporation. This information is not a trade secret under the Restatement of Torts for two reasons. First, C has not "used" the information in any manner, such as by producing vacuum cleaners. Second, C is not engaged in business. In contrast, this information would qualify for protection under the UTSA and probably under the DTSA as well.

Or imagine that D, a bus driver, accidentally learns that a famous star who regularly endorses a brand of peanut butter in television ads actually hates it. Again, this information would not qualify for trade secret protection under the Restatement test because D is not using it in a business. However, it could be a trade secret under the UTSA and DTSA assuming that it has potential economic value—for example, to a movie magazine that might pay for the information as part of a story.

Under the UTSA, information used by non-profit entities such as charitable, educational, governmental, and religious organizations also qualifies for protection as

39. Restatement of Torts § 757 cmt. b.

40. UTSA § 1 cmt.

41. 18 U.S.C. § 1836(b)(1). *See* § 4.04.

long as the other trade secret elements are satisfied.[42] One hurdle here would be showing that the secret has actual or potential economic value. However, information relating to donations, gifts, grants, and other sources of revenue would presumably meet this requirement. The same result would follow under the DTSA as long as the requisite link to commerce was established.

[3] Single-Event Information

Another facet of the Restatement of Torts approach was that the information had to be in "continuous use in the operation of the business."[43] Thus, "information as to single or ephemeral events in the conduct of a business" such as "the amount or other terms of a secret bid for a contract or the salary of certain employees, or the security investments made or contemplated, or the date fixed for the announcement of a new policy" did not qualify for protection.[44] However, many courts that otherwise followed the Restatement approach rejected the continuous use requirement.

Under the majority view today—as reflected in the UTSA and DTSA—information that is used only once or for a short period of time can be a trade secret. For instance, if car manufacturer E establishes a secret date for announcing a new model car or contractor F makes a confidential bid to construct a project, this information is eligible for protection even though it is not used continuously.

[4] Negative Information

Negative information—knowing what not to do—may have economic value. For instance, suppose G spends thousands of dollars researching a potential cure for a rare type of cancer, and eventually discovers that this approach will not work. G's knowledge has potential economic value because it could prevent other scientists from wasting money by investigating the same approach.

Many courts following the Restatement of Torts approach refused to protect negative information on the basis that it required "continuous use" of the information. As the court explained in *Materials Development Corp. v. Atlantic Advanced Metals, Inc.*, "the secret to be protected should be positive, not negative ... [E]quity will not protect knowledge as to mistakes to be avoided...."[45]

A UTSA comment recognizes that the Act protects negative information. It notes that a trade secret includes "information that has commercial value from a negative

42. The Restatement (Third) of Unfair Competition takes the same position; its definition covers information used in the operation of "businesses and other commercial enterprises" and "nonprofit entities...." Restatement (Third) of Unfair Competition § 39 cmt. d.

43. Restatement of Torts § 757 cmt. b.

44. *Id. See, e.g.,* Lehman v. Dow Jones & Co., 783 F.2d 285, 298 (2d Cir. 1986) (refusing to protect information relating to the acquisition of another company on the basis that it was not in continuous use).

45. 172 U.S.P.Q. 595, 606 (Mass. Super. Ct. 1971). *But see* Metallurgical Indus. Inc. v. Fourtek, Inc., 790 F.2d 1195, 1203 (5th Cir. 1986) ("Knowing what not to do often leads automatically to knowing what to do.").

viewpoint, for example the results of lengthy and expensive research which proves that a certain process will *not* work could be of great value to a competitor."[46] For instance, if H invests time and energy in trying to sell a type of new product to potential interested businesses—with no success—the resulting list of uninterested companies would be valuable to H's competitors. Competitors could use this information to avoid the uninterested companies and target their efforts on other potential customers.[47]

However, it is unclear whether the DTSA encompasses negative information. This is because the act only applies to information "related to" a product or service that is used or intended to be used in interstate or foreign commerce.[48] For instance, in the above hypothetical H might argue that his list of uninterested companies is "related to" a product he is trying to sell in interstate commerce. This relationship—while arguable—may be too thin to justify DTSA protection. On the other hand, courts generally interpret the Commerce Clause in an expansive manner.

[5] Ideas

Suppose J has a concept for an innovative product that she gives to K, a potential manufacturer; K uses the concept but refuses to compensate J. Alternatively, imagine that L has a concept for a new television show that he submits to television network M; M creates the new show, but pays nothing to L.

Under the Restatement of Torts approach, mere ideas did not qualify for trade secret protection because they were not being "used" in a business at the time of submission. Courts dealt with this situation by occasionally awarding relief based on tort, express contract, implied contract, restitution, or other theories, depending on the circumstances of the submission. Many states followed the rule that an idea could qualify for protection only if it was both concrete and novel. As a result, a distinction arose between trade secret law and "idea submission cases."

But an idea *can* be a trade secret under the UTSA and DTSA. As the Restatement (Third) of Unfair Competition explains, "[w]ith the rejection under the Uniform Trade Secrets Act ... of any requirement of use by the owner of a trade secret ... there is no longer a formal distinction between trade secrets and ideas that form the subject matter of the idea submission cases."[49]

An example is *Contour Design, Inc. v. Chance Mold Steel Co., Ltd.*, where the plaintiff developed a concept for an ergonomic computer mouse, which it disclosed to the defendant under a confidentiality agreement.[50] Plaintiff sued for misappropriation after the defendant began marketing a similar product, and the court granted a temporary restraining order. In its analysis, the court noted that (a) the UTSA protects a plaintiff who has not yet had an opportunity to use the secret and (b) "[a] number

46. UTSA § 1 cmt. (emphasis in original).
47. *Cf.* Hollingsworth Solderless Terminal Co. v. Turley, 662 F.2d 1324 (9th Cir. 1980).
48. 18 U.S.C. § 1836(b)(1). *See* § 4.04.
49. Restatement (Third) of Unfair Competition § 39 cmt. h.
50. 2010 WL 174315 (D.N.H. Jan. 14, 2010).

of courts have applied the Act 'to confidential disclosures of concepts, or as yet-untested, ideas for a new product or a new process.' "[51]

Even though an idea is a type of "information" under the UTSA and DTSA, the plaintiff in such a misappropriation lawsuit may have difficulty winning the case. When a person submits an idea to another without a confidentiality agreement, an employment relationship, or a preexisting business relationship, it is usually viewed as a gift. Thus, the plaintiff will probably be unable to prove that he exercised "reasonable" efforts to maintain its secrecy.[52]

[B] Elements Not Required

[1] Tangible Form

The information constituting a trade secret need not be memorialized in a writing or other tangible medium.[53] The initial draft of the UTSA included such a requirement, but this provision was deleted in later versions.[54] As the Washington Supreme Court explained in *Ed Nowogroski Insurance, Inc. v. Rucker*, "[t]he form of information, whether written or memorized, is immaterial under the ... Uniform Trade Secrets Act [which] makes no distinction about the form of trade secrets."[55] In contrast, the DTSA expressly provides that both "tangible" and "intangible" information qualify for protection.[56] As one court summarized, "it does not matter whether a copy of [the plaintiff's] drawing came out in a defendant's hand or in his head."[57]

For example, suppose restaurant owner N has a secret recipe. Because N has never reduced the recipe to writing, she orally discloses it to her chefs as needed. N's recipe qualifies for protection under the UTSA and DTSA—so long as it satisfies the other elements of a trade secret—even though it does not exist in tangible form.

However, the form of the information may still be relevant in certain cases where an employer sues a former employee for misappropriation. An employee's general knowledge and skill is not a trade secret of the employer.[58] In distinguishing between the two, courts are more likely to find a trade secret if the employee "appropriates some physical embodiment of the information such as written formulas, blueprints, plans, or lists of customers."[59]

---

51. *Id.* at *5 (citing 2 Roger M. Milgrim & Eric B. Bensen, Milgrim on Trade Secrets § 9.05[4] (2019)). *But see* Daktronics, Inc. v. McAfee, 599 N.W.2d 358, 361 (S.D. 1999) (holding that under the state's version of the UTSA a "concept" for a new product could not be a trade secret).

52. *See* § 2.05.

53. *See, e.g.*, Bridgestone/Firestone, Inc. v. Lockhart, 5 F. Supp. 2d 667, 680–81 (S.D. Ind. 1998) (protecting business information that was not memorialized in tangible form).

54. Sharon K. Sandeen, *The Evolution of Trade Secret Law*, 33 Hamline L. Rev. 493, 525 (2010).

55. 971 P.2d 936, 948 (Wash. 1999).

56. 18 U.S.C. § 1839(3).

57. Sperry Rand Corp. v. Rothlein, 241 F. Supp. 549, 563 (D. Conn. 1964).

58. *See* § 2.02[C].

59. Restatement (Third) of Unfair Competition § 42 cmt. d.

[2] Novelty

Trade secret decisions occasionally suggest—incorrectly—that novelty is required.[60] In *Kewanee Oil Co. v. Bicron Corp.*, the Supreme Court observed that:

> [S]ome novelty will be required [for a trade secret] if merely because that which does not possess novelty is usually known; secrecy, in the context of trade secrets, thus implies at least minimal novelty.[61]

Accordingly, courts occasionally suggest that a trade secret must provide at least a "slight ... advance" over existing knowledge.[62]

But statements like these are misleading: novelty is not necessary. Over 80 years ago, the Restatement of Torts noted that "[n]ovelty and invention are not requisite for a trade secret as they are for patentability."[63] Similarly, the Restatement (Third) of Unfair Competition explains: "Although trade secret cases sometimes announce a 'novelty' requirement, the requirement is synonymous with the concepts of secrecy and value...."[64] Neither the UTSA or DTSA require novelty.[65]

The *Kewanee Oil* dictum suffers from several problems in the modern era. First, the requirement that the secret have independent economic value obviates any need for a novelty analysis; a non-novel secret is worth nothing. Moreover, there is no need to require novelty as a proxy for secrecy, because secrecy is a necessary element for trade secret protection.

Finally, the Court's statement about non-novel information is overbroad. True, non-novel information *may be* generally known, but it is not *always* generally known. A core theme in the UTSA and DTSA is that multiple independent developers can obtain a trade secret in the same information.[66] Suppose that O and P are two of the many companies involved in aerospace research. O develops a valuable research process, which it keeps secret. Later P independently develops the same process. Even though P's process is not novel, it qualifies for protection because it is not "generally known" to or "readily ascertainable" by other companies in the field.

[3] Concreteness

Traditionally, courts followed the rule that an idea must be reduced to concrete form in order to be a trade secret. Under this approach, the law did not protect a vague and abstract concept until it was sufficiently defined or implemented—such as converting the idea for an invention into a working prototype. In practice, however, the line between an abstract idea and a "concrete idea" was often hazy. The Restatement

---

60. *See, e.g.*, Electro-Craft Corp. v. Controlled Motion, Inc., 332 N.W.2d 890, 899 (Minn. 1983) ("[S]ome novelty is required; mere variations on widely used processes cannot be trade secrets.").

61. 416 U.S. 470, 476 (1974).

62. *See, e.g.*, Anaconda Co. v. Metric Tool & Die Co., 485 F. Supp. 410, 422 (E.D. Pa. 1980).

63. Restatement of Torts § 757 cmt. b.

64. Restatement (Third) of Unfair Competition § 39 cmt. f.

65. Some courts still require novelty in idea submission cases. *See* § 2.02[A][5].

66. *See* § 2.04[B][1].

of Torts endorsed this concept by stating that a trade secret must be a "process or device" used continuously in a business, rather than a mere idea.[67]

The UTSA and DTSA abandon the concreteness standard. Both define a "trade secret" as a type of "information," without any requirement that it be either sharply defined or implemented in physical form.[68] Thus, an abstract idea could qualify for trade secret protection.

[C] Special Exception: Employee's General Knowledge and Skill

Suppose employee Q has knowledge and skill that relates to her particular job. If this information is "generally known" or "readily ascertainable," it would clearly not qualify for trade secret protection under the UTSA or DTSA. However, if the information does not fall within these categories, can it be a trade secret? And can Q accept a new job with another employer in the same industry where she will use this information?

Most jurisdictions have long recognized a special exception for an employee's general skill and knowledge. As the Restatement (Third) of Unfair Competition explains: "Information that forms the general skill, knowledge, training, and experience of an employee cannot be claimed as a trade secret by a former employer even when the information is directly attributable to an investment of resources by the employer in the employee."[69] The Restatement of Employment Law similarly provides that "information ... acquired by employees through their general experience, knowledge, training, or skills during the ordinary course of their employment" is not a trade secret.[70]

Without this exception, it would be difficult for an employee to accept a new job at another company in the same industry. The rule reflects a compromise between the legitimate need to protect employers and the importance of employee mobility in a market economy. As the Seventh Circuit observed in *AMP, Inc. v. Fleischhacker*:

> Our society is extremely mobile and our free economy is based upon competition. One who has worked in a particular field cannot be compelled to erase from his mind all of the general skills, knowledge and expertise acquired through his experience....[71]
>
> Any other rule would force a departing employee to perform a prefrontal lobotomy on himself or herself. It would disserve the free market goal of maximizing available resources to foster competition.... [I]t would not strike a

67. Restatement of Torts § 757 cmt. b.

68. However, the trade secret owner who sues for misappropriation has the burden of defining the secret with sufficient specificity; otherwise, the court cannot determine whether it qualifies for trade secret protection. Restatement (Third) of Unfair Competition § 39 cmt. d. *See* § 5.04[B].

69. Restatement (Third) of Unfair Competition § 42 cmt. d.

70. Restatement of Employment Law § 8.02.

71. 823 F.2d 1199, 1202 (7th Cir. 1987) (quoting ILG Industries v. Scott, 273 N.E.2d 393, 396 (Ill. 1971)).

> proper balance between the purposes of trade secrets law and the strong policy in favor of fair and vigorous business competition.[72]

The definition of a trade secret in the UTSA does not expressly recognize this exception. Since the overriding goal of the UTSA was to codify "the basic principles of common law trade secret protection,"[73] however, it seems likely that the drafters intended to retain the traditional exemption for an employee's general knowledge and skill. And decisions interpreting state versions of the UTSA have applied this exception. For example, in *Bendinger v. Marshalltown Trowell Co.* a trowel manufacturing company sued its former factory manager after he took a similar position with a competitor. Applying the state's version of the UTSA, the Arkansas Supreme Court reasoned that none of the plaintiff's trade secrets had been misappropriated because the defendant "is only using his *general* knowledge gained through his education and his twenty-seven years of experience in the trowel industry [which] poses no threat to [plaintiff's] trade secrets."[74]

Although the DTSA's trade secret definition is also silent on the issue, legislative history clearly indicates that Congress intended the exception to apply. The House Judiciary Committee report on the EEA states that it "is not intended to be used to prosecute employees who change employers or start their own companies using general knowledge and skills developed while employed."[75] The remedies section of the DTSA reflects this approach. It provides that an injunction against trade secret misappropriation cannot prevent a person from taking a new job merely based on "information the person knows."[76] Accordingly, decisions applying the DTSA recognize that an employee's general knowledge or skill is not a trade secret.[77]

For example, suppose that corporation R, which manufactures trucks, provides training so that employee S can operate a new state-of-the-art machine that only a few manufacturers are currently using. The knowledge S obtains in this training is not a trade secret. Or imagine that T, a new attorney at a law firm, gets valuable feedback from senior attorneys at the firm about how to improve her brief-writing skills. The resulting improvement in her skills cannot be a trade secret.

The line between general skill and knowledge, on the one hand, and a trade secret, on the other, is often difficult to draw. Some of the factors courts have considered in making this distinction are whether the information: (1) was disclosed to the employee by the employer or produced by the former employee's own efforts; (2) was contained in physical records taken from the employer or merely in the former employee's memory; (3) is used elsewhere in the industry or is peculiar to the former employer; and (4) solves a specific problem that others in the industry have been unable to solve.

72. *Id.* at 1205 (quoting Fleming Sales Co., Inc. v. Bailey, 611 F. Supp. 507, 514 (N.D. Ill. 1985)).

73. UTSA pref. note.

74. Bendinger v. Marshalltown Trowell Co., 994 S.W.2d 468, 475 (Ark. 1999) (emphasis in original).

75. H.R. Rep. No. 104-788, at 7 (1996).

76. 18 U.S.C. § 1836(b)(3)(A)(i)(I).

77. *See, e.g.*, United States v. Hsu, 155 F.3d 189, 196–97 (3d Cir. 1998).

§ 2.03 "Independent Economic Value"

[A] Overview

To qualify as a trade secret under the UTSA, information must derive "independent economic value, actual or potential, from not being generally known to, and not being readily ascertainable by proper means by, other persons who can obtain economic value from its disclosure or use."[78] The DTSA standard is almost identical.[79]

What is "independent economic value"? The term "independent" means that the information must have value that is separate and apart from its value to the trade secret owner; that is, it must also have value to *others*.[80] The legislative history of the UTSA suggests that the drafters believed that "economic value" was synonymous with "commercial value."[81] As the Iowa Supreme Court observed in *US West Communication, Inc. v. Office of Consumer Advocate*, secret information "that would be useful to a competitor and require cost, time and effort to duplicate is of economic value."[82] Some cases suggest that the independent economic value requirement codifies the Restatement factor that the information have "value"—that it provides a "competitive advantage" over other businesses.[83]

As a practical matter, many courts seem to presume that this element is satisfied by the mere existence of a lawsuit, because a rational plaintiff would only sue to protect information that has value. But the value element is more complex than this presumption suggests. First, the value must arise "from" the relative secrecy of the information. Suppose that U's tire factory uses an obsolete secret device; the device has economic value to U because it allows the plant to function, not because it is a secret. Accordingly, it cannot be protected as a trade secret.[84] Second, the information must be valuable both to the trade secret claimant and to "other persons." U's obsolete secret device has no economic value to other tire manufacturers or anyone other than U.[85]

In *United States v. Hanjuan Jin*, the district court analyzed the type of evidence used to prove this element.[86] It observed that the degree to which the information conferred an economic advantage on the owner, together with the cost and effort

78. UTSA § 1(4).

79. 18 U.S.C. § 1839(3)(B).

80. *See* George S. May Int'l Co. v. Int'l Profit Assoc., 628 N.E.2d 647, 653 (Ill. App. 1993) (information "must be sufficiently secret to impart economic value to both its owner and its competitors because of its relative secrecy").

81. Sandeen, *supra* note 54, at 526.

82. 498 N.W.2d 711, 714 (Iowa 1993).

83. *See, e.g.*, Electro-Craft Corp. v. Controlled Motion, Inc., 332 N.W.2d 890, 900 (Minn. 1983).

84. *See* Buffets, Inc. v. Klinke, 73 F.3d 965, 969 (9th Cir. 1996) (job manuals were not trade secrets because "while it may have been reasonable to conclude that [the plaintiff] obtained value from the manuals, there is little to suggest that any value was obtained from the manuals being kept secret").

85. *See, e.g.*, Optic Graphics, Inc. v. Agee, 591 A.2d 578 (Md. App. 1991) (information was not a trade secret because it was useful only to plaintiff).

86. 833 F. Supp. 2d 977 (N.D. Ill. 2012).

necessary to develop the information, were helpful criteria.[87] Further, the court noted that in some situations the value of the secret "is evident in the circumstances of the offense, such as a defendant's acknowledgement that the secret is valuable or the asking price set by a defendant for the trade secret."[88]

How much economic value must the information have? As yet, there is no clear answer to this question because neither the UTSA nor DTSA addresses the issue. Some courts fill this gap by using the standard adopted by the Restatement (Third) of Unfair Competition.[89] Under this approach, the information must provide an "advantage" over others who do not possess such information: "The advantage, however, need not be great. It is sufficient if the secret provides an advantage that is more than trivial."[90]

In sum, the exact parameters of "independent economic value" are uncertain. As the *Hanjuan Jin* court observed, "this is a fact-intensive analysis for which there are no bright-line rules."[91] Accordingly, one authority warns: "Imaginative lawyers and courts will continue to have a field day in defining ... 'independent economic value'... as used in ... the Uniform Act."[92]

[B] Actual Value

Actual value is often established through direct evidence. For instance, in *Metallurgical Industries Inc. v. Fourtek, Inc.* the plaintiff proved value in part through testimony by its vice president that customers regarded the zinc powder produced by its secret process "as a better product than that [produced] by the coldstream process used by others."[93] Often the most convincing direct evidence is that the defendant has used the plaintiff's information to successfully provide the same service or product to customers. Suppose that V, a car dealership, has a database containing secret information about its past customers. If employees of W, a competing dealership, appropriate and use such information to sell cars to V's customers, this provides compelling evidence of its value.

Actual value can also be proven by circumstantial evidence, such as: (1) the time and money that the plaintiff invested to develop the secret; (2) the plaintiff's use of the information; (3) the willingness of others to pay for the information; and (4) the defendant's efforts to obtain the information.[94]

87. *Id.* at 1009.
88. *Id.* at 1010.
89. *See, e.g.*, Copart, Inc. v. Sparta Consulting, Inc., 277 F. Supp. 3d 1127, 1153 (E.D. Cal. 2017).
90. Restatement (Third) of Unfair Competition § 39 cmt. e.
91. *Hanjuan Jin*, 833 F. Supp. 2d at 1010.
92. Melvin F. Jager, Trade Secrets Law § 3:35 (2019).
93. 790 F.2d 1195, 1201 (5th Cir. 1986).
94. *See, e.g.*, Editions Play Bac, S.A. v. Western Pub. Co., Inc., 31 U.S.P.Q.2d 1338 (S.D.N.Y. 1999) (willingness of two publishers to pay plaintiff for right to market educational game was sufficient evidence of independent economic value to preclude summary judgment on issue). *See also* Restatement (Third) of Unfair Competition § 39 cmt. e.

[C] Potential Value

The plaintiff in a trade secret case may have trouble proving that the information has actual value. For example, if X develops an idea for a new product, with the hope of selling the product to the public in the future, X may find it difficult to prove that the idea has actual value. Therefore, a plaintiff need only prove that the information has "potential" value.

For instance, in *Altavion, Inc. v. Konica Minolta Systems Laboratory, Inc.*, the California Court of Appeal held that the design concepts underlying plaintiff's innovative barcode system had potential value because the defendant (1) expressed "serious interest" in purchasing plaintiff's technology and, when negotiations failed, (2) applied for patents that covered the technology.[95]

Another example is *University Accounting Service, LLC v. Schulton*, where defendant Schulton, a former employee, took information about plaintiff's customers when he left the company. After the plaintiff sued for misappropriation, Schulton moved for summary judgment on the basis that the information had no economic value.[96] Although the names of the customers were publicly known, the court observed that other data about them had potential value, including "customer-specific preferences and priorities."[97] Otherwise, the court reasoned, "there would be no reason why Schulton would have taken them with him when he left his employment."[98] It concluded that a "rational finder of fact could conclude that this information gives [the plaintiff] a potential business advantage sufficient to qualify as a trade secret."[99]

Yet the precise meaning of "potential" value is far from clear and will undoubtedly be the subject of future litigation.

§ 2.04 Not "Generally Known" and Not "Readily Ascertainable by Proper Means"

[A] Relative Secrecy

The most obvious requirement for trade secret protection—as the name of the doctrine implies—is secrecy. As the Supreme Court observed in *Kewanee Oil Co. v. Bicron Corp.*, "[t]he subject of a trade secret must be secret...."[100] Yet absolute secrecy is not essential. The law requires only *relative secrecy*.

For example, the UTSA and DTSA reflect the common law principle that "more than one person can be entitled to trade secret protection with respect to the same

95. 171 Cal. Rptr. 3d 714, 744 (App. 2014).

96. 2019 WL 2425122 (D. Or. June 10, 2019).

97. *Id.* at *5.

98. *Id.*

99. *Id.*

100. 416 U.S. 470, 475 (1974).

information."[101] Information may be a trade secret even if two or more companies in the same industry know about it, as long as it is not "generally known" within that industry. Further, even if only one person actually knows the information, it will not qualify for protection if others could readily ascertain it.

In practice, the owner of a trade secret must often disclose it to others in order to benefit from the information. For instance, if company Y manufactures a product that embodies a trade secret, it will need to reveal the secret to its employees, and potentially to suppliers, distributors, licensees, and franchisees as well. A trade secret that is disclosed in a limited and controlled manner will still meet the relative secrecy requirement.[102]

In order to qualify for protection as a trade secret under the UTSA and DTSA, the information must derive value "from not being generally known to, and not being readily ascertainable" by "proper means by," other persons who can obtain economic value from its disclosure or use.[103] In addition to the requirements that the information not be "generally known" or "readily ascertainable," both approaches recognize a third limitation: an employee's general knowledge and skill cannot be protected as a trade secret.[104]

As a practical matter, many courts appear to ignore the distinction between "generally known" and "readily ascertainable" information—because the evidence used to establish each one overlaps to some extent. For instance, in *Basic American, Inc. v. Shatila* the Idaho Supreme Court used the Restatement of Torts factors to help interpret the state's version of the UTSA; it commented that all six factors "address the issue of whether the information in question is generally known or readily ascertainable."[105]

The analysis below examines the level of secrecy necessary for a trade secret to *arise*. Chapter 6 explores when a trade secret will *end* due to lack of secrecy.

[B] Not "Generally Known"

[1] Overview

The requirement that information not be "generally known" concerns what other persons *actually* know, not what they might *potentially* know in the future. Suppose that Z has a secret formula for making an innovative cocktail that others could easily duplicate after tasting the drink; but she has not yet provided any of these cocktails

101. UTSA pref. note.

102. *See* § 2.05.

103. UTSA § 1(4)(i); 18 U.S.C. § 1839(3)(B). As originally drafted, the EEA trade secret definition referred to information that was not generally known to or readily ascertainable by "the public." The legislative history of the DTSA shows that the reason this language was stricken and replaced by "another person who can obtain economic value from the disclosure or use of the information" was to bring the "Federal definition of a trade secret into conformity" with the UTSA definition. Sen. Rep. No. 114-220, at 10 (2016).

104. *See* § 2.02[C].

105. 992 P.2d 175, 184 (Idaho 1999).

to others. The formula is not generally known because no one beyond Z is aware of it—at least for now.

Under the Restatement of Torts approach, trade secret protection did not extend to "[m]atters of public knowledge or of general knowledge in an industry."[106] The UTSA/DTSA requirement that the information not be "generally known" expresses almost the same concept. Accordingly, case law developed under the Restatement is helpful in determining the meaning of "generally known."

What if information claimed to be a trade secret is only slightly different from what is generally known? As the court explained in *Microbix Biosystems, Inc. v. Biowhitakker, Inc.*:

> [A]s a matter of common sense, generally known information need not be *exactly* the same as the alleged trade secret. If, as here, there is no substantial difference between the alleged trade secret and what is generally known, there is no protectable trade secret.[107]

In a situation like this where there is no significant difference, of course, the information would presumably also lack protection because it has no economic value.

Whose knowledge is relevant? While the Restatement considered both the "public" and any relevant "industry," the UTSA and DTSA consider a narrower group: other persons who can obtain economic value from its disclosure or use. Depending on the circumstances, this group might include the companies in a particular industry or large segments of the public. The UTSA drafters explained that:

> The language "not being generally known to ... other persons" does not require that information be generally known to the public for trade secret rights to be lost. If the principal persons who can obtain economic benefit from information are aware of it, there is no trade secret. A method of casting metal, for example, may be unknown to the general public but readily known within the foundry industry.[108]

Under this approach, information that is known to some participants within an industry—but not all of the "principal persons"—may qualify for protection. As the UTSA drafters noted: "Because a trade secret need not be exclusive to confer a competitive advantage, different independent developers can acquire rights in the same trade secret."[109] Suppose that only ten companies are involved in mining uranium. If only three of those companies, for example, are aware of an innovative procedure for such mining, it is eligible for protection as a trade secret. On the other hand, if most companies know about the procedure, it is not a trade secret.

But consider this factual wrinkle. Assume instead that nine of the ten companies independently develop the same mining procedure, but none of the companies know

---

106. Restatement of Torts § 757 cmt. b.

107. 172 F. Supp. 2d 665, 674 (D. Md. 2000) (emphasis in original).

108. UTSA § 1 cmt.

109. *Id.*

that the others have done so. If such widespread industry knowledge cannot be proven, then the information will be treated as a trade secret—even though it should not be.

[2] Proving this Element

Proving a negative is notoriously difficult. Accordingly, courts often rely on circumstantial evidence in concluding that certain information is not generally known.

Some courts in UTSA states have used the Restatement of Torts factors to make this determination. Two factors are particularly important: "the amount of effort or money expended by him in developing the information" and "the extent of measures taken by him to guard the secrecy of the information." First, if a business has devoted strenuous efforts or large sums of money to develop certain information, this suggests that the information was not generally known; if it were, the business would have no need to expend this effort or money. In one case, for instance, the plaintiff claimed a trade secret in a process for producing hash brown potatoes. The court stressed that the plaintiff had devoted almost six years to developing the process, which it would not have done if the process were generally known.[110] Second, when a business owner has undertaken measures to guard the secrecy of the claimed trade secret, this shows that the owner believes that the information is not generally known.

Other factors that courts have considered on this point include: (a) statements by the defendant or by experts about the novelty of the information; (b) the willingness of others to pay for the information; (c) the defendant's use of improper means of acquisition; and (d) the issuance of a patent based on the information.

An illustrative case is *Learning Curve Toys, Inc. v. PlayWood Toys, Inc.*, where a toy designer sued a manufacturer for misappropriating its concept for a "noise-producing toy railroad track."[111] The Seventh Circuit reversed the trial court's JNOV for the defendant manufacturer, finding that there was substantial evidence to show that the concept "was not generally known outside of [plaintiff] PlayWood's business."[112] The plaintiff's expert witness testified that the concept was "unique" in the toy industry, and would allow a seller to "differentiate itself from a host of competitors who [were] making a generic product."[113] The court also noted that the defendant was the first seller to put such a track on the market, more than a year after the plaintiff developed the concept. Finally, the court stressed that the defendant had successfully obtained a patent on the toy, which indicated that the concept was sufficiently novel to qualify for patent protection.

Direct evidence can also be used to show that particular information is generally known, especially within a particular industry. An example is *Noah v. Enesco Corporation*, where the court found that plaintiff's concept for figurines of "animals inter-

---

110. *Basic American*, 992 P.2d at 185.

111. 342 F.3d 714, 723 (7th Cir. 2003).

112. *Id.*

113. *Id.*

acting with each other" after leaving Noah's Ark was generally known in the giftware industry, because other companies had previously sold "similar depictions."[114] Similarly, if employees from six of the eight firms in a particular industry testify that their firms know the information, it is generally known in the industry.

[C] Not "Readily Ascertainable by Proper Means"

[1] Overview

The requirement that information not be "readily ascertainable by proper means" concerns what other persons might *potentially* know in the future, not what they *actually* know.[115] Recall Z's secret formula for making an innovative cocktail, which others could easily duplicate if they tried. The formula is readily ascertainable, even though it is not generally known. Thus, it cannot qualify for trade secret protection. The fact that no other person has actually figured out the formula is irrelevant.

As a rule, information in the public domain cannot be a trade secret. As the Supreme Court explained in *Bonito Boats v. Thunder Craft Boats, Inc.*, "concepts within the public grasp, or those so obvious that they readily could be, are the tools of creation available to all."[116] However, a compilation of data from the public domain may qualify for protection.[117]

Under the Restatement of Torts approach, "a substantial element of secrecy must exist, so that, except by the use of improper means, there would be difficulty in acquiring the information."[118] The UTSA/DTSA requirement that the information not be readily ascertainable by proper means expresses the same basic concept. Thus, courts have used case law developed under the Restatement to help interpret this standard.

[2] Not "Readily Ascertainable"

The UTSA and DTSA do not define the term "readily ascertainable." However, the UTSA offers examples in a comment:

> Information is readily ascertainable if it is available in trade journals, reference books, or published materials. Often, the nature of a product lends itself to being readily copied as soon as it is available on the market.[119]

The comment then provides an illustration where information is not readily ascertainable: if reverse engineering a particular product would be "lengthy and expen-

---

114. 911 F. Supp. 299, 301, 304 (N.D. Ill 1995).

115. Some courts influenced by the Restatement approach effectively ignore this requirement by imposing liability for misappropriation—even when the information is readily accessible—if the defendant acquired it by improper means. *See* §4.01[C].

116. 489 U.S. 141, 156 (1989).

117. *See* §2.04[D].

118. Restatement of Torts §757 cmt. b. However, some courts following this approach found misappropriation when improper means were used to obtain it, even if the information was readily ascertainable.

119. UTSA §1 cmt.

sive."[120] At bottom, the term "readily ascertainable" is ambiguous. As the Vermont Supreme Court noted in *Dicks v. Jenson*, there is no "standard benchmark" for determining when it is met.[121]

Most jurisdictions broadly agree that whether information is readily ascertainable depends on the "degree of time, effort, and expense required of a defendant to acquire or reproduce the alleged trade secret information by other proper means."[122] Thus, if acquiring such information from examination of a competitor's product would be "difficult, costly, or time-consuming," it is not readily ascertainable.[123] In practice, the application of this standard is a fact-intensive inquiry.

For example, in *Buffets, Inc. v. Klinke* the Ninth Circuit held that recipes for "staples such as BBQ chicken and macaroni and cheese" were not trade secrets, noting that "very little effort would be required to 'discover' them" because they were "little more than typical American fare."[124]

In contrast, the Eighth Circuit concluded in *AvidAir Helicopter Supply, Inc. v. Rolls-Royce Corp.* that a manufacturer's "information letters" which helped repair shops overhaul helicopter engines were protected as trade secrets, because duplicating the information would require "a substantial investment of time, effort, and energy."[125] Similarly, the court in *Fireworks Spectacular, Inc. v. Premier Pyrotechnics, Inc.* held that the identities of potential customers for fireworks and other information contained in plaintiffs' customer lists was not readily ascertainable.[126] It stressed that plaintiffs had invested "a great amount of time, effort, and expense" in developing the information, "including hundreds of hours of 'cold-calling.'"[127]

Other factors that courts have considered in determining whether information is "readily ascertainable" include: (1) the extent of the plaintiff's efforts, money, and time in developing the information; (2) plaintiff's precautions against disclosure; (3) the willingness of others to pay for the information; and (4) the defendant's use of improper means of acquisition.[128]

As a rule, information that the public can access with relative ease—such as information in a reference book—is readily ascertainable. For instance, in *Krafft v. Downey* the Pennsylvania Supreme Court held that a process for transferring photographic images to flagstone was not a trade secret because the process "was ascer-

120. *Id.*

121. 172 Vt. 43, 49 (2001).

122. Amoco Prod. Co. v. Laird, 622 N.E.2d 912, 918 (Ind. 1993). *See also, e.g.*, Fireworks Spectacular, Inc. v. Premier Pyrotechnics, Inc., 147 F. Supp. 2d 1057 (D. Kan. 2001); Marshall v. Gipson Steel, Inc., 806 So. 2d 266 (Miss. 2002).

123. Restatement (Third) of Unfair Competition § 39 cmt. f.

124. 73 F.3d 965, 968 (9th Cir. 1996).

125. 663 F.3d 966, 973 (8th Cir. 2011).

126. 147 F. Supp. 2d 1057 (D. Kan. 2001).

127. *Id.* at 1066.

128. Restatement (Third) of Unfair Competition § 39 cmt. f; Editions Play Bac, S.A. v. Western Publishing Co., 31 U.S.P.Q.2d 1338 (S.D.N.Y 1993) (citing cases).

tainable to anyone with access to the internet, a bookstore, or the library."[129] On the other hand, information contained in a source that the public is unlikely to access, such as an obscure publication, does not meet this standard. Thus, information in a book written in French that sold only 50 copies or an article published in an Alaskan newspaper with 100 subscribers and no online presence is not readily ascertainable.

Further, even information contained in easily accessed publications may not be readily ascertainable under some circumstances. The Restatement notes that "the theoretical possibility of reconstructing the secret from published materials containing scattered references to portions of the information" does not mean that the secret is readily ascertainable.[130] For example, if A's secret process for purifying copper ore could be pieced together only by assembling data fragments from 20 different published articles, the process is not readily ascertainable.

The principles discussed above should logically apply to information posted on the internet, as the *Krafft* court suggested. Much like the contents of a reference book, relevant information on the internet can usually be located without undue effort, time, or cost. However, if information is posted only for a brief period of time or in a manner that makes it difficult to locate—for instance, if it is not indexed by a search engine or only appears on the password-protected portion of a website—then it is not readily ascertainable.[131]

Information contained in a U.S. patent or a published patent application is normally seen as readily accessible.[132] The reason is that "patents are intended to be widely disclosed" and, therefore, "[p]ublished patent applications are in fact studied by inventors in the relevant field."[133] However, there is some question about whether information in foreign patents should treated in the same manner. For instance, it may well be that a patent issued in Chile or Iceland is more akin to an obscure magazine article, than a published reference book. In this context, it is important to note that information in foreign patents is considered as "prior art" to determine whether an invention satisfies the patent elements of novelty and nonobviousness. Yet this approach may not apply to trade secrets because the requirements for patent protection are much more rigorous.[134]

In contrast, a number of cases held that information in court records is not readily ascertainable because it is unlikely to be noticed. As the Fourth Circuit noted in *Hoechst Diafoil Co. v. Nan Ya Plastics Corp.*, "widely-disseminated sources" such as

---

129. 68 A.3d 329, 338 (Pa. 2013).

130. Restatement (Third) of Unfair Competition § 39 cmt. f.

131. *Cf.* DVD Copy Control Ass'n, Inc. v. Bunner, 10 Cal. Rptr. 3d 185, 192 (App. 2004) (internet posting does not terminate a trade secret if it is "sufficiently obscure or transient or otherwise limited").

132. Restatement (Third) of Unfair Competition § 39 cmt. f ("[I]nformation that is disclosed in a patent ... does not qualify for protection...."). The same is true for documents comprising the "prosecution history" or "file wrapper" for the patent, including correspondence between the applicant and the U.S. Patent and Trademark Office.

133. BondPro Corp. v. Siemens Power Generation, Inc., 463 F.3d 702, 707 (7th Cir. 2006).

134. *See* § 3.02[B] (discussing the differences between trade secrets and patents).

trade journals, reference books, and other published materials are "qualitatively different from the files of a single district court."[135] Similarly, in *Gates Rubber Co. v. Bando Chemical Industries, Ltd.*, the court stressed that there was no evidence that "a competitor had access to or learned of the [information in the court records] during the period after the hearing and before the record was sealed."[136]

As a general matter, information contained in most government records—while available to the public in theory—is not readily ascertainable. Bids for government contracts, applications for land use permits, or requests for certain kinds of licenses, for example, may contain sensitive information but are unlikely to be read by ordinary citizens.

[3] "Proper Means"

The UTSA and DTSA do not define the term "proper means." Instead, a UTSA comment provides examples that offer limited guidance. It states that "[p]roper means *include*":

- Discovery by independent invention;
- Discovery by "reverse engineering," that is, by starting with the known product and working backward to find the method by which it was developed;
- Discovery under a license from the owner of the trade secret;
- Observation of the item in public use or on public display; and
- Obtaining the trade secret from published literature.[137]

Notably, the approved methods in these examples do not involve criminal, tortious, or unethical behavior. This is significant because a comment to the UTSA observes that "[o]ne of the broadly stated policies behind trade secret law is 'the maintenance of standards of commercial ethics.' "[138] This suggests that illegal or unethical methods would not be "proper means."

Although the UTSA attempts to define "improper means"—the logical counterpart of "proper means"—this definition merely consists of examples.[139] Its § 1(1) explains that " 'improper means' *includes* theft, bribery, misrepresentation, breach or inducement of a breach of a duty to maintain secrecy, or espionage through electronic or other means."[140] This non-exclusive list of examples falls short of a usable definition. Moreover, a comment to this section states that "[a] complete catalogue of improper means is not possible."[141] At a minimum, however, these examples imply that at least certain types of criminal, tortious, or unethical conduct would not be "proper means."

---

135. 174 F.3d 411, 419 (4th Cir. 1999).
136. 9 F.3d 823, 849 (10th Cir. 1993).
137. UTSA § 1 cmt. (emphasis added).
138. *Id.* (citing Kewanee Oil Co. v. Bicron Corp., 416 U.S. 470 (1974)).
139. *See* § 4.02[D] for a detailed analysis of "improper means."
140. UTSA § 1(1) (emphasis added).
141. *Id.*

The DTSA follows the same pattern, providing similar examples of improper means rather than a specific definition.[142]

The Restatement (Third) of Unfair Competition helpfully states that where a trade secret is acquired through "conduct that is itself a tortious or criminal invasion of the trade secret owner's rights, the acquisition ordinarily will be regarded as improper."[143] However, it cautions that the acquisition of a trade secret "can be improper" even where the method is "not independently wrongful."[144] At least under some circumstances, then, an acquisition method that is not "wrongful" may still be "improper."

[D] Combinations of Information

A combination of information can be a trade secret, even if each individual component is generally known or readily ascertainable, as long as the combination as a whole qualifies for protection. As one court explained:

> Combinations of public information from a variety of different sources when combined in a novel way can be a trade secret. It does not matter if a portion of the trade secret is generally known, or even that every individual portion of the trade secret is generally known, as long as the combination of all such information is not generally known.[145]

For example, in *Metallurgical Industries Inc. v. Fourtek, Inc.*, the plaintiff sought trade secret protection for modifications it made to its carbide reclamation furnaces: the installation of chill plates, multiple crucibles, pump filters, and unitary graphite heating elements.[146] It argued that the "process, taken as a whole, is a trade secret in the carbide business."[147] In turn, the defendants observed that all of these devices were "well known to modern manufacturing" and, accordingly, that the overall process "can be no secret, either."[148] However, the Fifth Circuit ruled for the plaintiff on the basis that this combination was not generally known in the industry.

Experian Information Solutions, Inc. v. Nationwide Marketing Services, Inc. also illustrates the point.[149] There plaintiff claimed a trade secret in a compilation of over 250 million names and addresses that it "gathered from generally available sources that are matters of public knowledge."[150] In reversing summary judgment for the defendant, the Ninth Circuit held that the plaintiff had established a triable issue of fact

---

142. 18 U.S.C. § 1839(6)(A).

143. Restatement (Third) of Unfair Competition § 43 cmt. c.

144. *Id.*

145. 02 Micro Int'l Ltd. v. Monolithic Power Sys., Inc., 420 F. Supp. 2d 1070, 1089–90 (N.D. Cal. 2006).

146. 790 F.2d 1195 (5th Cir. 1986).

147. *Id.* at 1198.

148. *Id.* at 1202.

149. 893 F.3d 1176 (9th Cir. 2018).

150. *Id.* at 1188.

that its information was not readily ascertainable by competitors, because the verification procedures it used gave the data a high degree of "reliability and accuracy."[151]

§ 2.05 Reasonable Efforts to Maintain Secrecy

[A] Overview

Under the UTSA and DTSA, information is protected as a trade secret only if the owner made reasonable efforts to keep it secret.[152] Thus, the UTSA defines a trade secret, in part, as information that "is the subject of efforts that are reasonable under the circumstances to maintain its secrecy."[153] The DTSA expresses the same concept in slightly different phrasing, requiring that "the owner ... has taken reasonable measures to keep such information secret."[154]

The requirement of reasonable efforts is a change from the Restatement of Torts approach. Under the Restatement, "the extent of measures taken by [the owner] to guard the secrecy of the information" is a relevant factor "considered in determining" whether a trade secret exists, but is not always necessary.[155]

Interestingly, the Restatement (Third) of Unfair Competition follows the older Restatement of Torts view. It does not require the owner to make reasonable efforts—or indeed any efforts—to maintain secrecy.[156] Instead, it merely notes that "[p]recautions taken to maintain the secrecy of information are relevant in determining whether the information qualifies for protection as a trade secret."[157]

Obviously, the owner who intentionally discloses the secret to the public cannot meet the UTSA/DTSA standard.[158] Yet in virtually all cases, the owner has taken some steps to protect the secret. Whether these steps constitute reasonable efforts to maintain secrecy is a question of fact, dependent on the circumstances of the particular case. There is no standard list of precautions that will always satisfy the standard. The safeguards that are adequate in one situation may be inadequate in another.

Under the UTSA and DTSA, the trade secret owner must take reasonable steps to protect its information against misappropriation by both *outsiders,* such as business competitors, and *insiders,* such as employees, suppliers, customers, licensees, and others with whom it has a business relationship. In the ordinary course of business, an owner may be able to exploit the secret only by disclosing it to employees or others.

151. *Id.*
152. The rationale for this requirement is not entirely clear. *See* § 11.05.
153. UTSA § 1(4)(ii).
154. 18 U.S.C. § 1839(3)(A).
155. Restatement of Torts § 757 cmt. b.
156. Restatement (Third) of Unfair Competition § 39.
157. *Id.* cmt. g.
158. *See* § 6.02[B].

After all, if B owns a large factory that uses a secret process, certain employees must know the secret. It is well settled that controlled disclosure to employees and other insiders is permitted.[159]

In evaluating the owner's efforts to protect secrecy, courts usually consider two categories of safeguards: (1) physical security measures; and (2) confidentiality procedures. Physical security measures such as computer passwords, data encryption, document storage vaults, fencing, guards, trash protocols, and video surveillance help to protect secrets—particularly from outsiders who might obtain them by burglary, espionage, or other improper means. Confidentiality procedures apply to employees and related businesses; these procedures signal to "employees and to others that certain information is secret and should not be disclosed."[160] They include confidentiality agreements, document markings, employee manuals, exit interviews for departing employees, policy statements, restrictions on document access, and other measures designed to prevent a breach of the duty to maintain secrecy.

[B] Defining "Reasonable" Efforts

The reasonableness of the owner's efforts "depends on a balancing of costs and benefits that will vary from case to case."[161] Because this turns on the circumstances of the particular case, the UTSA and DTSA do not provide clear guidance on the meaning of the standard.

The UTSA drafters note that "reasonable efforts to maintain secrecy have been held to include advising employees of the existence of a trade secret, limiting access to a trade secret on [a] 'need to know basis,' and controlling plant access."[162] This list of examples is not a useful template because it fails to consider the circumstances of individual cases.

More helpfully, the same UTSA comment explains that courts "do not require that extreme and unduly expensive procedures be taken to protect trade secrets against flagrant industrial espionage."[163] It supports this point by citing *E.I. duPont deNemours & Co., Inc. v. Christopher.*[164] In *DuPont,* the Fifth Circuit reasoned that a corporation building a new plant was not required to install a temporary roof over the site in order to preclude aerial photographs that could be used to deduce its secret process:

> We should not require a person or corporation to take unreasonable precautions to prevent another from doing that which he ought not to do in the first place. Reasonable precautions against predatory eyes we may require, but an impenetrable fortress is an unreasonable requirement, and we are not

159. UTSA § 1 cmt. ("It follows that reasonable use of a trade secret including controlled disclosure to employees and licensees is consistent with the requirement of relative secrecy.").

160. Electro-Craft Corp. v. Controlled Motion, Inc., 332 N.W.2d 890, 902 (Minn. 1983).

161. Rockwell Graphic Systems, Inc. v. DEV Industries, Inc., 925 F.2d 174, 179 (7th Cir. 1991).

162. UTSA § 1 cmt.

163. *Id.*

164. 431 F.2d 1012 (5th Cir. 1970).

> disposed to burden industrial inventors with such a duty in order to protect the fruits of their efforts.[165]

The legislative history of the EEA, the predecessor to the DTSA, strikes the same theme as the UTSA comment quoted above:

> The definition of trade secret requires that the owner of the information must have taken objectively reasonable and active measures to protect the information from becoming known to unauthorized persons....[166]
>
> The fact that the owner did not exhaust every conceivable means by which the information could be kept secure does not mean that the information does not satisfy this requirement. Rather, a determination of the "reasonableness" of the steps taken by the owner to keep the information secret will vary from case to case and be dependent on the nature of the information in question.[167]

In practice, courts generally use a cost-benefit analysis to assess whether the owner's efforts were reasonable. The factors used in this analysis vary widely from case to case. For example, in *Matter of Innovative Construction Systems, Inc.*, the Seventh Circuit observed: "In essence, this requires an assessment of the size and nature of [the owner's] business, the cost to it of additional measures, and the degree to which such measures would decrease the risk of disclosure. What may be reasonable measures in one context may not necessarily be so in another."[168]

The Restatement (Third) of Unfair Competition notes that relevant factors include "the foreseeability of the conduct through which the secret was acquired and the availability and cost of effective precautions against such an acquisition, evaluated in light of the economic value of the trade secret."[169]

Suppose C owns a small mountain resort. What steps should she take to protect the secrecy of her customer list? In theory, the information might be misappropriated by either competitors or employees. C should take simple physical security precautions, such as ensuring that the list cannot be easily seen by customers or other visitors and locking the office at night. C should also adopt basic confidentiality procedures: informing her employees that the list is a trade secret, having them execute confidentiality agreements, marking the list as confidential, and adopting computer security protocols for electronic versions of the list. Given the size, nature, and location of C's business, the value of the list, and the cost of more intensive precautions (such as guards or video surveillance), C would probably not be required to do more.[170]

---

165. *Id.* at 1017. On the other hand, since high-resolution aerial photos are now widely available today, perhaps a modern court would expect an owner in DuPont's position to take additional precautions.

166. H.R. Rep. No. 104-788, at 7 (1996).

167. *Id.* at 12–13.

168. 793 F.2d 875, 884 (7th Cir. 1986).

169. Restatement (Third) of Unfair Competition § 43 cmt. c.

170. *Cf.* Dicks v. Jensen, 768 A.2d 1279 (Vt. 2001) (holding that resort owner failed to take reasonable precautions for customer list where employees did not sign confidentiality agreements and names of tour groups were posted where any office visitor could see them).

The modern trend toward storing data in the "cloud" presents a special challenge. Almost all decisions analyzing reasonable efforts have involved trade secrets located in a place controlled by the owner—either in tangible form (such as a document in an office file) or in electronic form (in a company server). But the storage of data in offsite servers means that many trade secrets are now under the control of third parties. Presumably, reasonable efforts in this context might include: (1) a company policy on the types of data that can be stored in the cloud; (2) a confidentiality agreement with the vendor; (3) physical security measures at the server site; and (4) virtual security protocols for those servers, such as data encryption, multiple layers of authentication, and safeguards against employees downloading data onto personal devices. Future decisions will undoubtedly provide guidance on how the reasonable efforts standard will apply to cloud storage.

In practice, the reasonable efforts standard is difficult for courts to apply. First, in many cases judges could legitimately disagree about whether a particular set of precautions was sufficient. This leads to close cases where the result might easily have gone the other way.

Second, there is a significant risk of hindsight bias—the human tendency to believe that past events could have been predicted at the time. It is important to remember how the issue of reasonable efforts arises in litigation. When an owner sues for misappropriation, the efforts it took to maintain secrecy have *proven* to be unsuccessful; someone was able to obtain the secret. The owner always could have taken additional precautions that would have prevented the loss. In this context, the owner must prove that its *unsuccessful* efforts were sufficient to meet the *reasonable* efforts standard.[171] In a related context, the Supreme Court cautioned that "[a] factfinder should be aware ... of the distortion caused by hindsight bias and must be cautious of arguments reliant upon *ex post* reasoning."[172]

[C] Illustrative Decisions

Two key decisions help to define the boundary between reasonable measures and inadequate efforts: *Rockwell Graphic Systems, Inc. v. DEV Industries, Inc.*[173] and *Electro-Craft Corp. v. Controlled Motion, Inc.*[174] Each involves a large manufacturing company; the first produced printing presses, the second electric motors.

In *Rockwell*, each printing press part was depicted in a "piece part drawing," which included information on manufacturing methods, alloys, tolerances, and other sub-

---

171. At the same time, the defendant who contests the issue is in an awkward position. It must argue that the owner should taken greater precautions to prevent the defendant—or whoever the defendant received the secret through—from misappropriating the secret. In effect, the defendant says: "You should have made it harder for me to get the secret!" Particularly in a jury trial, this is a difficult argument for the defendant to make.

172. KSR Int'l Co. v. Teleflex Inc., 550 U.S. 398, 421 (2007) (discussing nonobviousness in patent law).

173. 925 F.2d 174 (7th Cir. 1991).

174. 332 N.W.2d 890 (Minn. 1983).

jects that could not be learned by merely inspecting the part. Copies of these drawings were sometimes given to subcontractors who manufactured parts. Rockwell used these physical security measures: (1) guards protected the fenced plant; (2) the drawings were kept in a vault; and (3) authorized employees had to sign drawings out of the vault and return them later. It also employed confidentiality procedures: (1) employees with access to the drawings signed nondisclosure agreements; (2) the drawings were stamped "confidential;" and (3) subcontractors who received copies of the drawings were required to sign nondisclosure agreements, which obligated them to return the copies after the order was filled. However, Rockwell did not prohibit subcontractors from copying the drawings; nor did it enforce the requirement that they return the copies. As a result, "tens of thousands of copies of these drawings [were] floating around outside Rockwell's vault, and many of these outside the company altogether."[175]

Rockwell sued DEV, a competing press manufacturer, and two of DEV's employees, who had previously worked for Rockwell, for trade secret misappropriation. DEV had 100 copies of Rockwell's piece part drawings; it claimed to have acquired them from Rockwell customers or vendors.[176] The district court granted summary judgment for the defendants on the basis that Rockwell had failed to take reasonable precautions. However, the Seventh Circuit reversed, finding that Rockwell had presented enough evidence to create a question of fact. It observed:

> Obviously Rockwell took some precautions, both physical (the vault security, the security guards ...) and contractual, to maintain the confidentiality of its piece part drawings. Obviously it could have taken more precautions. But at a cost, and the question is whether the additional benefit in security would have exceeded that cost. We do not suggest that the question can be answered with the same precision with which it can be posed, but neither can we say that no reasonable jury could find that Rockwell had done enough....[177]

In contrast, the *Electro-Craft Corp.* court held that the plaintiff (EEC) failed to take reasonable precautions to protect secrecy, and reversed the trial court's judgment in its favor. The background facts were similar to those in *Rockwell*: EEC manufactured motors; the trade secrets at issue were the "dimensions, tolerances, adhesives, and manufacturing processes" of its motor;[178] and it claimed that former employees had taken its trade secrets, started a new company, and used the information to develop competing motors.

Like Rockwell, EEC took some steps to protect its secrets: employing security guards; screening its publications for confidential information; and having some employees sign confidentiality agreements. But the court found that its physical security measures were insufficient: (1) many plant entrances were unguarded and unlocked;

175. *Rockwell*, 925 F.2d at 177.

176. This was a difficult claim to sustain since a security guard had caught one of the defendants —then a Rockwell employee—actually "removing piece part drawings from Rockwell's plant." *Id.* at 176.

177. *Id.* at 180.

178. *Electro-Craft*, 332 N.W.2d at 898.

(2) employees were not required to wear badges; (3) "[d]iscarded drawings and plans for motors were simply thrown away, not destroyed;" and (4) drawings and other documents were not kept in a central or locked location.[179]

More importantly, the court held that ECC's confidentiality procedures were fatally lax:

> ... EEC treated its information as if it were not secret. None of its technical documents were marked "Confidential," and drawings, dimensions, and parts were sent to customers and vendors without special marking. Employee access to documents was not restricted. ECC never issued a policy statement outlining what it considered to be secret. Many informal tours were given to vendors and customers without warnings as to confidential information. Further, two plants each had an "open house" at which the public was invited to observe manufacturing processes.[180]

Rockwell and *Electro-Craft Corp.* illustrate the difficulty that courts experience in applying the reasonable efforts standard. In each case, the trial court and the appellate court reached different decisions based on the same facts.

---

179. *Id.* at 902. However, the court found that these weak physical security measures were not fatal to plaintiff's suit, because the evidence "did not indicate that industrial espionage is a major problem" in the industry. *Id.*

180. *Id.* at 903.

Chapter 3

Trade Secret Interface with Other Doctrines

§ 3.01 Introduction

American law has traditionally recognized three main categories of intellectual property: patents, copyrights, and trademarks. In recent decades, trade secrets have evolved into an equally important fourth category. An amorphous fifth category—usually called confidential or proprietary information—governs the extent to which the law protects information that does not qualify for protection under the first four categories.

It is important to understand the relationship between trade secrets and these other doctrines. Most importantly, the outer boundaries of patent, copyright, and trademark law help to determine the scope of trade secret law, despite a certain amount of overlap. Chapter 2 explained what a trade secret *is*; this chapter helps to explain what a trade secret *is not*.

The evolution of trade secret law will be influenced by how these other doctrines develop over time. If we envision intellectual property law as a unified field, then the expansion or contraction of one doctrine will inevitably impact the others.

Finally, as a practical matter, the attorney who is familiar with the comparative strengths and weaknesses of each doctrine is best able to advise a client about the optimum form of protection. For example, a computer program might be protected by patent, copyright, or trade secret law—or even as confidential or proprietary information.

§ 3.02 Patent Law

[A] Overview

Patent law protects a broad variety of inventions: novel and nonobvious products of human ingenuity that serve a useful purpose. These can range from cutting-edge medicines to robotic technologies to more workaday inventions, like specialized tools or eco-friendly disposable silverware.

The Intellectual Property Clause of the Constitution empowers Congress to "promote the Progress of Science and useful Arts, by securing for limited Times to … Inventors the exclusive Right to their respective … Discoveries."[1] As the Clause indicates, patent law is expressly utilitarian. Its purpose is to give inventors an economic incentive to create valuable new inventions, in the form of a time-limited monopoly. The Supreme Court explained in *Kewanee Oil Co. v. Bicron Corp.* that:

> The patent laws promote this progress by offering a right of exclusion for a limited period as an incentive to inventors to risk the often enormous costs in terms of time, research, and development. The productive effort thereby fostered will have a positive effect on society through the introduction of new products and processes of manufacture into the economy, and the emanations by way of increased employment and better lives for our citizens.[2]

The Patent Act provides that a person who "invents or discovers any new and useful process, machine, manufacture, or composition of matter, or any new and useful improvement thereof" may obtain a patent from the U.S. Patent and Trademark Office (PTO).[3] Five elements are necessary for a patent: (1) patentable subject matter; (2) utility; (3) novelty; (4) nonobviousness; and (5) description/enablement.[4] Patentable subject matter encompasses virtually any product or process, except for laws of nature, natural phenomena, and abstract ideas.[5] The utility and novelty elements are met where the invention is useful and new. Nonobviousness requires that the invention not be obvious to a person having ordinary skill in the particular field. Finally, the inventor must describe the invention in sufficient detail such that a skilled person could replicate it.

1. U.S. Const. art. I, § 8, cl. 8.
2. 416 U.S. 470, 480 (1974).
3. 35 U.S.C. § 101.
4. 35 U.S.C. §§ 101, 102, 103, 112.
5. *See, e.g.*, Alice Corp. Pty. Ltd. v. CLS Bank Int'l, 573 U.S. 208, 216 (2014).

The term of a patent is 20 years from the date of application. During this period, the patentee has the right within the United States to prevent anyone else from making, using, selling, offering for sale, or importing the invention. As a practical matter, this gives the patentee the exclusive right to use or sell the invention during the term.

Patent infringement is a strict liability offense, and few defenses are available. A patent is presumed to be valid, but an accused infringer may raise the defense that the patent is invalid.

[B] Differences from Trade Secret Law

Patent law and trade secret law are close cousins, in that both protect the exclusive right to valuable information and both reflect utilitarian theory. However, there are several significant differences between them. The biggest difference is that a trade secret must be *secret*, while a patented invention must be *disclosed* to the public. In addition:

- The standards for obtaining a patent are rigorous, while it is comparatively easy to gain trade secret protection.
- The scope of information covered by patent law is quite narrow, while trade secret law protects a broad range of information.
- A patent right arises only when the PTO approves a patent application, but a trade secret does not require government approval.
- Patent law provides more powerful protection than trade secret law (e.g., independent creation and reverse engineering are not defenses to patent infringement, but are defenses to trade secret misappropriation).
- Patent infringement is a strict liability offense, while trade secret misappropriation requires that the defendant have actual or constructive knowledge of wrongful acquisition.
- A patent has a fixed duration, while a trade secret might last forever.

[C] Overlap with Trade Secret Law

The vast majority of trade secrets do not qualify for patent protection. Yet there is considerable overlap between the two doctrines because a patentable invention might be covered by either one.

Virtually every patentable invention is initially protected as a trade secret. Consider inventor A, who secretly develops the world's first anti-gravity machine. Almost certainly, the information embodied in the machine is a trade secret. The information is valuable; it is not generally known to the public or readily ascertainable; and A took steps to keep it secret. At some point, A will decide whether to seek a patent or continue to rely on trade secret law.

The choice between patent law and trade secret law turns on two main factors. First, how likely is it that the patent will be granted? If patentability is highly probable, this factor will normally be dispositive. Where patentability is unclear, however, the inventor who applies for a patent takes a major risk.[6] Most patent applications are published 18 months after filing. If the application is denied, the inventor will lose both patent and trade secret protection, since the published application will be a public disclosure that destroys secrecy. In this situation, the inventor may decide to rely on trade secret law.

Second, which approach provides greater security for the inventor? Patent protection is more powerful, but may have a shorter duration. If the duration of trade secret protection will be significantly longer—because the risks of disclosure, independent creation, and reverse engineering are low—the inventor may prefer to rely on trade secret law. On other hand, the rate of technological change in the particular industry may be so rapid that the 20-year duration of a patent is more than sufficient.

[D] Preemption?

It is well settled that the federal Patent Act does not preempt state trade secret law. The leading decision on the point is *Kewanee Oil Co. v. Bicron Corp.*, where the Supreme Court held that Ohio's state trade secret law—based on the Restatement of Torts—was not preempted.[7]

The issue in *Kewanee Oil* was conflict preemption: whether the Ohio law "'clashes with the objectives of the federal patent laws.'"[8] The Court focused on three policies that underpin the patent laws: (1) to encourage inventors to create new products and processes; (2) to ensure that state law does not remove information from the public domain; and (3) to have inventors disclose the secrets of their inventions to the public. The Court quickly observed the Ohio law did not clash with the first two polices. It reasoned that "the patent policy of encouraging invention is not disturbed by the existence of another form of incentive to invention."[9] In addition, it noted that trade secret law did not remove information from the public domain.

However, the Court conceded that it was more difficult to reconcile the patent policy of disclosure with the trade secret requirement of nondisclosure. It noted that if a state law "were to cause a substantial risk that holders of patentable inventions would not seek patents, but rather would rely on the state protection, we would be compelled to hold that such a system could not constitutionally continue to exist."[10]

6. An example is seeking a patent on a business method. Although the PTO has issued a number of business method patents, their validity is questionable. The Supreme Court invalidated business method patents in two key decisions, but failed to provide standards for when such a patent should issue. *See id.* and Bilski v. Kappos, 561 U.S. 593 (2010).

7. 416 U.S. 470 (1974).

8. *Id.* at 480 (quoting Sears, Roebuck & Co. v. Stiffel Co., 376 U.S. 225, 231 (1964)). There is no serious argument that either express preemption or field preemption applies to state trade secret law.

9. *Id.* at 484.

10. *Id.* at 489.

The Court avoided this result with the dubious assertion that there was only a "remote" possibility an inventor with a patentable invention would rely on trade secret protection.[11] As a result, it concluded that trade secret law did not conflict with the patent policy of disclosure.

In closing, the *Kewanee Oil* court stressed that its decision was supported by the acquiescence of Congress to state trade secret laws:

> Trade secret law and patent law have co-existed in this country for over one hundred years.... Congress, by its silence over these many years, has seen the wisdom of allowing the States to enforce trade secret protection. Until Congress takes affirmative action to the contrary, States should be free to grant protection to trade secrets.[12]

The Court revisited the *Kewanee Oil* rationale in *Bonito Boats, Inc. v. Thunder Craft Boats, Inc.*[13] With hindsight, it identified three factors which were central to its conclusion that Ohio trade secret law "did not conflict with the federal policies of encouragement of patentable invention and the prompt disclosure of such innovations" that underpin patent law.[14] First, trade secret law is consistent with the patent policy of keeping public domain information in the public domain. Second, this law provides weaker protection than patent law, particularly because it permits independent creation and reverse engineering. Finally, trade secret law safeguards the fundamental right of privacy, which the patent laws do not address. Notably, the *Bonito Boats* Court did not repeat the assertion that inventors were highly unlikely to rely on trade secret law rather than obtain a patent.

§ 3.03 Copyright Law

[A] Overview

Copyright law protects a broad range of artistic works such as books, dances, movies, music, plays, poetry, and sculpture—and computer programs as well. The policy basis for copyright law, like patent law, is expressly utilitarian. The relevant portion of the Intellectual Property Clause of the Constitution authorizes Congress to "promote the Progress of Science and useful Arts, by securing for limited Times to Authors ... the exclusive Right to their respective Writings...."[15] The Supreme Court explained in *Mazer v. Stein* that:

> The economic philosophy behind the clause empowering Congress to grant ... copyrights is the conviction that encouragement of individual effort by per-

11. *Id.* at 490.
12. *Id.* at 493.
13. 489 U.S. 141 (1989).
14. *Id.* at 155.
15. U.S. Const. art. I, § 8, cl. 8.

sonal gain is the best way to advance public welfare through the talents of authors....[16]

A copyright arises automatically, without any government action, when (1) an original (2) work of authorship is (3) fixed in a tangible medium of expression.[17] In this context, originality means that the work reflects at least a modicum of creativity and was independently created by the author, not copied.[18] A work of authorship includes categories such as literary works; pictorial, graphic, and sculptural works; and architectural works.[19] Finally, fixation requires that the work be set forth in a tangible medium (such as a piece of paper, a computer disk, or videotape) for a period of more than transitory duration.

The basic copyright term is measured by the life of the author plus 70 years. During this period, the author and her successors have the exclusive rights to reproduce the work, to prepare derivative works based on the original, and to distribute copies of the work to the public, among other rights.

Copyright infringement is a strict liability offense. However, the fair use doctrine permits others to make limited use of the copyrighted work in creating new works (especially transformative works) where this does not harm the market for the original work or its derivatives. And if a person creates a new work that is similar to a preexisting copyrighted work without knowledge of the earlier work, she is insulated from liability by the independent creation doctrine.

The idea-expression dichotomy is a core principle in copyright. Copyright law protects the expression of an idea, not the idea itself. Thus, copyright does not extend to any "idea, procedure, process, system, method of operation, concept, principle, or discovery."[20] For example, if B writes a book about how to build a canoe in eight hours, anyone is free to use the method outlined in the book. And C may write a book in her own words about how to use B's method, as long as she does not take his protected expression.

[B] Differences from Trade Secret Law

Although copyright and trade secret law both reflect utilitarian theory, they are fundamentally different doctrines.

The most important distinction is that, broadly speaking, copyright law only protects the *form* in which information is expressed, while trade secret law protects the *content* of information.[21] For example, if company D has a secret business strategy

16. 347 U.S. 201, 219 (1954).

17. 17 U.S.C. § 102(a).

18. *See* Feist Publications, Inc. v. Rural Tel. Service Co., Inc., 499 U.S. 340, 358 (1991).

19. 17 U.S.C. § 102(a).

20. 17 U.S.C. § 102(b).

21. In rare situations, both might protect the content of an opinion or judgment. For example, in CDN Inc. v. Capes, 197 F.3d 1256 (9th Cir. 1999), the court held that estimates of the values of collectable coins were copyrightable because they resulted from a complex process of judgment, and

set forth in a memorandum, trade secret law protects the strategy itself, while copyright law only protects the wording used to describe the strategy. Accordingly, if E steals the memorandum and uses his own words to disclose the strategy to D's competitor, he is liable for trade secret misappropriation but not for copyright infringement. Other differences include:

- Copyright law encompasses both private and publicly distributed works, while trade secret law requires secrecy.
- Copyright law requires that the information be fixed in a tangible medium, but trade secret law does not.
- Copyright infringement is a strict liability offense, while trade secret misappropriation requires that the defendant have actual or constructive knowledge of wrongful acquisition.
- A copyright has a fixed duration, while a trade secret might last forever.

[C] Overlap with Trade Secret Law

In certain situations, *either* copyright law or trade secret law could provide effective protection. For example, suppose that F's factory uses a secret process that is described in a company manual. If G steals one of the manuals, makes 20 copies, and distributes them to his workers, he is liable for trade secret misappropriation; G acquired the information by improper means and disclosed it to others. G is also liable under copyright law for copying the text of the manual—the manner in which the information was expressed.

Another example is computer software. Software is initially written in source code, which human programmers can understand. It is then translated into computer readable object code—a series of ones and zeros—which humans cannot understand. Assume that H develops a secret computer program that she uses in her business. Copyright law protects the source code and object code against reproduction, as they are both considered to be "literary works."[22] Similarly, assuming that they are not readily ascertainable and the required secrecy is maintained, the source code and object code both qualify for protection as trade secrets.

The copyright-trade secret interface can be particularly important where a product containing proprietary software is sold on the open market (such as a car or a "smart" appliance), because the doctrines may provide overlapping protection. A buyer might be able to determine the object code embodied in the product. However, copyright law prevents him from copying or using that code, except to the extent allowed by fair use. He could try to reverse engineer the object code in order to determine the

---

thus constituted a type of literary work expressed in numbers. Trade secret law would similarly protect such estimates as long as they were kept relatively secret.

22. *See, e.g.*, Apple Computer, Inc. v. Franklin Computer Corp., 714 F.2d 1240, 1249 (3d Cir. 1983).

source code; but if the source code is not readily ascertainable, it is protected as a trade secret.

[D] Preemption?

The federal Copyright Act expressly preempts state law in certain situations. It provides that "all legal or equitable rights that are equivalent to any of the exclusive rights within the general scope of copyright ... in works of authorship that are fixed in a tangible medium of expression and come within the subject matter of copyright ... are governed exclusively by this title."[23] In analyzing the first element, courts consider whether the state law cause of action is essentially about unauthorized copying of the work (and thus preempted) or whether it requires one or more extra elements (not preempted).[24]

The extent to which copyright law preempts state trade secret law is not entirely clear. Most circuits find no preemption on the theory that the rights are not equivalent because trade secret misappropriation requires an *extra element*: acquisition through a breach of a duty to maintain secrecy or by other improper means. As the Fifth Circuit summarized in *GlobeRanger Corp. v. Software AG United States of America, Inc.*, "[b]ecause trade secret law protects against not just copying but also any taking that occurs through breach of a confidential relationship or other improper means, all ten circuits that have considered trade secret misappropriation claims have found them not preempted by the Copyright Act."[25]

Yet a handful of cases have found preemption. An example is *Relational Design & Technology, Inc. v. Data Team Corp.*, where plaintiff alleged that defendants acquired and used secret information that they knew or had reason to know was "acquired under circumstances giving rise to a duty to maintain its secrecy."[26] The court ruled that the plaintiff's trade secret claim was preempted because it pleaded that "one act constituted both misappropriation of trade secrets and copyright infringement."[27]

The Copyright Act has no preemptive effect on the Defend Trade Secrets Act because it is a federal statute. A number of cases asserting claims under both statutes have been brought in federal courts.

---

23. 17 U.S.C. § 301(a). The second element—works within "the subject matter of copyright"—is interpreted broadly. It includes all works "of a *type*" covered by the Copyright Act, "even if federal law does not afford protection to them," for example, because they lack sufficient originality. ProCD, Inc. v. Zeidenberg, 86 F.3d 1447, 1453 (7th Cir. 1996) (emphasis in original).

24. *See, e.g.*, Stromback v. New Line Cinema, 384 F.3d 283, 302–05 (6th Cir. 2004).

25. 836 F.3d 477, 486 (5th Cir. 2016). *See also* Restatement (Third) of Unfair Competition § 39 cmt. c rep. note ("The preemptive effect of federal copyright law as delineated in § 301 of the Copyright Act does not extend to state trade secret protection, even when the trade secrets are embodied in works of authorship, provided that the state cause of action is premised upon improper acquisition or breach of confidence.").

26. 1992 WL 97799, at *2 (D. Kan. Apr. 16, 1992).

27. *Id.*

§ 3.04 Trademark Law

Trademark law and trade secret law are polar opposites. A trademark is a name, word, or symbol used in the marketplace so that consumers can identify the source of particular goods.[28] By definition, it must perform its function in a *public* setting. In contrast, a trade secret consists of valuable information that is relatively secret; it must be used in a *private* setting. Accordingly, there is no appreciable overlap between these two bodies of law.

Yet a trademark might be used to supplement trade secret protection. Suppose J develops a secret formula for a consumer product, like a mouthwash. Over time, J develops a robust market for the mouthwash using a brand name as a trademark. During this period, trade secret law protects the formula. At some point, the formula becomes public, and trade secret protection is lost. Competitors can now duplicate the mouthwash. But they cannot market it under J's trademark. As a practical matter, consumers may continue to buy J's brand name product since they cannot be certain that competing products use the same formula.[29]

§ 3.05 Confidential or Proprietary Information Law

[A] Overview

If information is not a trade secret and not covered by some other intellectual property law doctrine, then it is in the public domain where anyone may use it freely. Patent and copyright law somewhat overlap with trade secret law, as discussed earlier in this chapter. Beyond this point, is there any other doctrine protecting information that does *not* qualify for trade secret protection? The answer is a limited and tentative "yes"—confidential or proprietary information.

The terms "confidential information" and "proprietary information" are widely used. For example, employers often ask employees to sign nondisclosure agreements that contain language like this: "Employee agrees not to disclose to others any confidential or proprietary information of Employer that she may acquire or originate during her employment."[30] Further, federal and state laws sometimes require that agencies safeguard confidential or proprietary information that businesses submit to government agencies.[31]

---

28. 15 U.S.C. § 1127.

29. *Cf.* Warner-Lambert Pharm. Co. v. John J. Reynolds, Inc., 178 F. Supp. 655 (S.D.N.Y. 1959) (licensee required to pay royalties for continued use of Listerine formula even after formula became public).

30. *See, e.g.*, Johnson Controls, Inc. v. Guidry, 724 F. Supp. 2d 612, 616 (W.D. La. 2010).

31. *See, e.g.*, 42 U.S.C. § 9211 (requiring protection for "trade secrets and other proprietary information" submitted by wind energy businesses).

But what are confidential information and proprietary information? These terms seem to mean the same thing, but they are rarely defined with precision. For example, Black's Law Dictionary provides a circular definition of "proprietary information": "Information in which the owner has a protectable interest."[32]

In practice, some authorities seem to take the position that these terms mean "trade secrets."[33] This approach is flawed since confidential or proprietary information that is—for example—readily ascertainable by members of the public is not a trade secret. The better view is that the terms have an independent—if somewhat fuzzy—meaning. In general, they refer to valuable confidential business information that does not qualify for trade secret protection.[34] In effect, confidential or proprietary information is midway on a spectrum, with trade secrets at one end and public domain information at the other.[35] For simplicity, the discussion below uses the term "proprietary information."

For example, suppose that company K develops a unique machine that it considers to be confidential, but does not make "reasonable efforts" to maintain secrecy. Information about that machine is not a trade secret, but might be proprietary information. Or suppose that ten companies are engaged in mining uranium. If six of the companies know about an innovative process for such mining, it cannot qualify for trade secret protection because it is "generally known." But if these companies keep the information confidential, it could be proprietary information.

It is generally accepted that proprietary information can be protected by contract, within certain limits. However, states disagree on whether non-contract claims may be brought for the misappropriation of such information.[36]

[B] Differences from Trade Secret Law

Proprietary information—by definition—does not qualify for trade secret protection, so there is no substantive overlap between these doctrines

Contract law can be used to safeguard proprietary information. In *Decision Insights, Inc. v. Sentia Group, Inc.*, the Fourth Circuit acknowledged that a nondisclosure agree-

---

32. Black's Law Dictionary 1474 (Bryan A. Garner ed., 11th ed. 2019).

33. *See, e.g.*, Affinity Partners, Inc. v. Drees, 1996 WL 1352635, at *4 (Norfolk Sup. Ct. Jan. 6, 1996) ("There is no meaningful distinction between 'trade secrets' and 'confidential information.'").

34. *See, e.g.*, Unisource Worldwide, Inc. v. Valenti, 196 F. Supp. 2d 269, 278–79 (E.D.N.Y. 2002) (enforcing agreement not to disclose "confidential information" even though the information was readily ascertainable and thus not a trade secret).

35. *See generally* Robert Unikel, *Bridging the "Trade Secret" Gap: Protecting "Confidential Information" Not Rising to the Level of Trade Secrets*, 29 Loy. U. Chi. L.J. 841 (1998). *See also* Chris Montville, Note, *Reforming the Law of Proprietary Information*, 56 Duke L.J. 1159 (2007).

36. Interestingly, Restatement of Torts § 759 imposes liability for procuring "information about another's business" by improper means in order to advance "a rival business interest." Comment b to this section states it applies to covered information "whether or not it constitutes a trade secret." Only a handful of courts have relied on this provision.

ment covering "any confidential or proprietary information ... owned or used" by the plaintiff would protect information that did not qualify for trade secret status.[37]

The Restatement of Employment Law recognizes that an employer may use a nondisclosure agreement to protect both "trade secrets ... and *other protectable confidential information that does not meet the definition of trade secret*."[38] Of course, the scope of any nondisclosure agreement is a fact-intensive question. But the Restatement offers helpful guidance on the meaning of "proprietary information" as the term is used in such agreements:

> Courts will generally protect nonpublic commercial information that provides a clear economic advantage to the employer by virtue of its confidentiality, provided that the restrictive covenant is otherwise reasonable ... and the information has been treated as confidential by the employer.[39]

In addition, a variety of common law theories—including conversion, interference with prospective business advantage, restitution, unfair competition, and unjust enrichment—might conceivably apply where one party misappropriates proprietary information belonging to another, if they are not preempted.

[C] Preemption or Displacement?

The Uniform Trade Secrets Act does not affect "contractual remedies, whether or not based upon misappropriation of a trade secret."[40] Accordingly, contract law may be used to protect proprietary information.

On the other hand, most courts conclude that the UTSA displaces non-contract claims concerning both trade secrets and proprietary information.[41] A minority of states take the opposite view, thus allowing the owner of proprietary information to sue on non-contract theories such as the common law doctrines mentioned above. In these states, the definition of proprietary information varies widely.

The UTSA provides that it "displaces conflicting tort, restitutionary, and other law of this State providing civil remedies for misappropriation of a trade secret," except for certain exceptions.[42] Most courts reason that this language precludes non-contract claims relating to *both* trade secrets and proprietary information, due to the UTSA goal of national uniformity.[43] As the New Hampshire Supreme Court explained in *Mortgage Specialists, Inc. v. Davey:*

---

37. 416 F. App'x 324, 332 (4th Cir. 2011). *See generally* § 8.03[C][2].

38. Restatement of Employment Law § 8.07(b)(1) (emphasis added).

39. *Id.* cmt. b.

40. UTSA § 7(b)(1).

41. In practice, "preemption" and "displacement" are often used interchangeably. However, preemption technically occurs when a federal law supersedes a state law pursuant to the Supremacy Clause of the Constitution. See U.S. Const. art. VI, § 2.

42. UTSA § 7(a).

43. *See, e.g.*, BlueEarth Biofuels, LLC v. Hawaiian Elec. Co., Inc., 235 P.3d 310, 319–24 (Haw. 2010).

> [V]iewed in the context of the overall legislative scheme and construed in a manner that effectuates the purpose of making uniform the law among States ... the [New Hampshire version of the UTSA] preempts claims that are based upon the unauthorized use of information, regardless of whether that information meets the statutory definition of a trade secret.[44]

However, a minority of courts find no displacement or preemption, based on the plain language of an exception in the UTSA. It states that the UTSA "does not affect ... other civil remedies that are not based upon misappropriation of a *trade secret*."[45] These courts reason that because proprietary information is—by definition—different from a trade secret, non-contract claims are not precluded.

Burbank Grease Services, LLC v. Sokolowski is an example of the minority approach.[46] In that case, plaintiff's former employee used its "confidential information" while working for a new employer.[47] The trial court held that plaintiff's tort claims based upon misappropriation were preempted. But the Wisconsin Supreme Court interpreted the state's version of the UTSA as only displacing tort claims relating to trade secrets: "Therefore, any civil tort claim not grounded in a trade secret, *as defined in the statute*, remains available to Burbank."[48]

The potential impact of the DTSA on proprietary information is less clear. 18 U.S.C. § 1838 provides that the act "shall not be construed to preempt or displace any other remedies, whether civil or criminal, provided by ... State ... law for the misappropriation of a trade secret." The legislative history states that this language should be not interpreted as preventing plaintiffs from raising "state law tort or contract claims" to "prevent the further misuse of a trade secret."[49]

Setting aside the preclusion issue, the protection of non-trade secret proprietary information raises important policy concerns. Trade secret law reflects a balance among four core policies: protecting commercial morality, encouraging innovation, protecting free competition, and promoting labor mobility.[50] The minority approach to proprietary information strikes a different balance, which somewhat undercuts the last two policies. It inhibits free competition by preventing competitors from using non-trade secret information. And, in some cases, it hinders employees from leaving to start new companies because they have no clear guidance about which information they may use, and thus risk being sued by former employers.

---

44. 904 A.2d 652, 664 (N.H. 2006).

45. UTSA § 7(b)(2) (emphasis added).

46. 717 N.W.2d 781 (Wis. 2006).

47. The trial court found that the "confidential information" was not protected by the state's trade secret statute because "the information did not meet the statutory definition of a trade secret." *Id.* at 787.

48. *Id.* at 793–94 (emphasis in original).

49. H.R. Rep. No. 104-788, at 13 (1996).

50. *See* § 1.03.

Chapter 4

Misappropriation of Trade Secrets

§ 4.01 Introduction

[A] Wrongful Conduct

Anyone is free to acquire, disclose, or use a trade secret owned by another unless his conduct is deemed to be improper—a *misappropriation* of the secret.[1] Today most courts use the standards set forth in the Uniform Trade Secrets Act and Defend Trade Secrets Act to determine civil liability in trade secret disputes. The UTSA approach generally codifies the prior case law on misappropriation, and the DTSA approach closely tracks the UTSA.

The UTSA provides that "[a]ctual or threatened misappropriation may be enjoined" and that "a complainant is entitled to recover damages for misappropriation."[2] Similarly, under the DTSA "[a]n owner of a trade secret that is misappropriated may bring a civil action" to obtain an injunction and/or damages.[3] The DTSA also authorizes the court to enjoin threatened misappropriation.[4]

Trade secret misappropriation is not a strict liability offense, unlike copyright and patent infringement. A person who utilizes copyrighted material or a patented inven-

1. This chapter examines civil liability for misappropriation. Criminal liability is discussed in Chapter 9.

2. UTSA §§ 2(a), 3(a). Remedies for misappropriation are discussed in Chapter 7.

3. 18 U.S.C. § 1836(b)(1), (b)(3). Under the DTSA, an "owner" is "the person or entity in whom or in which rightful legal or equitable title to, or license in, the trade secret is reposed." 18 U.S.C. § 1839(4).

4. 18 U.S.C. § 1836(b)(3)(A)(i).

tion without the consent of the owner is liable regardless of whether he knew or should have known that his conduct was an infringement. In contrast, liability for trade secret misappropriation generally requires proof that the secret was obtained through some form of wrongful conduct. In other words, liability turns on the circumstances under which the secret was obtained and the defendant's knowledge of those circumstances.

For example, assume that A manufactures a product using a patented process. If B, who holds a patent on that process, sues A for infringement, B will win even if A had no idea that the process was patented. However, a slight change to the hypothetical alters the result. If A manufactures a product using a secret but unpatented process and B sues A for misappropriation of its trade secret, B will win only if it can prove that A knew or should have known that the secret was wrongfully obtained from B.

In practical terms, this distinction means that proving wrongful use of a trade secret is far more difficult and fact sensitive than proving patent infringement. And the misappropriation element can make trade secret litigation more personal than an analogous patent infringement suit. The trade secret owner must show that the defendant effectively stole the trade secret—or obtained it from one who did—in order to prevail.

[B] UTSA/DTSA Definition

The UTSA and DTSA share the same definition of the term "misappropriation":

> (i) acquisition of a trade secret of another by a person who knows or has reason to know that the trade secret was acquired by improper means; or
>
> (ii) disclosure or use of a trade secret of another without express or implied consent by a person who
>
> > (A) used improper means to acquire knowledge of the trade secret; or
> >
> > (B) at the time of disclosure or use, knew or had reason to know that his knowledge of the trade secret was
> >
> > > (I) derived from or through a person who had utilized improper means to acquire it;
> > >
> > > (II) acquired under circumstances giving rise to a duty to maintain its secrecy or limit its use; or
> > >
> > > (III) derived from or through a person who owed a duty to the person seeking relief to maintain its secrecy or limit its use; or
> >
> > (C) before a material change of his position, knew or had reason to know that it was a trade secret and that knowledge of it had been acquired by accident or mistake.[5]

---

5. UTSA § 1(2); 18 U.S.C. § 1839(5). This is the UTSA definition of the term. The DTSA definition is identical in substance, but varies slightly in wording. Although both definitions use the term "improper means," they define this term somewhat differently. *See* § 4.02[D][1], [4][b].

This chapter explores each element of the definition in detail. At this point, however, it is helpful to focus on three major aspects of the definition:

- *Acquisition v. disclosure or use*: The definition provides different liability standards for acquisition of a trade secret, on the one hand, and disclosure or use of the secret, on the other hand. The chapter follows this format, first examining misappropriation by acquisition and then by disclosure or use.
- *Manner of acquisition*: Liability for acquisition, disclosure, and use arises from three ways the trade secret could be acquired from its owner: (a) "improper means;" (b) "breach of duty;" or (c) "accident or mistake."
- *Knowledge*: Liability attaches only where the defendant either "knew" or "had reason to know" certain information about how the secret was acquired from its owner.

In practice, most misappropriation cases arise from the *use* of a trade secret—rather than its mere acquisition or disclosure—because the trade secret owner is most likely to suffer harm when the information is actually used by another. Occasionally, a use theory will be paired with a disclosure theory—for example, where one defendant improperly discloses a trade secret to another defendant, who uses it. The most common misappropriation scenario occurs when an employee breaches a duty to maintain secrecy. For example, suppose C legally obtains a trade secret from his employer D, but then changes jobs and begins working for E, one of D's competitors. C discloses the secret to E. E, knowing that it is a trade secret, begins using the information in her business. On these facts, C is liable for wrongful disclosure, and E is liable for wrongful use.

[C] Compared to Restatement of Torts

Under the Restatement of Torts, the mere *acquisition* of a trade secret was not actionable. The Restatement did impose liability in a related but narrower situation: where a person "for the purpose of advancing a rival business interest, procures by improper means information about another's business."[6] Accordingly, liability for wrongful acquisition is much broader under the UTSA/DTSA approach.

The Restatement provided that the *disclosure* or *use* of a trade secret could be wrongful:

> One who discloses or uses another's trade secret, without a privilege to do so, is liable to the other if
>
> (a) he discovered the secret by improper means, or
>
> (b) his disclosure or use constitutes a breach of confidence reposed in him by the other in disclosing the secret to him, or

6. Restatement of Torts § 759.

> (c) he learned the secret from a third person with notice of the facts that it was a secret and that the third person discovered it by improper means or that the third person's disclosure of it was otherwise a breach of his duty to the other, or
>
> (d) he learned the secret with notice of the facts that it was a secret and that its disclosure was made to him by mistake.[7]

This section served as the foundation for the UTSA/DTSA definition of misappropriation by disclosure or use discussed above. It is roughly parallel to the UTSA/DTSA approach, but with a different organization and somewhat different terminology.

One interesting difference between the Restatement and UTSA/DTSA approaches arises when a defendant discloses or uses secret information that was *actually* obtained by improper means even though it *could have* been obtained by proper means. This is a misappropriation under the Restatement according to some courts; but is not a misappropriation under the UTSA or DTSA.

For instance, suppose that F, an employee of G, uses G's secret customer list in his job. F then takes a new job with H and uses the list to sell to H's customers. Even if F could have easily obtained the same list by searching the internet, he is liable for misappropriation under the Restatement approach. As the Second Circuit stated in *Franke v. Wiltschek*:

> It matters not that defendants could have gained their knowledge from a study of the expired patent and plaintiffs' publicly marketed product. The fact is that they did not. Instead they gained it from plaintiffs via their confidential relationship, and in so doing incurred a duty not to use it to plaintiffs' detriment.[8]

A federal court subsequently explained: "*Franke* simply supports the uncontroversial proposition that 'it is no defense in an action [for misappropriation of trade secrets] that the process in question *could have* been developed independently, without resort to information gleaned from the confidential relationship.'"[9] Here, as elsewhere, the Restatement approach reflects the view that the rationale for trade secret law is preservation of commercial morality rather than the protection of property rights.

In contrast, F is not liable under the UTSA or DTSA because the customer list is readily ascertainable, and, accordingly, is not a trade secret.[10]

---

7. *Id.* § 757.

8. 209 F.2d 493, 495 (2d Cir. 1953).

9. Broker Genius, Inc. v. Zalta, 280 F. Supp. 3d 495, 518 n.15 (S.D.N.Y 2017) (quoting Imperial Chem. Indus. Ltd. v. Nat'l Distillers & Chem. Corp., 342 F.2d 737, 743 (2d Cir. 1965)) (emphasis in original).

10. *See* § 2.04[C]. *See, e.g.*, MEI-GSR Holdings, LLC v. Peppermill Casinos, Inc., 416 P.3d 249, 254 (Nev. 2018) ("[W]e hold that a defendant's acquisition of information by *improper means* does not preclude the defendant from demonstrating that the information is readily ascertainable by other persons.") (emphasis in original).

[D] Compared to Restatement (Third) of Unfair Competition

The misappropriation standard set forth in § 40 of the Restatement (Third) of Unfair Competition generally follows the UTSA/DTSA formulation, though it uses slightly different language.[11] A comment following this section helpfully explains that "the rules governing trade secrets as stated in this Restatement are ... intended to be consistent with and applicable to actions under the Uniform Trade Secrets Act."[12]

§ 4.02 Wrongful Acquisition of Trade Secret

[A] Overview

The UTSA and DTSA both impose liability for the improper acquisition of a trade secret. Under both statutes, the "acquisition of a trade secret of another by a person who knows or has reason to know that the trade secret was acquired by improper means" is a "misappropriation" of the secret.[13]

Suppose J finds a handwritten note on a public sidewalk; J reads the note and discovers that it contains a valuable trade secret owned by K. On these facts, J has acquired a trade secret owned by another person—but cannot be sued for misappropriation because J did not obtain it by improper means. On the other hand, if J obtains the note by the illegal act of burglarizing K's home, J is liable for misappropriation *even if J never uses the information or discloses it to another.*

Why is liability imposed for the mere acquisition of a trade secret? First, this approach helps to prevent illegal use of the secret, and thus safeguards owners from harm. If a person like J is deterred from obtaining the secret in the first place, there is no danger that J will use it himself or pass it on to one of K's competitors who will do so. Second, in some situations it may be difficult to prove that a defendant has actually used another's trade secret (particularly given the expansive definition of "use" applied in the trade secret context),[14] but possible to prove that the defendant acquired the secret illegally. In this situation, acquisition liability is a proxy for use liability.

It is vital to understand that only *wrongful* acquisition of a trade secret is actionable. If L holds a trade secret, L's employees, licensees, subcontractors, and many others may all be given legal access to the secret. All of them acquire the secret, but none of them does so by improper means.

Improper means such as bribery, burglary, espionage, fraud, or theft are sometimes used to obtain trade secrets. But wrongful acquisition cases are usually less dramatic.

---

11. Restatement (Third) of Unfair Competition § 40.
12. *Id.* cmt. a.
13. UTSA § 1(2)(i); 18 U.S.C. § 1839(5)(A).
14. *See* § 4.03[C].

The most common situation — by far — involves the employee who takes a new job. Suppose that M learns one of N's trade secrets in the ordinary course of working for N. On these facts, M legally obtained the secret. M then takes a new job and voluntarily discloses the secret to O, her new employer, who knows that M obtained it from N. M's disclosure would be viewed as a breach of her duty to maintain secrecy. Therefore, O acquired the information by improper means.

Unsurprisingly, the remedies that the trade secret owner can obtain for wrongful acquisition are limited. If the defendant never used or disclosed the secret, the plaintiff did not suffer any actual harm and thus cannot obtain compensatory damages.[15] The most likely remedy is an injunction that bars the defendant from using the secret or disclosing it to others.

[B] "Acquisition"

The UTSA and DTSA do not define the term "acquisition." The leading case analyzing its meaning is *AUA Private Equity Partners, LLC v. Soto*, where the federal district court applied the plain-language approach.[16] The court relied on Black's Law Dictionary, which defines the term as "the gaining of possession or control over something."[17] Using this standard, it concluded that the plaintiff had adequately pleaded a claim for wrongful acquisition under the DTSA by alleging that the defendant, its former employee, had uploaded plaintiff's trade secrets "from her work laptop to her personal cloud-based storage," where she had possession and control of the information.[18]

Under this standard, P wrongfully acquires a trade secret if it: (1) steals a confidential drawing from Q's factory; (2) obtains a secret customer list from one of R's employees; or (3) hacks into S's computer system and downloads a proprietary formula.

A person who inadvertently comes into possession of a trade secret, however, is not liable for wrongful acquisition. As one court observed, the word "acquire" "implies more than passive reception; it implies pointed conduct intended to secure dominion over the thing."[19] Thus, if chef T's secret recipe accidentally blows off a restaurant counter and into customer U's open purse without U's knowledge, there is a good argument that U did not "acquire" the trade secret. Moreover, liability for mere acquisition requires that the information be obtained by improper means, which indicates that it must be the result of intentional conduct. That said, where a party

---

15. *But see* Food Serv. of America, Inc. v. Carrington, 2013 WL 4507593, at *14 (D. Ariz. Aug. 23, 2013) (suggesting that the plaintiff could recover the expenses it incurred in reviewing the documents that the defendant had misappropriated).

16. 2018 WL 1684339 (S.D.N.Y. Apr. 5, 2018).

17. *Id.* at *5.

18. *Id.* at *7. *See also* Silvaco Data Systems v. Intel Corp., 109 Cal. Rptr. 3d 27, 40 (App. 2010) (defendant's acquisition of software written in machine-readable object code was not acquisition of the underlying source code that constituted plaintiff's trade secrets).

19. *Silvaco Data Systems*, 109 Cal. Rptr. 3d at 40.

obtains a trade secret by accident or mistake, she may be liable for misappropriation based on later use or disclosure. For example, U could be sued for wrongful use if she discovered the recipe in her purse and utilized it in her own restaurant, knowing that it was T's recipe.[20]

[C] "Knows or Has Reason to Know"

[1] Generally

A defendant is liable for misappropriation by acquisition under the UTSA and DTSA only if he "knows or has reason to know" that the trade secret was obtained from its owner through improper means.[21] The first portion of this standard is an *actual knowledge* test. The second portion is a *constructive knowledge* test: the defendant is liable if a reasonable person would know the information based on the circumstances of the situation, even if the plaintiff cannot prove that he had actual knowledge.

Case law generally interprets this standard to require that the defendant must know or have reason to know that both (a) the information was a trade secret and (b) improper means were used to acquire it,[22] though some courts appear to conflate these requirements. Both the actor who directly acquired the trade secret from its owner and any third parties who later obtain the secret from that actor may be liable.

In applying this standard, it is not necessary to prove that the defendant knew the information met the legal definition of a trade secret. As the court observed in *United States v. Hanjuan Jin*, it need only be shown that "the defendant was aware that the information had the general attributes of a trade secret—that it was valuable to its owner because it was not generally known and that the owner had taken measures to protect it."[23]

The Restatement of Torts observes that frequently the two types of knowledge required for liability "are mutually dependent and notice of the one is also notice of the other. Thus, if the actor knows that the information proffered to him by one person is the trade secret of another he is put on inquiry as to the former's authority to disclose the information."[24] Conversely, if the defendant actually knows or should know that the information was obtained by an improper method, he may be charged with constructive notice that it is a trade secret.

---

20. *See* § 4.03[E][4].

21. UTSA § 1(2)(i); 18 U.S.C. § 1839(5)(A).

22. *See, e.g.*, Data General Corp. v. Grumman Sys. Support Corp., 825 F. Supp. 340, 360 (D. Mass. 1993).

23. 833 F. Supp. 2d 977, 1014 (N.D. Ill. 2012) (interpreting the EEA before adoption of the DTSA).

24. Restatement of Torts § 757 cmt. m. Because the Restatement did not impose liability for mere acquisition of a trade secret, this provision directly applies only to actions for wrongful disclosure or use. But the approach should logically extend to wrongful acquisition actions as well.

[2] Knowledge of Person Obtaining Secret from Owner

Suppose that V, W's employee, has access to industrial drawings as a routine part of his job. Every drawing bears a warning at the top of each page in large red print that says: CONFIDENTIAL—DO NOT REMOVE FROM PREMISES. V smuggles three of the drawings outside of W's factory by hiding them in his coat.

On these facts, V is clearly liable for wrongful acquisition. First, V had clear notice from the red warning that the drawings were intended to be kept secret; and the fact that he smuggled them out of the plant is additional circumstantial evidence of this knowledge. In fact, it is likely that W took other measures to maintain the secrecy of this information, including having V sign a standard nondisclosure agreement. In virtually any situation where an employer undertakes reasonable measures to maintain secrecy—which is required for the information to be protected as a trade secret[25]—its employees will have either actual or constructive notice of secrecy. Again, it is not necessary that a person in V's position be familiar with the legal definition of a "trade secret" or realize that the drawings meet that standard. Second, the manner in which V took the drawings out of the plant shows that he knowingly engaged in theft. There is no reason that V would hide them in his coat if he were acting in good faith.

[3] Knowledge of Third Parties

Now assume that V takes a new job with X, one of W's competitors, and gives X secret information about the content of the drawings. V's disclosure breaches his duty to maintain secrecy. X may now be liable for wrongful acquisition, even though it did not directly obtain the information from W.

In many situations, a third party like X may not have actual knowledge of V's wrongful appropriation. But a third party will often be charged with constructive knowledge because it had "reason to know" based on the circumstances of the case. As one court summarized, a defendant may be on notice that information offered by one person is actually a trade secret held by another when "a reasonable person would have been put on inquiry and an inquiry pursued with reasonable diligence would have disclosed that the information provided to the defendant was actually wrongfully obtained from another."[26]

Factors used to determine whether a defendant had reason to know include: (a) its familiarity with industry customs or practices that suggest the disclosure is unauthorized; (b) the extent of its knowledge of the disclosing party's relationship with the trade secret owner; and (c) its knowledge of any precautions against disclosure taken by the owner.[27]

An example is *Rohm and Hass Co. v. Adco Chemical Co.*,[28] where the plaintiff sued for wrongful acquisition of a process for producing a paint ingredient. The evidence

25. *See* § 2.05.
26. C & F Packing Co., Inc. v. IBP, Inc., 1998 WL 1147139, at *6 (E.D. Ill. Mar. 16, 1998).
27. Restatement (Third) of Unfair Competition § 40 cmt. d.
28. 689 F.2d 424 (3d Cir. 1982).

established that: (a) defendants had unsuccessfully attempted to duplicate the process for years; (b) they then hired Harvey, one of plaintiff's former technicians who was familiar with the process, and asked him to duplicate one of the plaintiff's products made with the process; (c) Harvey "handed them the Process ... almost as soon as he walked in the door;"[29] (d) the defendants knew that his experience with paints could only have come from his work for the plaintiff; and (e) they never asked Harvey about the origin of the process. The Third Circuit reasoned that these facts "left it all but impossible to avoid the conclusion that defendants knew Harvey had revealed to them something that plaintiff had tried very hard to keep secret."[30]

Similarly, in *Experian Information Solutions, Inc. v. Nationwide Marketing Services, Inc.*, someone stole Experian's compilation of consumer names and addresses, and later sold them to Nationwide, a competitor that used the information.[31] Nationwide asserted that it had no reason to know the information was stolen, and the trial court granted its summary judgment motion. The Ninth Circuit reversed, finding that the following evidence created a question of fact: (a) Nationwide paid "less than 1% of the market rate" for a license to use the data; (b) it obtained ownership through an invoice, rather than obtaining limited use rights through a written agreement; and (c) Nationwide's president had "prior experience that should have put him on notice of an improper acquisition."[32]

[D] "Improper Means"

[1] Generally

[a] Lack of Comprehensive Definition

A person who acquires a trade secret by proper means may use it freely. For example, if Y discovers Z's trade secret by reading about it in a newspaper or deducing it while observing Z's publicly available product, Y is not liable for misappropriation.

Yet the line between "proper means" and "improper means" may be difficult to discern. While there is broad agreement that certain types of acts are "improper means," there is no comprehensive definition of the term. Instead, authorities primarily attempt to explain the term through examples.

The Restatement (Third) of Unfair Competition provides the most helpful explanation:

> "Improper" means of acquiring another's trade secret ... include theft, fraud, unauthorized interception of communications, inducement of or knowing participation in a breach of confidence, and other means either wrongful in themselves or wrongful under the circumstances of the case.[33]

---

29. *Id.* at 430.
30. *Id.* at 431.
31. 893 F.3d 1176 (9th Cir. 2018).
32. *Id.* at 1189.
33. Restatement (Third) of Unfair Competition § 43.

It is generally accepted that criminal acts, tortious acts, or breaches of confidentiality duties are all improper means. The UTSA states that the term "includes theft, bribery, misrepresentation, breach or inducement of a breach of a duty to maintain secrecy, or espionage through electronic or other means."[34] The Restatement of Torts offers similar examples in explaining the term, such as using "physical force to take a secret formula" or making "fraudulent misrepresentations to induce disclosure."[35] The theme that links these examples is that they are all inherently *wrongful acts*. For example, if A obtains B's trade secret by breaking into B's office or tapping B's phone line, A acquires it by improper means.

But beyond these categories, what other acts constitute "improper means"? A comment to the UTSA definition cites the Restatement of Torts for the proposition that "[a] complete catalogue of improper means is not possible."[36] The Restatement (Third) of Unfair Competition similarly agrees that "[i]t is not possible to formulate a comprehensive list of the conduct that constitutes 'improper' means of acquiring a trade secret."[37] The principal uncertainty is when *lawful acts* can constitute improper means, as discussed in more detail below.[38]

The definition of "improper means" is relevant to both basic categories of misappropriation: (1) wrongful acquisition of a trade secret; and (2) improper disclosure or use of that secret. For convenience, it is discussed here in the context of wrongful acquisition.

[b] Examples of Proper Means

In theory, the definition of "improper means" might be clarified by examining acquisition methods that are considered to be "proper means." A comment to the UTSA states that proper means include:

- Discovery by independent invention;
- Discovery by "reverse engineering," that is, by starting with the known product and working backward to find the method by which it was developed;
- Discovery under a license from the owner of the trade secret;
- Observation of the item in public use or on public display; and
- Obtaining the trade secret from published literature.[39]

Yet this list is less helpful than it appears. If the information can be obtained from observation of an item in public use, from reverse engineering without undue effort,

34. UTSA § 1(1). The basic DTSA definition is identical to the UTSA definition. 18 U.S.C § 1839(6)(A).

35. Restatement of Torts § 757 cmt. f.

36. UTSA § 1 cmt.; Restatement of Torts § 757 cmt. f.

37. Restatement (Third) of Unfair Competition § 43 cmt. c.

38. *See* § 4.02[D][4].

39. UTSA § 1 cmt. In contrast, the DTSA merely specifies that "reverse engineering, independent derivation, and any other lawful means" are not "improper means." 18 U.S.C. § 1839(6)(B).

or by reading published literature, then it is very likely not a trade secret at all—because it is "readily ascertainable."[40] Further, an owner who has licensed the use of its trade secret to another party would never be able to sue that party for wrongful acquisition.

Once these methods are set aside, only two items on the list are potentially relevant: discovery of the trade secret by independent invention or reverse engineering in situations where the information is not readily apparent. Accordingly, the list does not offer much guidance on the definition of improper means.

[2] Breach of Duty to Maintain Secrecy

[a] Generally

The most common type of misappropriation involves the breach of a duty to maintain secrecy. The UTSA and DTSA both provide that "breach or inducement of a breach of a duty to maintain secrecy" constitutes improper means.[41] But neither one defines a "duty to maintain secrecy." As a result, its scope is determined by case law governing the duty of confidentiality.

Broadly speaking, a duty of confidentiality can arise from any of three sources: (i) an express contract; (ii) an implied duty based on the facts and circumstances surrounding a particular relationship; or (iii) operation of law.

Trade secret owners commonly use an *express contract*—usually in the form of a nondisclosure agreement—to create a clear duty to maintain secrecy. The Restatement (Third) of Unfair Competition provides that this duty arises where a person makes "an express promise of confidentiality prior to the disclosure of the trade secret."[42] As a practical matter, any company with valuable trade secrets will require such contracts as part of the reasonable precautions it takes to preserve the secrecy of the information, and thus prevent the loss of trade secret protection.[43] A variety of parties involved in the company's business—including employees, contractors, subcontractors, suppliers, customers, licensees, and franchisees—may also be required to execute such contracts.

Absent an express contract, an *implied contract* to maintain secrecy may arise from the nature of the relationship between the trade secret owner and another party. As the Restatement explains, a duty of confidentiality arises where a trade secret is:

> disclosed to the person under circumstances in which the relationship between the parties to the disclosure or the other facts surrounding the disclosure justify the conclusions that, at the time of the disclosure,
>
> (1) the person knew or had reason to know that the disclosure was intended to be in confidence, and

---

40. *See* § 2.04[C].
41. UTSA § 1(1); 18 U.S.C. § 1839(6)(A).
42. Restatement (Third) of Unfair Competition § 41(a).
43. *See* §§ 2.05, 8.03[C].

(2) the other party to the disclosure was reasonable in inferring that the person consented to an obligation of confidentiality.[44]

Circumstances that are relevant in determining whether the recipient of a trade secret has such an implied duty include the customs in the business or industry, precautions taken by the trade secret owner to maintain secrecy that are known to the recipient, whether the recipient solicited the disclosure, and whether the parties have an ongoing relationship.[45]

Finally, a duty to maintain secrecy may arise by *operation of law.* The classic example is where one party owes a fiduciary duty to another, since this relationship imposes a duty of confidentiality on the fiduciary. Thus, for example, attorney C who receives trade secret information from client D must keep the information secret. Other fiduciaries, such as agents, guardians, and trustees, have the same obligation.

It is important to understand that *inducing* a breach of duty to maintain secrecy is also improper. This scenario arises most commonly when an employer convinces a new employee to disclose a trade secret owned by his former employer. Virtually any conduct aimed at convincing a person to breach his duty can be viewed as inducement.

[b] Employees

An employee with access to trade secrets is almost always bound by a duty of confidentiality, by either express contract, implied contract, or operation of law. Thus, if she knows or has reason to know that information received from her employer is confidential, she may not disclose it. For example, suppose that E knowingly discloses one of her employer's trade secrets to F, a third party. E obtained the information lawfully, so she is not liable for wrongful acquisition.[46] Because E's disclosure is probably a breach of duty, however, F would be liable for wrongful acquisition as long as he knew or had reason to know that E breached her duty.

Today many companies mandate that new employees sign nondisclosure agreements or similar contracts.[47] Such an agreement typically (i) states that the employee will acquire secret or confidential information during the course of his employment and (ii) prohibits him from disclosing it except as necessary to perform his work for the employer. Courts routinely enforce these agreements against current and former employees.

---

44. Restatement (Third) of Unfair Competition §41(b).

45. *Id.* §41 cmt. b.

46. But E is liable for wrongful disclosure. She knew or should have known that her knowledge of the secret was acquired under circumstances giving rise to a duty to maintain its secrecy. UTSA §1(2)(ii)(B)(II); 18 U.S.C. §1839(5)(B)(ii)(II). Arguably, E would also be liable for wrongful acquisition if she had somehow taken personal possession of it. *See, e.g.*, AUA Private Equity Partners, LLC v. Soto, 2018 WL 1684339 (S.D.N.Y. Apr. 5, 2018) (employee liable for wrongful acquisition when she emailed trade secrets to her personal account in violation of the employer's policy).

47. *See* §8.03[C].

Under some circumstances, a court will find that employees are bound by an implied nondisclosure agreement based on the facts of their relationship. An example is *Winston Research Corp. v. Minnesota Mining and Manufacturing Co.*,[48] where the court observed that "an agreement not to disclose might be implied from [the employer's] elaborate efforts to maintain the secrecy of its development program, and the employees' knowledge of these efforts and participation in them."[49]

Finally, even absent an express or implied contract, the general rule is that many employees are bound by a duty of confidentiality as a matter of law.[50] The Restatement of Employment Law provides:

> Employees in a position of trust and confidence with their employer owe a fiduciary duty of loyalty to the employer in matters related to their employment. Other employees who come into possession of the employer's trade secrets owe a limited fiduciary duty of loyalty with regard to those trade secrets.[51]

A comment to the Restatement (Third) of Unfair Competition echoes that theme:

> [A]n employee is subject to a duty of loyalty applicable to all conduct within the scope of the employment.... The duty of loyalty ... includes a duty not to disclose the employer's confidential information to others.[52]

This duty continues after the employment relationship has ended. Accordingly, a former employee is barred from disclosing the former employer's trade secrets.

Some decisions appear to question whether employment creates a duty of confidentiality as a general matter.[53] But as the Restatement comments, these cases are "often better understood as resting on the absence of a protectable trade secret."[54] Where an employee has no reason to believe that particular information is confidential, his disclosure of the information is not a breach of duty. For example, in *Electro-Craft Corp. v. Controlled Motion, Inc.*, the Minnesota Supreme Court found no liability for misappropriation, in part, because the plaintiff never told its employees what information should be kept confidential.[55]

[c] Parties to Business Transactions

One recurring problem is whether an implied duty of confidentiality exists between parties who are negotiating a business transaction, such as a sale, lease, supply contract, license, or franchise agreement. In general, when a party discloses a trade secret to another without first obtaining an express nondisclosure agreement, there

48. 350 F.2d 134 (9th Cir. 1965).

49. *Id.* at 140.

50. *See, e.g.*, Surgidev Corp. v. Eye Tech., Inc., 648 F. Supp. 661, 695 (D. Minn. 1986).

51. Restatement of Employment Law § 8.01(a).

52. Restatement (Third) of Unfair Competition § 42 cmt. b.

53. *See, e.g.*, Shatterproof Glass Corp. v. Guardian Glass Co., 322 F. Supp. 854, 869–70 (E.D. Mich. 1970).

54. Restatement (Third) of Unfair Competition § 42 cmt. c.

55. 332 N.W.2d 890, 903 (Minn. 1983).

is a risk that the recipient may be able to use the information freely, without liability for misappropriation. As the Supreme Court noted in *Ruckelshaus v. Monsanto Co.*, "[i]f an individual discloses his trade secret to others who are under no obligation to protect the confidentiality of the information, or otherwise publicly discloses the secret, his property right is extinguished."[56] But depending on the circumstances, a duty of confidentiality may exist when such a disclosure is made during the course of business negotiations.

The issue sometimes arises in situations where the proposed transaction concerns information that is valuable because it is secret. Suppose G is negotiating to sell its business to H, and most of its value stems from trade secrets. H needs to know the secrets in order to determine their value; but if G discloses the secrets, H has no need to buy them.[57] Ideally, the parties would enter into an express agreement by which H promises not to use the secrets or disclose them to another prior to purchasing them. However, in many cases this does not occur.

In the landmark decision of *Smith v. Dravo Corp.*, the Seventh Circuit held that a duty of confidentiality arose in this situation.[58] Plaintiffs' business was an early pioneer in the development of standardized cargo containers for transporting goods by rail or ship. After defendant expressed interest in buying the business, plaintiffs provided the defendant with information about their "secret designs, plans and prospective customers."[59] However, the negotiations broke down, and the defendant ultimately began (i) manufacturing containers that incorporated features from plaintiffs' designs and (ii) selling its containers to some of the plaintiffs' prospective customers. On appeal, the court reasoned that the defendant owed an implied duty of confidentiality:

> Here plaintiffs disclosed their design for one purpose, to enable defendant to appraise it with a view in mind of purchasing the business. There can be no question that defendant knew and understood this limited purpose. Trust was reposed in it by plaintiffs that the information thus transmitted would be accepted subject to that limitation.[60]

On the other hand, in many situations an owner who voluntarily discloses a trade secret has no recourse when the other person uses the information for its own benefit. An example is *Smith v. Snap-On Tools Corp.*,[61] where the plaintiff invented a new type of ratchet, sent information about it to the defendant, and then sued for misappro-

---

56. 467 U.S. 986, 1002 (1984).

57. This dilemma is known as Arrow's information paradox.

58. 203 F.2d 369 (7th Cir. 1953). *See also* Phillips v. Frey, 20 F.3d 623, 630–32 (5th Cir. 1994) (prospective buyer of business who learned trade secret during negotiations had a duty to maintain secrecy).

59. *Smith*, 203 F.2d at 373. Under modern law, there would be a strong argument that the design of plaintiffs' containers did not qualify for trade secret protection because it was readily ascertainable; at the time of the case, anyone could purchase one of the containers from plaintiffs' company and inspect it.

60. *Id.* at 376.

61. 833 F.2d 578 (5th Cir. 1987).

priation after the defendant began selling the same ratchet. Reasoning that "one party's disclosure of an alleged trade secret to another does not automatically create a confidential relationship," the Fifth Circuit concluded that the defendant was not liable for misappropriation.[62] It implied that the outcome might be different if (i) the defendant "actively solicited" the information from the plaintiff or (ii) the plaintiff made it clear that "the disclosure was intended as part of a course of negotiations aimed at creating a licensing agreement or entering into a similar business transaction."[63]

[3] Criminal and Tortious Acts

Criminal and tortious acts are classic examples of improper means. As noted above, the UTSA and DTSA expressly recognize that conduct such as bribery, fraud, and theft will be viewed as improper means.[64]

If J acquires K's trade secret by burglarizing K's office, tapping K's phone line, bribing K's employee, or hacking into K's computer system, J's criminal activities constitute improper means.

A variety of tortious acts—ranging from fraud to unfair competition—are also viewed as improper means. Thus, if J acquires K's secret by fraudulently claiming to be a customer, inducing one of K's employees to breach her duty of confidentiality, or trespassing onto K's property, these acts are improper means.

[4] Lawful Acts as "Improper Means"

[a] State Law

Can lawful acts constitute "improper means"? As a matter of state law, the answer is a clear "yes"; there is general agreement that lawful acts may be improper means under some circumstances. However, authorities offer only vague guidance on when this will occur.

A comment to Restatement of Torts § 757 explains that "[i]n general, [improper means are] means which fall below the generally accepted standards of commercial morality and reasonable conduct."[65] The implication is that certain lawful acts are covered. Similarly, a comment to the UTSA specifies that "[i]mproper means could include otherwise lawful conduct which is improper under the circumstances."[66] More directly, the Restatement (Third) of Unfair Competition states that improper means include means that are not inherently wrongful but are "wrongful under the circumstances of the case."[67]

---

62. *Id.* at 580.

63. *Id.*

64. *See, e.g.*, AUA Private Equity Partners, LLC v. Soto, 2018 WL 1684339, at *7 (S.D.N.Y. Apr. 5, 2018) (employee who uploaded employer's trade secrets from "her work laptop to her personal cloud-based storage" acquired the information by theft and in breach of her duty to maintain secrecy).

65. Restatement of Torts § 757 cmt. f.

66. UTSA § 1 cmt.

67. Restatement (Third) of Unfair Competition § 43.

[b] Rejection by DTSA?

The outcome is less certain under the DTSA. While its basic definition of "improper means" is identical to the UTSA definition above, the DTSA adds a subparagraph (B) which provides that the term "does not include reverse engineering, independent derivation, or *any other lawful means of acquisition.*"[68] On its face, this language seems to state that lawful acts cannot be improper means. Under this approach, the acquisition of a trade secret by any method that does not involve a breach of duty to maintain secrecy, a criminal act, or tortious conduct would be permissible.

The scant legislative history on the issue may imply that Congress did not intend this outcome. The House Report notes that the basic definition of "improper means" in the DTSA is "identical" to the UTSA definition.[69] It explains the purpose of the added subparagraph as follows: "Subparagraph (B) serves to clarify that reverse engineering and independent derivation of the trade secret do not constitute improper means."[70] The report does not discuss the "any other lawful means of acquisition" phrase, which may indicate that this language was not seen as significant. It would be anomalous to suggest that Congress intended to narrow the traditional meaning of "improper means" without addressing the issue in the legislative history.

The question of whether lawful methods can ever constitute improper means under the DTSA must await judicial resolution. Until that occurs, the issue will remain unsettled.

[c] *E.I. duPont deNemours & Co. v. Christopher*

The leading case on when lawful conduct can constitute improper means is *E.I. duPont deNemours & Co. v. Christopher*,[71] which the Fifth Circuit decided in 1970. A UTSA comment cites *DuPont* as its only example of "otherwise lawful conduct which is improper under the circumstances."[72]

The case arose when DuPont was constructing a new plant designed to produce methanol by a "highly secret but unpatented process."[73] At the request of a third party, the defendants flew over the plant and took aerial photographs of the "parts of the process ... exposed to view from directly above the construction area," without trespassing into DuPont's airspace.[74] DuPont sued for trade secret misappropriation, alleging that the photographs would allow a skilled person to determine the process.

In upholding the trial court ruling in favor of DuPont, the Fifth Circuit cited the Restatement of Torts standard that improper means were "means which fall below

68. 18 U.S.C § 1839(6)(B) (emphasis added).
69. H.R. Rep. No. 114-529, at 14 (2016).
70. *Id.*
71. 431 F.2d 1012 (5th Cir. 1970).
72. UTSA § 1 cmt.
73. *DuPont*, 431 F.2d at 1013.
74. *Id.*

the generally accepted standards of commercial morality and reasonable conduct."[75] It explained:

> [W]e realize that industrial espionage of the sort here perpetrated has become a popular sport in some segments of our industrial community. However, our devotion to free wheeling industrial competition must not force us into accepting the law of the jungle as the standard of morality expected in our commercial relations. Our tolerance of the espionage game must cease when the protections required to prevent another's spying cost so much that the spirit of inventiveness is dampened. Commercial privacy must be protected from espionage which could not have been reasonably anticipated or prevented.... Perhaps ordinary fences and roofs must be built to shut out incursive eyes, but we need not require the discoverer of a trade secret to guard against the unanticipated, the undetectable, or the unpreventable methods of espionage now available.
>
> ... To require DuPont to put a roof over the unfinished plant to guard its secret would impose an enormous expense to prevent nothing more than a school boy's trick.... We should not require a person or corporation to take unreasonable precautions to prevent another from doing that which he ought not to do in the first place.... "Improper" will always be a word of many nuances, determined by time, place, and circumstances. We therefore need not proclaim a catalogue of commercial improprieties. Clearly, however, one of its commandments does say "thou shall not appropriate a trade secret through deviousness under circumstances in which countervailing defenses are not reasonably available."[76]

As this passage indicates, *DuPont* touches on several themes, each of which could help to define "improper means": commercial morality; cost-benefit analysis; and reasonableness under the totality of the circumstances.

[d] Modern Approaches

The UTSA provides scant guidance on when lawful conduct will be viewed as improper means. Its comment discussing the issue stresses the commercial morality theme: "One of the broadly stated policies behind trade secret law is 'the maintenance of standards of commercial ethics.' "[77]

But the meaning of commercial morality is undefined. While perhaps laudable as a policy goal, it is not linked to an objective standard that judges can utilize to decide concrete cases. Absent such a standard, reasonable people may differ as to whether particular conduct is commercially acceptable. Moreover, concepts of commercial morality may vary among different industries and may change over time.

---

75. *Id.* at 1016.

76. *Id.* at 1016–17.

77. UTSA § 1 cmt. (quoting Kewanee Oil Co. v. Bicron Corp., 416 U.S. 470 (1974)).

The most comprehensive modern approach to the issue comes from the Restatement (Third) of Unfair Competition, which echoes the *DuPont* themes:

> The propriety of the acquisition must be evaluated in light of all the circumstances of the case, including whether the means of acquisition are inconsistent with accepted principles of public policy and the extent to which the acquisition was facilitated by the trade secret owner's failure to take reasonable precautions against discovery of the secret by the means in question.[78]

Yet the Restatement standard is also difficult to apply in practice. First, as noted above, because the concept of commercial morality is undefined, a person cannot know in advance whether his planned conduct is proper. This can only be determined after the fact, when a judge utilizes a multi-factor test to assess whether the conduct was "improper" under the circumstances at the time.

Second, linking "improper means" to the extent that the plaintiff has taken precautions to maintain secrecy conflates two different liability elements. In order to establish that a trade secret exists in the first place, the plaintiff must show that she made "reasonable" efforts to maintain its secrecy, given the circumstances of the case.[79] Incorporating this standard into the separate element of improper means creates a circularity problem. The plaintiff who establishes that she holds a valid trade secret has already proven, by definition, that she took reasonable precautions. As a result, considering the element again, this time in the test for misappropriation, would make no difference in the outcome of the case.

Third, changes in technology mean that reasonable precautions against acquisition will change over time—perhaps more rapidly than the judiciary can process. Take, for example, the plane surveillance in *DuPont*. Today a private individual can purchase a drone equipped with a camera for less than $100. The idea that such a drone might be used for industrial surveillance is hardly difficult to anticipate. Does that mean that *DuPont* is no longer good law for the factual scenario it dealt with?

Finally, setting aside these problems, combining commercial morality and reasonable precautions into a single test is unworkable. Suppose the defendant's conduct violates a clear norm of commercial morality, but arguably the plaintiff did not take reasonable steps to maintain secrecy. In a situation like this where these factors point in different directions, it would be difficult for a court to decide whether improper means were used.

A few courts have taken a different approach to the issue based on statutory interpretation. The leading decision is *Systems 4, Inc. v. Landis & Gyr, Inc.*,[80] where the plaintiff and defendant both submitted secret bids for a new building system at the National Gallery of Art. There, a National Gallery employee mistakenly gave a closed box containing plaintiff's bid to an employee of the defendant, who later opened it

78. Restatement (Third) of Unfair Competition § 43 cmt. c.

79. UTSA § 1(4); 18 U.S.C. § 1839(3)(A); *see also* § 2.05.

80. 8 F. App'x 196 (4th Cir. 2001).

and read the bid. The district court granted summary judgment against plaintiff in its suit for misappropriation, and the Fourth Circuit affirmed. In reaching this result, the court utilized the UTSA definition of "improper means" by identifying a common theme linking the examples listed in the definition. The court observed that they are all types of "intentional conduct involving some sort of stealth, deception or trickery."[81] Applying its standard to the case, the court reasoned that the defendant's employee received the box through inadvertence since it was closed when it was obtained, not through any form of stealth, deception, or trickery.

[e] Sample Situations

Suppose that L, one of M's employees, discards a copy of M's customer list in the trash. N, a competitor, searches through the trash bins outside M's plant at night and finds the list. Has N used improper means? A few cases have considered whether such conduct is acceptable.[82] In some jurisdictions, this would be viewed as conversion, and hence the use of improper means.[83] But under the law of most states, a person who leaves trash at the curb for pickup by a garbage truck has no reasonable expectation of privacy in its contents. Nonetheless, it can be argued that N's conduct is improper because searching through trash is inconsistent with commercial morality and necessarily includes an element of stealth.[84]

Next, assume that N attends a trade convention and encounters L in a bar. N buys L a glass of wine and begins asking questions about M's business, without any intent to induce L to breach confidences. L then blurts out M's most valuable trade secret. In this situation, N did not use improper means. Merely asking questions—without any element of trickery—is a standard research technique used widely by businesses.[85] On the other hand, if N purchases seven rounds of drinks before L discloses the secret, an argument can be made that N's conduct violates commercial norms. The same result follows if L disclosed the secret after only one drink, if N knew that L was on medication that made him particularly susceptible to alcohol.

What if N, pretending to be a potential customer, contacts M to ask for a demonstration of M's product? During the demonstration at M's factory, N sees an unusual combination of equipment and is able to discern a trade secret about M's process.

---

81. *Id.* at 200.

82. If the documents containing the secret were not shredded or otherwise destroyed, the trade secret owner may have failed to take reasonable precautions to protect the information and thereby lost trade secret protection.

83. *See, e.g.*, Tennant Co. v. Advance Machine Co., Inc., 355 N.W.2d 720, 725 (Minn. App. 1984) (defendant was liable for conversion because it removed plaintiff's discarded customer lists from dumpster).

84. Reflecting this view, the Connecticut definition of "improper means" expressly includes "searching through trash." Conn. Gen. Stat. § 35-51(a).

85. On these facts, N would probably be liable for misappropriation if he used or disclosed the information to others because he would have reason to know it was a trade secret and that it was obtained by accident or mistake. *See* § 4.03[E][4].

On these facts, N used improper means.[86] His misrepresentation of his identity is inconsistent with commercial morality.

Alternatively, suppose that N is taking a train from New York to DC to visit a customer. N notices that L (one of M's employees) is seated one row in front of him. During the train ride, L makes a call on his cell phone to M's headquarters and mentions secret information, which N overhears. Did N use improper means? No. On these facts, N has taken no affirmative action to obtain the information. N is in much the same position as a person who finds a piece of paper on the sidewalk with a trade secret written on it or who views secret industrial equipment from a public street.[87] A person in N's situation is not required to inform other people about his presence in order to avoid overhearing trade secrets. On the other hand, there might be a stronger case against N if he discovered the trade secret by leaning over the seat in front of him to peek at L's open laptop screen. Moreover, N would be hard pressed to avoid liability if he covertly opened L's laptop while L was sleeping or purchasing a snack from the dining car.

[f] Reflections on Lawful Acts as Improper Means

The doctrine that lawful acts can constitute improper means—and thus justify liability for misappropriation—reflects the traditional view that the purpose of trade secret law is to preserve commercial morality as seen in the Restatement and the Restatement (Third) of Unfair Competition. The UTSA adopts this view as well, though with somewhat less force, while the DTSA arguably ignores it.

In contrast, if we view the purpose of trade secret law as protecting property rights in order to encourage innovation, there is little or no justification for the doctrine. As discussed above, the standard for determining when lawful acts constitute "improper means" is badly flawed. Because it is hard for courts to administer the standard, its results are unpredictable. In turn, this uncertainty tends to discourage innovation. Businesses routinely collect information about their competitors to discover market opportunities or obtain other commercial advantages. Under the traditional standard, it is difficult for businesses and others to know when their competitive conduct complies with the law.

As the justification for trade secret law gradually shifts away from preserving commercial morality toward protecting property rights, it is possible that at some point lawful acts will no longer be viewed as improper means.

[E] Proving Wrongful Acquisition

It is often difficult for the trade secret owner to provide direct evidence of wrongful acquisition. The owner of a jewel, for example, can easily discover if it has been

86. However, M may have failed to take reasonable precautions to safeguard its trade secret.

87. Again, N would not be able to use or disclose this information to others.

stolen—simply because it is missing—and the defendant who physically possesses the jewel can be prosecuted for theft. But information is intangible. The holder of a trade secret may not be able to prove that it has been taken by anyone, since he still has possession of the information. And it is difficult to prove that a particular defendant possesses an intangible item.

As one court explained:

> Misappropriation … can rarely be proved by convincing direct evidence. In most cases plaintiffs must construct a web of perhaps ambiguous circumstantial evidence from which the trier of fact may draw inferences which convince him that it is more probable than not that what plaintiffs allege happened did in fact take place. Against this often delicate construct of circumstantial evidence there frequently must be balanced defendants and defendants' witnesses who directly deny everything.[88]

As a result, wrongful acquisition must often be established through circumstantial evidence. An example is *Pioneer Hi-Bred International v. Holden Foundation Seeds, Inc.*,[89] where plaintiff alleged that the defendant employed improper means to acquire the genetic make-up of the plaintiff's hybrid seed corn and then used this information to develop two seed lines. In response, defendant asserted that its seed lines were independently derived from an earlier line that it owned, called L 120.

At trial, plaintiff relied on circumstantial evidence to prove wrongful acquisition. This evidence demonstrated that the defendant: (1) actively tried to obtain plaintiff's genetic material for years; (2) searched farms for stray plants containing this material; (3) developed seed lines that experts concluded were probably derived from plaintiff's material; (4) kept deficient records for the development of the seed lines at issue, in contrast to its prior meticulous records on other seed work; and (5) discarded all of the L 120 seed which it claimed was the independent source of the seed lines at issue before it could be tested.[90] The trial court held that this showing was sufficient to shift the burden to the defendant to prove that its seed lines were lawfully acquired, a burden that the defendant was unable to meet.

On appeal, the Eighth Circuit approved the burden-shifting approach. It commented that "[a]n inference of misappropriation from limited facts is especially warranted in situations such as this where the secret itself is so unique that any form of duplication would probably be improper."[91]

---

88. Greenberg v. Croydon Plastics Co., Inc., 378 F. Supp. 806, 814 (E.D. Pa. 1974). *But see* Kadant, Inc. v. Seeley Mach., Inc., 244 F. Supp. 2d 19, 38 (N.D.N.Y. 2003) (rejecting plaintiff's argument that the court should infer acquisition by improper means on the basis that defendants could not have developed competing products so quickly unless they had stolen plaintiff's trade secrets).

89. 35 F.3d 1226 (8th Cir. 1994).

90. *Id.* at 1239.

91. *Id.* at 1240.

§ 4.03 Wrongful Disclosure or Use of Trade Secret

[A] Overview

In many situations, a person is free to disclose or use a trade secret owned by another. Suppose O tells his friend P about a recipe for a new type of cocktail, and P has no reason to believe that the recipe is a secret or that O obtained it improperly. Even if the recipe qualifies for trade secret protection, P is entitled to share it with others or use it freely herself.

But disclosure or use of a trade secret without the consent of the trade secret owner may be a misappropriation. This turns on the circumstances under which the secret was obtained from its owner and the defendant's actual or constructive knowledge of those circumstances. For instance, if P in the hypothetical above knew that O obtained the recipe from his employer, who took precautions to keep it secret, P is liable for misappropriation if she uses the recipe.

The UTSA and DTSA both impose liability for the *disclosure* or *use* of a trade secret. Under both statutes, the term "misappropriation" includes:

> Disclosure or use of a trade secret of another without express or implied consent by a person who
>
> (A) used improper means to acquire knowledge of the trade secret; or
>
> (B) at the time of disclosure or use, knew or had reason to know that his knowledge of the trade secret was
>
> (I) derived from or through a person who had utilized improper means to acquire it;
>
> (II) acquired under circumstances giving rise to a duty to maintain its secrecy or limit its use; or
>
> (III) derived from or through a person who owed a duty to the person seeking relief to maintain its secrecy or limit its use; or
>
> (C) before a material change of his position, knew or had reason to know that it was a trade secret and that knowledge of it had been acquired by accident or mistake.[92]

Notice that three of the key concepts that define liability for disclosure or use were discussed earlier in the chapter: (1) "knows or has reason to know;"[93] (2) "improper means;"[94] and (3) "breach of duty."[95]

---

92. UTSA § 1(2)(ii). The DTSA definition is substantively identical, but varies slightly in wording. 18 U.S.C. § 1839(5)(B)(ii).

93. *See* § 4.02[C]. *See also* DPT Lab., Ltd. v. Bath & Body Works, Inc., 1999 WL 33289709, at *6 (W.D. Tex. Dec. 20, 1999) (noting that defendant "should have known" that the product samples it received from plaintiff were to be held in confidence, even though they were not covered by the specific terms of the confidentiality agreements between them).

94. *See* § 4.02[D].

95. See § 4.02[D][2].

[B] "Disclosure"

The term "disclosure" is not defined in the UTSA or DTSA. However, the Restatement (Third) of Unfair Competition explains: "Any conduct by the actor that enables another to learn the trade secret, including the sale or transfer of goods or other tangible objects from which the trade secret can be obtained, is a 'disclosure' of the secret. . . ."[96] For example, Q discloses R's trade secret if she: (1) emails R's confidential customer list to S; (2) hands a copy of R's secret formula to S; (3) tells S about an unsuccessful research approach that R tried; or (4) sells one of R's secret prototype products to S.

But in *Gibson-Homans Co. v. Wall-Tite, Inc.*, the court held that no disclosure occurred when one of the defendants merely "thumbed through" a notebook containing plaintiff's secret formulas, since the defendant was not a chemist and "it is clear that an untrained person could not utilize or impair the commercial value of the formulas."[97] It explained that neither the text or legislative history of the UTSA suggested that every "casual reference to a trade secret, made in the company of persons who are unable to use or derive value from the secret, constitutes a 'misappropriation.' "[98]

The defendant's motive for disclosure is irrelevant except in rare cases where a privilege is recognized.[99] For example, in *Southwestern Energy Co. v. Eickenhorst*, the defendant (an attorney) had previously filed a class action lawsuit against the plaintiffs using secret information that she learned from them pursuant to a confidentiality agreement while representing a prior client in a different matter. On these facts, court reasoned that the complaint stated a claim for disclosure under the state's version of the UTSA, even though the defendant did not disclose the information for "competitive reasons."[100] The court explained:

> The Act is designed to prevent [disclosure] to third parties irrespective of motive so that the owner of the trade secret may reasonably maintain its secrecy. If the Act allowed the information to pass freely into the public arena so long as the messenger had no anti-competitive reasons, then the Act would provide no real protection at all.[101]

The disclosure of a trade secret to the public effectively destroys the secret.[102] By definition, information cannot qualify for continued protection as a trade secret once it is "generally known" by others.[103] This type of disclosure causes direct and immediate harm to the trade secret owner that justifies an award of compensatory damages.[104]

96. Restatement (Third) of Unfair Competition § 40 cmt. c.
97. 1992 WL 512411, at *5 (C.D. Cal. Oct. 27, 1992).
98. *Id.* at *4.
99. *See* § 6.05.
100. 955 F. Supp. 1078, 1085 (W.D. Ark. 1997).
101. *Id.*
102. *See* § 6.02.
103. *See* § 2.04[B].
104. For a discussion of remedies, see Chapter 7.

In contrast, disclosure of a secret to one person or a small group of people may not terminate the trade secret because it is still not "generally known." Although such a private disclosure will increase the risk of both additional disclosure and unauthorized use in the future, compensatory damages may be difficult to prove.[105] As a result, the remedy for private disclosure will often be an injunction rather than damages. However, both the UTSA and DTSA provide that in lieu of any other method for determining damages, damages for disclosure may be measured by a "reasonable royalty."[106]

Finally, suppose that T, a vice-president of company U, is about to start a new job at V, a competing company, and it is likely that T will disclose U's trade secrets to V. Some states follow the controversial *inevitable disclosure doctrine*, under which a court will issue an injunction to bar a former employee like T from taking the new position.[107]

[C] "Use"

[1] Generally

The term "use" is not defined in the UTSA or DTSA. The case law interpreting the term, however, indicates that its scope is extremely broad. As a California court explained in *PMC, Inc. v. Kadisha*: "Employing the confidential information in manufacturing, production, research or development, marketing goods that embody the trade secret, or soliciting customers through the use of trade secret information, all constitute use."[108]

Even more broadly, the Restatement (Third) of Unfair Competition provides: "As a general matter, any exploitation of the trade secret that is likely to result in injury to the trade secret owner or enrichment to the defendant is a 'use'...."[109]

[2] Direct Use

The classic example of direct use occurs when the defendant incorporates the plaintiff's trade secret into its own product or process without changing it in any way. Suppose that W holds a trade secret in a particular process used in refining copper ore; if X adopts the same process in its own refinery, X has used the secret. Similarly, X uses a trade secret if he utilizes Y's secret cola recipe to make a competing cola. The same result follows if X solicits business from customers on Z's secret customer list.

---

105. Restatement (Third) of Unfair Competition § 40 cmt. c.

106. UTSA § 3(a); 18 U.S.C. § 1836(b)(3)(B)(ii). *See, e.g.*, StorageCraft Tech. Corp. v. Kirby, 744 F.3d 1183, 1186 (10th Cir. 2014) (using this standard where a former director disclosed one of the corporation's secrets "to a rival company in a fit of retaliatory pique without any desire for personal riches"). *See* § 7.04[C].

107. This doctrine is discussed in § 7.02[C][2].

108. 93 Cal. Rptr. 2d 663, 673 (App. 2000).

109. Restatement (Third) of Unfair Competition § 40 cmt. c.

The defendant need not use all of the trade secret; merely using a substantial portion is enough to trigger liability.[110] For example, if A's secret process has two steps and B incorporates one of those steps into his own process, B has used the secret.

Yet at some point the link between the plaintiff's trade secret and the defendant's conduct becomes so tenuous that it cannot be viewed as a "use." In *Silvaco Data Systems v. Intel Corp.*, the California Court of Appeal reasoned that merely "using a product does not constitute a 'use' of trade secrets employed in its manufacture."[111] The case arose when two of plaintiff's former employees formed their own company and sold software to Intel that contained the plaintiff's object code; the object code in that software was derived from source code, which plaintiff asserted was a trade secret.[112] In response to the plaintiff's argument that Intel "used" the source code when it ran the software program, the court stated: "One who bakes a pie from a recipe certainly engages in the 'use' of the latter; but one who eats the pie does not, by virtue of that act alone, make 'use' of the recipe in any ordinary sense...."[113]

[3] Indirect Use (aka Substantial Derivation)

More commonly, actionable use occurs when a defendant exploits the trade secret in an indirect manner. It is not necessary that the defendant use the secret in its original form. The Restatement notes that a defendant is liable for using the secret "with independently created improvements or modifications if the result is substantially derived from the trade secret."[114]

An example is *Mangren Research and Development Corp. v. National Chemical Co., Inc.*, where the plaintiff created a new "mold release agent" that helped prevent rubber and plastics from sticking to industrial molds; the key ingredient was a particular type of polytetrafluoroethylene (PTFE).[115] The plaintiff fired one of its chemists, who later developed a competing product for the defendant. In the ensuing litigation, the defendant argued that it had not used the plaintiff's secret formula because (a) many of the ingredients in its product were different and (b) it employed a different type of PTFE. Upholding the jury verdict in favor of the plaintiff, the Seventh Circuit agreed that the defendant's product was substantially derived from the plaintiff's trade secret. It stressed that the defendant's PTFE had the same key characteristics as the plaintiff's ingredient: a "highly degraded PTFE with a low molecular weight and low tensile strength."[116] The court continued: "[I]f trade secret law were not flexible enough to encompass modified or even new products that are substantially

110. *Id.*

111. 109 Cal. Rptr. 3d 17, 41 (App. 2010).

112. Programmers write programs in source code, which humans can understand. In turn, a specialized program translates the source code into object code, which machines can read. Software sold to end users contains object code, not source code.

113. *Silvaco Data Systems*, 109 Cal. Rptr. 3d at 41.

114. Restatement (Third) of Unfair Competition § 40 cmt. c.

115. 87 F.3d 937 (7th Cir. 1996).

116. *Id.* at 944.

derived from the trade secret of another, the protections that the law provides would be hollow indeed."[117]

On the other hand, the Restatement makes clear that "if the contribution made by the trade secret is so slight that the actor's product or process can be said to derive from other sources of information or from independent creation, the trade secret has not been 'used.'"[118]

Under some circumstances, a use occurs when the defendant utilizes a trade secret only for information purposes, without seeking to duplicate any part of the plaintiff's product or process. Similarly, when a trade secret consists of negative information—knowing what not to do—employing this information as a starting point for research, to accelerate existing research, or to avoid development expenses are all actionable uses.

Yet in some situations, a broad interpretation of use would unreasonably interfere with market competition, as illustrated by *Omnitech International, Inc. v. Clorox Co.*[119] There Omnitech provided trade secret information concerning its pesticide products to Clorox pursuant to an express confidentiality agreement so that Clorox could evaluate purchasing Omnitech's business; but Clorox bought a different pesticide company instead. Omnitech then sued on the theory that Clorox had considered the trade secret information in evaluating its purchase of the other company. The Fifth Circuit rejected Omnitech's claim that this was a "use" of the information:

> Certainly "misappropriation" of a trade secret means more than simply using knowledge gained through a variety of experiences, including analyses of possible target companies, to evaluate a potential purchase. To hold otherwise would lead to one of two unacceptable results: (i) every time a company entered into preliminary negotiations for a possible purchase of another company's assets in which the acquiring company was given limited access to the target's trade secrets, the acquiring party would effectively be precluded from evaluating other potential targets; or (ii) the acquiring company would, as a practical matter, be forced to make a purchase decision without the benefit of examination of the target company's most important assets—its trade secrets.[120]

[D] "Without Express or Implied Consent"

The UTSA and DTSA both require that the plaintiff prove the improper disclosure or use occurred without its "express or implied consent."[121] Express consent is rarely an issue; the trade secret holder who clearly agreed to its disclosure or use by another party is not in a position to complain. The issue sometimes surfaces, however, where

117. *Id.*
118. Restatement (Third) of Unfair Competition § 40 cmt. c.
119. 11 F.3d 1316 (5th Cir. 1994).
120. *Id.* at 1325.
121. UTSA § 1(2)(ii); 18 U.S.C. § 1839(5)(B).

the plaintiff has licensed the use of the trade secret but contends that the defendant's use exceeded the scope of the license.

Implied consent is sometimes inferred from the circumstances of the case, particularly where the relationship between the parties is close but informal. For example, assume company C regularly shares trade secret information with its supplier D in the ordinary course of business. If C never warns D not to use the information without C's permission, it may be difficult in later litigation for C to overcome D's claim that it received implied consent.

[E] Source of Trade Secret Knowledge

[1] Generally

A defendant is liable under the UTSA and DTSA for disclosing or using a trade secret without the owner's consent in three basic situations:

- *Improper means*: he "used improper means to acquire knowledge of the trade secret"[122] *or* "knew or had reason to know" that his knowledge was "derived from or through a person" who had utilized "improper means to acquire" it.[123]
- *Breach of duty*: he "knew or had reason to know" that his knowledge of the secret was "acquired under circumstances giving rise to a duty to maintain" its secrecy or limit its use *or* was "derived from or through a person who owed a duty to the person seeking relief to maintain" its secrecy or limit its use.[124]
- *Accident or mistake*: "before a material change" in his position, he "knew or had reason to know" that it was a trade secret and that knowledge of it had been acquired by "accident or mistake."[125]

[2] "Improper Means"

Two categories of defendants are liable for the disclosure or use of a trade secret acquired by *improper means*: (a) the wrongful actor who directly obtains the secret from the owner; and (b) those who learn the secret from the wrongful actor, if they have the requisite knowledge. As discussed above, "improper means" include criminal and tortious conduct, breach or inducement of a breach of duty to maintain secrecy, and—at least under the UTSA—lawful acts that are wrongful under the circumstances of the case.[126]

First, disclosure or use of the secret by the wrongful actor—the person who used improper means to acquire knowledge of the trade secret—is a misappropriation.[127]

---

122. UTSA § 1(2)(ii)(A); 18 U.S.C. § 1839(5)(B)(i).
123. UTSA § 1(2)(ii)(B)(I); 18 U.S.C. § 1839(5)(B)(ii)(I).
124. UTSA § 1(2)(ii)(B)(II), (III); 18 U.S.C. § 1839(5)(B)(ii)(I), (II).
125. UTSA § 1(2)(ii)(C); 18 U.S.C. § 1839(5)(B)(iii).
126. *See* § 4.02[D].
127. UTSA § 1(2)(ii)(A); 18 U.S.C. § 1839(5)(B)(i).

This overlaps with the rule that acquisition of a secret by improper means is a misappropriation, which is discussed earlier in this chapter.[128]

Suppose that E and F are competing toy manufacturers. G illegally hacks into E's computer system, learns one of E's secret processes, and discloses it to F. G's conduct is a form of theft, which constitutes improper means. On these facts, G is liable for *disclosure* of a trade secret obtained by improper means.[129]

Second, disclosure or use of the secret by a person who knew or had reason to know that it was derived from or through a person who acquired it by improper means is also a misappropriation. In the above hypothetical, assume that F began using the secret process in its factory, knowing that G acquired the secret by theft. In this situation, F is liable for wrongful *use* of a trade secret.

[3] Breach of "Duty to Maintain Its Secrecy"

Two categories of defendants are liable for the disclosure or use of a trade secret acquired by a person who is under a *duty to maintain its secrecy*: (a) the actor who legally obtained the secret from the owner; and (b) those who learn the secret from that actor, if they have the requisite knowledge. In this situation, the actor who obtained the information from the trade secret owner acquired it by proper means.[130]

First, disclosure or use of a trade secret by a person who acquired it under circumstances giving rise to a duty to maintain its secrecy or limit its use is a misappropriation. The law governing when such a duty to maintain secrecy arises is discussed in detail earlier in this chapter.[131] The classic example of a person subject to a duty to maintain secrecy is an employee who signed a nondisclosure agreement.

Suppose H, a toy manufacturer, employs J as a quality control engineer; J signs an agreement promising not to disclose H's trade secrets. In the course of his employment, J learns about a secret process that H uses in its plant. J obtained this information legally, so he is not liable for wrongful acquisition. But assume that J now discloses the secret to his new employer K, who also manufactures toys. On these facts, J is liable for *disclosure* of a trade secret in violation of his duty to maintain secrecy.

A common scenario involves the employee who properly obtains a trade secret, memorizes it, and later discloses it to a new employer. Courts uniformly hold that the form in which the secret is acquired is irrelevant to liability. As one panel observed, "[u]sing memorization ... does not transform that trade secret from confidential in-

---

128. *See* §4.02[D].

129. G is also liable for acquisition of the trade secret by improper means.

130. The breach of a duty to maintain secrecy has two separate roles. As discussed earlier in the chapter, such a breach is relevant to determine if a trade secret was *wrongfully* acquired. In that context, it is one type of improper means. *See* §4.02[D][2]. However, as used in this context it helps to define when disclosure or use of a *legally* acquired secret is a misappropriation. The provisions governing liability for disclosure or use treat such a breach of duty as a category separate and apart from improper means.

131. *See* §4.02[D][2].

formation into non-confidential information."[132] In the example above, J is liable even if he merely memorized the secret.

Second, disclosure or use of a trade secret by a person who knew or had reason to know that it was derived from or through a person who owed a duty to the person seeking relief to maintain its secrecy is also misappropriation. In the above hypothetical, assume that K begins using the process in his factory, knowing that J was under a duty to maintain its secrecy. H now sues K. In this situation, K is liable for *use* of a trade secret derived from a person (J) who owed a duty to maintain secrecy.

In this kind of lawsuit, the new employer's actual or constructive knowledge that a breach of duty occurred is a core issue. Particularly where the new employer is aware that (a) the employee formerly worked for a company in the same industry and (b) the valuable information provided by the employee is the type of information that he had access to at that company, an inference may arise that the new employer should have inquired about its origin.

[4] "Accident or Mistake"

Trade secrets are sometimes obtained by accident or mistake. For example, a government agency might inadvertently release a corporation's secret test data to a member of the public or a business owner could carelessly leave a secret drawing in the back seat of a taxi where a later passenger finds it.

A person who acquires a trade secret by *accident or mistake* is liable for misappropriation under the UTSA and DTSA under narrow circumstances—only if before a material change of his position, he knew or had reason to know that (a) it was a trade secret and (b) his knowledge of it was acquired by accident or mistake.[133]

Assume that L, while walking down the street, discovers a piece of paper that contains a handwritten recipe for a dessert. L has no reason to believe that the recipe is a trade secret or that he acquired it by mistake. On these facts, L is free to disclose the recipe to others or to use it himself, even though it is actually a trade secret owned by M.

Suppose instead that M quickly notifies L that the recipe is a trade secret. At this point, L may not disclose or use the recipe; such "notice suffices to make ... [L] a misappropriator thereafter."[134]

However, if L materially changes his position before receiving notice—for instance, by building a new factory to manufacture the dessert—he is in a different situation. The UTSA and DTSA authorize the court to order that a party like L pay a reasonable

---

132. Stampede Tool Warehouse, Inc. v. May, 651 N.E.2d 209, 217 (Ill. App. Ct. 1995).

133. UTSA § 1(2)(ii)(C); 18 U.S.C. § 1839(5)(B)(iii). *See, e.g.*, Williams v. Curtiss-Wright Corp., 681 F.2d 161 (3d Cir. 1982).

134. UTSA § 2 cmt.

royalty for continued use of the secret, instead of issuing an injunction prohibiting its future use.[135]

Whenever a trade secret is obtained through accident or mistake, it is important to consider the possibility that the information does not qualify for legal protection. As a rule, if the owner fails to take reasonable precautions to maintain the secrecy of her information, it is no longer a trade secret.[136] In some circumstances, the fact that the secret was discovered by accident or mistake may be evidence of the owner's failure to take such precautions. A comment to the UTSA explains that the "type of accident or mistake that can result in a misappropriation" by a good-faith acquirer requires "conduct by a person seeking relief that does not constitute a failure of efforts that are reasonable under the circumstances to maintain its secrecy."[137]

[F] Proving Unauthorized Disclosure or Use

[1] Generally

Unauthorized disclosure or use of a trade secret is sometimes proven by direct evidence, such as emails or witness testimony. But often this must be proven by circumstantial evidence. As one court explained in a trade secret decision: "In most cases plaintiffs must construct a web of perhaps ambiguous circumstantial evidence from which the trier of fact may draw inferences which convince him that it is more probable than not that what plaintiffs allege happened did in fact take place."[138]

[2] Disclosure

In many cases, disclosure can be proven by witness testimony or documentary evidence. N might testify that he overheard O tell P's trade secret to Q. Or the plaintiff could introduce into evidence an email from R that disclosed the secret to S.

More commonly, disclosure is proven by circumstantial evidence. For instance, in *UniRAM Technology, Inc. v. Taiwan Semiconductor Manufacturing Co.* plaintiff alleged that the defendant improperly disclosed trade secrets to Monolithic Systems Technology; defendant opposed plaintiff's motion for summary judgment on the basis that there was no evidence of such disclosure.[139] However, plaintiff was able to show that: (a) defendant knew plaintiff's trade secrets; (b) defendant owned shares in Monolithic; (c) Monolithic owed "tens of millions of dollars" to defendant, but was a "failed player" in the relevant market; (d) "top officials at both companies met to find a solution" to this problem; and (e) shortly thereafter, defendant and Monolithic were working jointly to develop a process that "mirrored" plaintiff's

135. UTSA § 2(b); 18 U.S.C. § 1833(b)(3)(A)(iii). *See* § 7.03[C].

136. *See* § 6.02.

137. UTSA § 1 cmt. *See also* Restatement (Third) of Unfair Competition § 40(b)(4).

138. Greenberg v. Croydon Plastics Co., Inc., 378 F. Supp. 806, 814 (E.D. Pa. 1974).

139. 617 F. Supp. 2d 938 (N.D. Cal. 2007).

secret technology.[140] The court found that this was enough circumstantial evidence to create a genuine issue of fact for trial.

[3] Use

In some cases, proving that the defendant used the secret through direct evidence is simple. Suppose T steals a confidential list containing customer data from her employer U and is hired by U's competitor V, where she tries to sell V's products to companies on the list. Witnesses might testify that they saw T referring to the list during her sales calls, which would establish use.

But use is often more difficult to prove. For example, W might manufacture a product that is quite similar to X's product, but deny that he is using any of X's trade secrets. The Restatement (Third) of Unfair Competition explains that "proof of the defendant's knowledge of the trade secret together with substantial similarities between the parties' products or processes may justify an inference of use by the defendant."[141] The defendant can then try to rebut this inference with its own proof.

Sokol Crystal Products, Inc. v. DSC Communications Corp. illustrates the point.[142] The case arose when plaintiff Sokol agreed to supply a telecommunications device to Granger, defendant DSC's predecessor, pursuant to a contract that prohibited Granger from using plaintiff's trade secrets. One of Granger's engineers later worked with a subsidiary company to develop its own version of the device. When Sokol sued the defendant for illegally using its trade secrets in manufacturing the device, it was unable to present any direct evidence of use. Since Granger had "access to Sokol's trade secrets" and Granger's "product was similar to Sokol's," the Seventh Circuit agreed the jury could infer that Granger used the secrets.[143] The defendant might have rebutted this inference by proving independent development, but was unable to do so.

Conversely, in *Kadant, Inc. v. Seeley Machine, Inc.*, the defendants were able to rebut the inference.[144] Defendants, who had access to plaintiff's secret information about how to manufacture certain parts related to papermaking machines, established a competing business and began selling similar parts. Plaintiff argued that "the only way defendants could develop, market, and sell their products in so short of time" was by using its trade secrets.[145] But the plaintiff lost because the defendants established that "the plaintiff's products were simple, consisting of non-technical and few parts, [and] that reverse engineering would take little time."[146]

---

140. *Id.* at 944.
141. Restatement (Third) of Unfair Competition § 40 cmt. c.
142. 15 F.3d 1427 (7th Cir. 1994).
143. *Id.* at 1432.
144. 244 F. Supp. 2d 19 (N.D.N.Y. 2003).
145. *Id.* at 38.
146. *Id.*

§ 4.04 Special Requirement for DTSA Liability: Link to Interstate or Foreign Commerce

[A] Overview

An important difference between the UTSA and DTSA is that a misappropriation action may be brought under the DTSA only "if the trade secret is related to a product or service used in, or intended for use in, interstate or foreign commerce."[147] This requirement must be satisfied in order for a court to have subject matter jurisdiction.

The Constitution does not grant Congress express authority to adopt legislation related to trade secrets, unlike copyrights and patents.[148] In enacting the DTSA, Congress relied upon the Commerce Clause, which permits it "[t]o regulate Commerce with foreign Nations, and among the several States, and with the Indian Tribes."[149]

The jurisdictional reach of the DTSA remains undefined. The closest parallel statute in intellectual property law is the Lanham Act, which is the basis for federal regulation of trademarks pursuant to the Commerce Clause. But the scope of that act is coextensive with the power of Congress to regulate commerce; it applies to "all commerce which may lawfully be regulated by Congress."[150] Thus, while that act cannot affect purely intrastate activities, it does apply to intrastate activities that "substantially" affect interstate or foreign commerce.[151] The DTSA, in contrast, arguably has a narrower jurisdictional scope. It does not apply to *all* commerce that Congress may lawfully regulate.

[B] Relation to Product or Service

One DTSA jurisdictional requisite is that the trade secret must be "related to a product or service." But how close must this relationship be? The few decisions on the point suggest that courts will take a broad view of the requirement. For example, *Blue Star Land Services, LLC v. Coleman* held that trade secrets in the form of oil field maps and rig schedules were sufficiently related to oil, a product intended for shipment in interstate commerce.[152]

Future disputes about the closeness of the required relationship are likely to arise in a variety of situations, including (1) negative information and (2) basic research. It is well settled that "knowing what not to do" is a protectable trade secret under the UTSA. But such negative information may not have a sufficiently close relationship

147. 18 U.S.C. § 1836(b)(1).

148. The Intellectual Property Clause of the Constitution authorizes Congress to regulate copyrights and patents, regardless of any impact on commerce. U.S. Const. art. I, § 8, cl. 8.

149. *Id.* cl. 3.

150. 15 U.S.C. § 1127.

151. United States v. Lopez, 514 U.S. 549, 559 (1995).

152. 2017 WL 6210901 (W.D. Okla. Dec. 8, 2017).

to a future product or service under the DTSA. Similarly, because basic research—by definition—seeks to expand humanity's knowledge in a general sense, not to develop a product or service, the information it produces might not qualify for DTSA protection, even if such information has potential value.

[C] Actual or Intended Use in Interstate or Foreign Commerce

The second jurisdictional requisite—that the product or service be "used in, or intended for use in, interstate or foreign commerce"—further limits the scope of the DTSA. Under this test, trade secrets relating to products or services used, or intended for use, only in intrastate commerce will not qualify for protection, even if they substantially affect interstate or foreign commerce.

In *Yager v. Vignieri*, an early case on the issue, the court held that it had jurisdiction over plaintiff's claim that the defendant misappropriated trade secrets related to his plastic surgery practice because some of the patients travelled from their New Jersey homes to a New York office to use plaintiff's services.[153] It stressed that this interpretation was appropriate because Congress "crafted the commerce language in the DTSA to 'reach broadly in protecting against the theft of trade secrets.'"[154] But even if other courts agree that this language should be interpreted broadly, it would not encompass purely intrastate activities. For example, if bar owner Y uses a secret recipe to make a "special" cocktail but serves only in-state customers, presumably Y could not sue for misappropriation under the DTSA.

§ 4.05 Liability of Third Parties

Suppose that Z misappropriates A's trade secret. Under what circumstances can third party B—who did not perform any act of misappropriation—be held liable for Z's conduct? In intellectual property law, the concept of secondary liability governs when a non-actor such as B is liable for the conduct of another actor. The principal type of secondary liability recognized in trade secret law is vicarious liability. If B is Z's employer, B may be secondarily liable for Z's misappropriation.[155]

Most jurisdictions recognize that an employer may be vicariously liable when one of its agents or employees misappropriates a trade secret. An example is *Advanced Systems, Inc. v. Huber*, where two employees of defendant Livingston & Haven obtained

---

153. 2017 WL 4574487 (S.D.N.Y. Oct. 12, 2017).

154. *Id.* at *2 (quoting United States v. Agrawal, 726 F.3d 235, 244 n.7 (2d Cir. 2013)). *See also* DTSA § 5(3), 130 Stat. 376, 384 (2016) (expressing the "sense of Congress" that the DTSA "applies broadly to protect trade secrets from theft").

155. In addition, under narrow circumstances the officers and directors of a corporation may be held liable for the corporation's misappropriation even though they had no role in it. *See, e.g.*, PMC, Inc. v. Kadisha, 93 Cal. Rptr. 2d 663 (App. 2000).

confidential drawings, price data, and cost data from plaintiff's employee Huber, knowing that he had acquired it by improper means.[156] The two employees were personally liable because they acquired these trade secrets with knowledge that Huber obtained them by improper means. In addition, the court ruled that Livingston & Haven was vicariously liable for the conduct of its employees. It explained that:

> Under Pennsylvania law, an employer may be vicariously liable for its employee's intentional acts if the conduct (1) is similar in kind to that which the employee is hired to perform, (2) occurs "substantially within" the temporal and spatial scope of employment, and (3) is "actuated," at least in part, in service of the employer.[157]

All of these elements were satisfied on the facts of the case.

Yet vicarious liability for misappropriation is controversial. As discussed above, the UTSA provides that a party is not liable for misappropriation unless it knows or has reason to know that the trade secret was acquired improperly. Accordingly, a few courts conclude that the UTSA displaces vicarious liability.[158] But the majority view is that displacement does not apply because vicarious liability is not an independent cause of action. Rather, it is a doctrine that "assesses liability not because of the act giving rise to the claim but because of a certain status."[159]

---

156. Advanced Fluid Systems, Inc v. Huber, 295 F. Supp. 3d 467, 486 (M.D. Pa. 2018) ("We join the majority of federal and state courts and hold that [the Pennsylvania version of the UTSA] authorizes vicarious trade secret liability.").

157. *Id.* Most states utilize a similar list of elements to define vicarious liability.

158. *See, e.g.*, Infinity Products, Inc. v. Quandt, 810 N.E.2d 1028, 1034 (Ind. 2004).

159. Newport News Indus. v. Dynamic Testing, Inc., 130 F. Supp. 2d 745, 751 (E.D. Va. 2001).

Chapter 5

Trade Secret Litigation

§ 5.01 Introduction

A trade secret exists only so long as the information is secret.[1] Even fleeting disclosure—such as posting a defense company's missile diagrams on a personal blog or forwarding a company's customer list to competitors—could be enough to destroy the

1. *See* § 6.02.

trade secret forever. As a result, the fundamental difference that separates a trade secret lawsuit from ordinary litigation is the risk that the secret will be lost by disclosure.

When someone wrongfully acquires, discloses, or uses a trade secret, time is of the essence. The owner must take immediate action to safeguard the information against further misappropriation. The urgency inherent in a trade secret case colors the entire litigation process. The complaint must be filed as soon as possible and should raise the strongest cognizable claims in order to impress the court with the importance of the case and the necessity for injunctive relief. Moreover, the plaintiff should usually seek a temporary restraining order and/or a preliminary injunction to bar further disclosure or use, and the litigation should proceed expeditiously.

During the course of litigation, care must be taken to ensure that the secret is not disclosed. In an ordinary case, the pleadings and other documents filed with the court are available for anyone to inspect, and the pretrial proceedings and the trial are open to the public. Counsel for the plaintiff in a trade secret case will want to obtain protective orders covering both the pretrial and trial phases to protect the information against disclosure. Compliance with those orders must be monitored throughout the litigation.

§ 5.02 Counseling the Client

[A] Litigation Risks

The threshold question in all litigation is whether the cost of pursuing a suit outweighs the cost of either doing nothing or settling the matter amicably.[2] Careful consideration of alternatives to litigation is particularly important in trade secret disputes for two reasons: the potential loss of the trade secret and the emotional impact of litigation.

Litigation risks further disclosure of the trade secret—and perhaps its loss. At a minimum, the secret must be shared with the court, opposing counsel, witnesses, and potentially a jury. Although the court must take steps to protect the secret, no system is perfect and it is possible that the secret will be inadvertently disclosed.[3]

In addition, the emotional impact of trade secret litigation can be significant. Patent liability, for example, can exist regardless of whether the infringer knew it was using someone else's protected information. But trade secret liability depends on affirmative misappropriation: the defendant must know or should have known that it was wrongfully acquiring, disclosing, or using the secret. And because trade secrets,

2. As Abraham Lincoln advised: "Discourage litigation.... Point out ... how the nominal winner is often a real loser—in fees, expenses, and waste of time." Abraham Lincoln, *Notes for Law Lecture*, *in* 2 Complete Works of Abraham Lincoln 140 (John G. Nicolay & John Hay eds., 1894).

3. *See, e.g.*, Gov't Employees Ins. Co. v. Nealey, 262 F. Supp. 3d 153, 168–70 (E.D. Pa. 2017) (plaintiff lost its trade secrets by disclosing the information in documents supporting a removal motion that were filed with the court, but not under seal).

by definition, are kept secret, the plaintiff is often required to accuse a formerly trusted employee, friend, or business partner of theft. Such an accusation has the potential to destroy longstanding relationships.

[B] Alternatives to Litigation

Counsel in a trade secret case may encourage the potential plaintiff to consider whether a less public and adversarial alternative is preferable, particularly where there is no risk of further misappropriation. Three approaches might be explored.

First, the parties could consider arbitrating the dispute. Arbitration—that is, presenting a case before a panel of private judges selected and paid for by both sides—allows an adversarial presentation of evidence, and ultimately provides the parties with a clear decision on their rights. In addition, because the parties can agree to keep the details of the arbitration confidential, this method may avoid some of the potential pitfalls arising from a public trial. On the other hand, arbitration may create the same interpersonal problems as litigation and be equally expensive. Moreover, the arbitration process generally does not permit appeals, and therefore may be less useful when the law is unsettled.

Potential litigants might also consider mediation—that is, presenting a case before a neutral third party hired by the parties who can guide the course of negotiations. This approach facilitates confidentiality and minimizes interpersonal tensions. It also provides the parties with an intermediary who can offer a helpful perspective on the dispute. But mediation will not be productive if the parties are deadlocked, since it does not provide a definitive decision on liability.

A third approach is informal negotiation between the parties without an intermediary. This approach provides confidentiality, saves the cost of a mediator, and allows the parties to engage in a less confrontational manner. Informal negotiation may work well where the parties have an ongoing business relationship or another incentive to come to the table. However, many parties considering litigation are beyond the point where it could be helpful. Most trade secret disputes are eventually settled, but this usually occurs during the course of litigation.[4]

§ 5.03 Selecting the Forum

[A] Overview

If the client has resolved to pursue litigation, a threshold question is where to file suit. This question has three distinct parts: (1) personal jurisdiction; (2) the choice between state and federal court; and (3) venue.

---

4. One study revealed that only 6% of trade secret cases filed in federal court over a 19-year period were tried to judgment. Elizabeth A. Rowe, *Unpacking Trade Secret Damages*, 55 Hous. L. Rev. 155, 167 (2017).

[B] Personal Jurisdiction

The trade secret plaintiff usually has limited options on where to file, based on the location of the defendant's activities. The Supreme Court has long held that the Due Process Clause "limits the power of a state court to render a valid personal judgment against a nonresident defendant."[5] In turn, the law of the state in which a federal district court is located determines the scope of its personal jurisdiction.[6]

In practical terms, the safest approach is to sue in the state where the defendant lives, and, accordingly, is subject to general jurisdiction. For a human being (for example, a former employee), this would be his domicile—i.e., his "true, fixed and permanent home and place of habitation."[7] In the case of a corporation (for example, a rival business), the plaintiff could sue either in the defendant's principal place of business or its state of incorporation.[8]

For example, if company A plans to sue employee B, a longtime resident of Wisconsin, Wisconsin would be an appropriate place to file because it is presumably B's domicile. Similarly, if inventor C wishes to sue company D, which is incorporated in Delaware and has its principal place of business in Ohio, both Delaware and Ohio would have personal jurisdiction. What if inventor C wants to sue D in New Hampshire, where D's subsidiary is based? New Hampshire does not have general jurisdiction over the parent corporation in this situation, so long as "the subsidiary has preserved some semblance of independence from the parent...."[9]

That said, a party should conduct basic research before automatically filing in the defendant's state of residence. Does the state's trade secret case law particularly favor defendants? Are there unusual procedural quirks that might benefit a defendant, such as a requirement that the plaintiff disclose the trade secret at an early stage of the litigation? Has the state adopted the Uniform Trade Secrets Act or does it protect trade secrets using a different framework? To what extent does the state's version of the UTSA displace common law theories such as conversion, fraud, and unfair competition?[10]

If the defendant's state of residence is a disadvantageous forum, the plaintiff may consider whether it can establish personal jurisdiction in another state. For instance, if it can be shown that the suit "arise[s] out of or relate[s] to the defendant's contacts

---

5. *See, e.g.*, Bristol-Myers Squibb Co. v. Superior Court of California, 137 S. Ct. 1773, 1779 (2017).

6. *See, e.g.*, Spiegel v. Schulmann, 604 F.3d 72, 76 (2d Cir. 2010). *See also* Fed. R. Civ. P. 4(k)(1) (authorizing district courts to assert personal jurisdiction over non-resident defendants to the extent permitted by state law).

7. Martinez v. Bynum, 461 U.S. 321, 331 (1983); *see also* Goodyear Dunlop Tires Operations, S.A. v. Brown, 564 U.S. 915, 924 (2011) (describing the domicile as "the paradigm forum for the exercise of general jurisdiction").

8. *Goodyear*, 564 U.S. at 924.

9. 4A Charles Alan Wright & Arthur R. Miller, Federal Practice & Procedure: Federal Rules of Civil Procedure § 1069.4 (4th ed. 2019 update).

10. *See* § 6.07[C].

with" a particular state, a court can constitutionally exercise personal jurisdiction over the defendant for "issues deriving from, or connected with" those contacts.[11] Similarly, jurisdiction will lie if an individual defendant is physically present in a state at the time of service. And any defendant can consent to suit in a particular state—either expressly or by failure to object to personal jurisdiction at the appropriate time.

For example, even if company E is incorporated in Virginia and has its principal place of business in Utah, it could still be sued in Oregon if (1) the suit is based on E's conduct in Oregon or (2) E does not object to being sued there. Similarly, employee F who is domiciled in Kansas could be sued in Texas if (1) the suit arises out of F's behavior while temporarily working in San Antonio or (2) F is served while visiting a friend in El Paso.

[C] State or Federal Court?

Once the state is selected, the next question is whether to sue in state or federal court. While a litigant can always file in state court if personal jurisdiction exists, filing in federal court—as a general matter—requires either a federal claim or diversity of citizenship between the parties.[12] In the past, it was sometimes difficult for the plaintiff in a trade secret case to invoke federal court jurisdiction. But the 2016 enactment of the Defend Trade Secrets Act—coupled with its similarity to the UTSA—obviated this problem. Today a plaintiff who wishes to litigate in federal court can simply sue under the DTSA or raise both DTSA and UTSA claims.[13]

The state and federal systems each have their own advantages and disadvantages, many of which apply to any type of civil litigation. For example, state courts may be more plaintiff-friendly; and their dockets may be less crowded, allowing the plaintiff to obtain relief with less delay. In the context of trade secret litigation, one potential benefit of filing in state court is that the case will be adjudicated under state law. Given the relative ages of the UTSA and DTSA, state law will probably be more developed than federal law for some time and, accordingly, will provide a more predictable outcome.

However, discovery may be less robust in state courts than in federal courts. And state courts sometimes have idiosyncratic procedural rules. For example, California requires the plaintiff to identify trade secrets with "reasonable particularity" before discovery can commence; this limits the plaintiff's ability to expand its case if more violations are later discovered and increases the danger that the secrets will be dis-

11. *See, e.g.*, *Bristol-Myers*, 137 S. Ct. at 1780. *See also, e.g.*, Pictometry Int'l Corp. v. Air America Flight Ctr., LLC, 394 F. Supp. 3d 320 (W.D.N.Y. 2019) (finding personal jurisdiction over certain out-of-state defendants in DTSA suit).

12. *See* 28 U.S.C. § 1331 ("The district courts shall have original jurisdiction of all civil actions arising under the Constitution, laws, or treaties of the United States."); *id.* § 1332(a)(1) ("The district courts shall have original jurisdiction of all civil actions where the matter in controversy exceeds the sum or value of $75,000 ... and is between ... citizens of different States.").

13. This assumes that the plaintiff can satisfy the DTSA's commerce element. *See* § 4.04.

seminated to the public.[14] On the other hand, federal courts have the benefit of uniform procedural rules. In addition, because of the *Erie* doctrine, plaintiffs suing in federal court may be able to avoid unhelpful state procedural rules.[15]

[D] Venue

The final consideration when selecting a forum is the particular judicial district within the state where the suit will be filed, usually called venue.

In federal courts, venue is controlled by a statute that generally requires the plaintiff to sue in either (1) "a judicial district in which any defendant resides, if all defendants are residents of the State in which the district is located" or (2) "a judicial district in which a substantial part of the events or omissions giving rise to the claim occurred" (or "a substantial part of property that is the subject of the action is situated").[16] If no district satisfies either criterion, the plaintiff may file in "any judicial district in which any defendant is subject to the court's personal jurisdiction."[17]

At first glance, this rule may seem restrictive. In reality, however, it gives a trade secret plaintiff significant latitude. For example, suppose G is a small tech company located in Boston; its employee H misappropriates G's valuable search algorithm and transmits it to G's competitor J, in San Francisco; J conducts business throughout California. Under the venue statute, G could sue J in any of the four judicial districts in California or—if H transmitted the algorithm to J from his computer workstation in Boston—in the district of Massachusetts.

Like forum selection, venue selection requires the plaintiff to conduct additional research to determine the optimal location. For example, an important consideration is whether the district judges have particular expertise in the subject matter of the trade secret. A defense contractor might fare better in the Eastern District of Virginia—where the judges are routinely faced with complicated technology disputes springing from Northern Virginia's defense industry—while a small tech company might target the Northern District of California, which covers Silicon Valley.

Another consideration is the number of judges available in a given jurisdiction. A smaller number may give the plaintiff greater ability to control which judge is assigned to the case. Filing in a district with only two judges, for instance, provides a more predictable choice than filing in one with twenty judges. Yet a larger number of judges might mean less delay in case processing and quicker rulings.

There is no one-size-fits-all answer to the best venue for a trade secrets suit. A sophisticated plaintiff will make a case-by-case determination about where to file.

---

14. *See* Cal. Civ. Proc. Code § 2019.210.

15. *See* Erie R. Co. v. Tompkins, 304 U.S. 64 (1938); Hanna v. Plumer, 380 U.S. 460 (1965).

16. *See* 28 U.S.C. § 1391(b)(1)–(2). For venue purposes: (1) a natural person is deemed to reside in the judicial district where she is domiciled; and (2) a corporation or other entity sued as a defendant is deemed to reside in any judicial district "in which such defendant is subject to the court's personal jurisdiction with respect to the civil action in question…." 28 U.S.C. § 1391(c)(1), (2).

17. *Id.* § 1391(b)(3).

§ 5.04 Drafting the Complaint

[A] Overview

Once the trade secret plaintiff has decided where to sue—and thus knows which law will govern the case—the next logical step is to determine which claims to raise and what remedies to request.

In light of the fast-moving nature of trade secrets cases, the complaint is usually the plaintiff's best opportunity to lay out the case for the court. Effective complaints strike a balance between asserting independent legal theories—to ensure that the defendant cannot easily win a motion to dismiss—and crafting a readable, credible argument that can be easily understood by the court.

[B] Describing the Trade Secret

A frequent point of dispute between the parties during the early stages of a case is how much of the trade secret the plaintiff must reveal in its complaint. Taken to the extreme, of course, the average plaintiff would prefer to share *no* information about the secret beyond alleging its existence, fearing that the information might end up in the public domain. If there is any risk that the description of the trade secret in the complaint might lead to a credible argument that the secret has been lost through disclosure, plaintiff's counsel must take the steps necessary to file the complaint under seal.

The defendant will usually prefer that the purported trade secret be set out in full in the complaint. Although there may be some situations where this is not the case (for example, if the dispute is over the ownership of the trade secret, or the defendant employs a very similar trade secret that would also be subject to exposure), it is generally in the defendant's interest to have the trade secret defined as clearly as possible. This will allow the defendant to evaluate whether it can challenge the purported secret on the basis that it does not qualify for protection, for example, because the information is generally known.

The defendant can use several tools to press the plaintiff for a more detailed description of the secret. Most notably, the defendant can file a motion to dismiss on the ground that the plaintiff has failed to provide sufficient detail to state a claim for misappropriation.[18] As the Seventh Circuit observed in *Composite Marine Propellers v. Van Der Woude*, "[i]t is not enough to point to broad areas of technology and assert that something there must have been secret and misappropriated."[19]

Where the complaint only makes vague allegations about the secret, a defendant can also try to obtain more detail at the preliminary injunction stage. Requesting a preliminary injunction is often a practical necessity; but it also comes with a higher

18. *See* § 5.06[D].

19. 962 F.2d 1263, 1266 (7th Cir. 1992).

burden of proof, since the plaintiff must show a likelihood of success. If the plaintiff presents only minimal evidence about the metes and bounds of the secret, the defendant is well positioned to argue that the plaintiff has not met its burden; alternatively, the defendant may introduce evidence indicating the plaintiff cannot meet its burden.[20] Either approach forces the plaintiff to show its hand or risk losing the preliminary injunction motion.

Finally, a defendant may sometimes use state procedures to force the plaintiff to disclose additional information. For example, a California statute requires that "[i]n any action alleging the misappropriation of a trade secret under the Uniform Trade Secrets Act, ... the party alleging the misappropriation shall identify the trade secret with reasonable particularity" prior to "commencing discovery relating to the trade secret."[21] Federal courts have not only applied this state law rule,[22] but—interestingly—have held that it applies to claims under both the UTSA and DTSA, even though the California statute only refers to the UTSA.[23]

[C] Claims

[1] Misappropriation

Presumably, the complaint will include a claim for trade secret misappropriation under the UTSA or DTSA. The plaintiff must allege facts showing that: (a) it owns a trade secret; (b) the defendant misappropriated the secret; and (c) as a result, the plaintiff suffered damage.

As the law currently stands, there is no downside to asserting violations of both statutes; and if the UTSA and DTSA offer different and complementary relief based on the facts of the case, there may be a significant upside. For example, under state law punitive damages may be more or less generous than the double damages award provided under the DTSA.[24]

While early district court decisions interpreting the DTSA have generally held that—despite the slight differences in language[25]—its boundaries overlap with the UTSA,[26] there is one notable exception. The DTSA states that it applies only to trade secrets misappropriated after its enactment on May 11, 2016. If the misappropriation

---

20. *See, e.g.*, Deltek, Inc v. Iuvo Sys., Inc., 2009 WL 1073196, at *10 (E.D. Va. Apr. 20, 2009).

21. Cal. Civ. Proc. Code § 2019.210; *see also, e.g.*, Swarmify, Inc. v. Cloudflare, Inc., 2018 WL 2445515 (N.D. Cal. May 31, 2018).

22. *See* Lilith Games (Shanghai) Co. Ltd. v. uCool, Inc., 2015 WL 4149066, at *2 (N.D. Cal. July 9, 2015) (noting a split in authority on the issue and deciding that the state law procedure applies).

23. AlterG, Inc. v. Boost Treadmills LLC, 388 F. Supp. 3d 1133, 1144 & n. 1 (N.D. Cal. 2019).

24. *Compare* 18 U.S.C. § 1836(b)(3)(C) (punitive damages may not exceed two times the amount of compensatory damages) *with* Va. Code Ann. § 8.01-38.1 (punitive damages may not exceed $350,000) *and* Cal. Civ. Code § 3294 (no limit on punitive damages as long as plaintiff establishes by "clear and convincing evidence that the defendant has been guilty of oppression, fraud, or malice").

25. *See* §§ 2.01[B], 4.01[B].

26. *See, e.g.*, New Country Motor Cars of Palm Beach, LLC v. Beresford, 2019 WL 3890456, at *8 (S.D. Fla. May 3, 2019) ("The parties agree that the same standards that apply under []UTSA

occurred entirely before that date, the UTSA may be the only effective remedy.[27] What if some of the acts in question occurred before May 11, 2016, and some occurred afterward? Courts have held that the DTSA still applies to the later acts, even if they "involve trade secrets misappropriated" before May 11, 2016.[28]

[2] Breach of Contract

If the complaint asserts that the defendant acquired a trade secret under circumstances giving rise to a duty to maintain the secrecy of the information because the defendant signed—and later violated—a nondisclosure agreement, the defendant has likely committed a breach of contract. In order to establish this claim, the plaintiff must show that: (a) it had a contract with the defendant; (b) it performed its duties under the contract or performance was excused; (c) the defendant breached the contract; and (d) as a result, the plaintiff suffered damage.[29]

Suppose subcontractor K signs a nondisclosure agreement with contractor L, pledging not to reveal any secret information that L shares in the course of K's work under the subcontract. If K violates the agreement by disclosing L's secret to L's competitor M, K has both breached the agreement and misappropriated the secret.

[3] Other Common Law Claims

The plaintiff may also be able to assert a range of other common law claims, if the UTSA does not displace them in the particular jurisdiction.[30] Depending on the facts, causes of action based on breach of fiduciary duty, conversion, fraud, quantum meruit, quasi-contract, restitution, tortious interference, and unfair competition may be available.

For example, the conduct required to establish tortious interference with prospective economic advantage—i.e., committing "an independent and intentional legal wrong" with an intent to "interfere with the plaintiff's" "reasonable expectation of an economic benefit from a relationship with a third party" that "caused the expectation to fail"—may overlap with conduct that establishes misappropriation.[31] If N violates a nondisclosure agreement with O by using O's secret information to sell a competing product to O's regular customer P, N may be liable for both misappropriation and tortious interference.

---

apply under DTSA."); CMI Roadbuilding, Inc. v. Iowa Parts, Inc., 920 F.3d 560, 564 (8th Cir. 2019) (UTSA and DTSA employ "similar" standards).

27. *See* 18 U.S.C. § 1836(e) (DTSA applies to "any act [that] occurs on or after the date of the enactment of this Act"); *see also* Taoglas Group Holdings Ltd. v. 2J Antennas USA, Corp., 2019 WL 1239302, at *4 (S.D. Cal. Mar. 18, 2019) ("[B]y its terms, the DTSA applies only to acts of misappropriation on or after May 11, 2016.").

28. *See, e.g.*, *Taoglas*, 2019 WL 1239302, at *5; *accord* Avago Tech. U.S. Inc v. Nanoprecision Prods., 2017 WL 412524, at *9 (N.D. Cal. Jan. 31, 2017).

29. *See, e.g.*, Coles v. Glaser, 205 Cal. Rptr. 3d 922, 927 (App. 2016).

30. *See* § 6.07[C].

31. *See* Restatement (Third) of Torts: Liability for Economic Harm § 17 (Tentative Draft 2018).

[4] Other Intellectual Property Claims

Finally, the plaintiff should consider adding claims based on other intellectual property doctrines, particularly patent and copyright. Of course, patented information has been publicly disclosed, and thus cannot be a trade secret; and since copyright law only protects the manner in which information is expressed, not the content of the information, it overlaps with trade secret law only in narrow situations.[32]

However, there may be patent or copyright claims that are so closely related to the trade secret claims that the plaintiff either (a) must raise them now to avoid subsequent claim preclusion or (b) may choose to assert them because it would be inefficient to litigate them later. For instance, if tech company Q brings a trade secret suit against competitor R for improperly using its secret algorithm for driverless cars, Q should determine whether there are any related patent claims for driverless car technology that could be brought in the same case.[33]

[D] Parties

Despite the rush to file a trade secret suit and thereby stop misappropriation, the plaintiff must be careful to ensure that it names the right defendants. This is simple in the classic scenario where the only defendant is the plaintiff's ex-employee.

The issue becomes more complex when one or more of the defendants is a corporation or other entity with various subsidiaries or divisions, or if it is unclear precisely who has access to the trade secret. Naming the proper corporate party is crucial because, as a general matter, parent corporations are not liable for the actions of their subsidiaries unless exceptional circumstances are present.

§ 5.05 Timing the Lawsuit

Once the plaintiff determines where to file and what claims to assert in the complaint, the next question is when to file. While this question is case specific, several factors are usually considered.

The plaintiff must first assess the risk that the secret will be disclosed or used if suit is not filed. For example, if the potential defendant is a competitor who has possessed the secret for years without disclosing or using it, there may be little need to file quickly. More commonly, suit must be filed as soon as possible because unauthorized disclosure or use is imminent.

In addition, the plaintiff should evaluate how the timing affects the overall business context. Will immediate filing affect how the public perceives the suit? Will it make a difference to the success of settlement negotiations? Alternatively, would it be better to delay until a certain event—perhaps an industry conference or a final attempt at

---

32. *See* §§ 3.02[C], 3.03[C].

33. *See, e.g.*, Waymo LLC v. Uber Techs., Inc., 870 F.3d 1350 (Fed. Cir. 2017).

a compromise—occurs? If there are serious doubts about whether the complaint should be filed swiftly, the plaintiff might reconsider whether to file at all.

§ 5.06 Pretrial Issues

[A] Overview

Certain procedural questions arise in any civil lawsuit, such as dealing with various motions and determining the scope of discovery. However, a number of pretrial issues frequently recur in trade secret litigation.

[B] Protective Orders

The plaintiff in a trade secret case will usually want the court to enter a protective order covering the pretrial phase of the case. Even in cases between rival companies, it will normally be in the interests of both sides to seek such an order.

The UTSA and DTSA require the court to protect trade secrets during litigation. The UTSA provides that "a court shall preserve the secrecy of an alleged trade secret by reasonable means;"[34] and the DTSA states that "the court shall enter such orders and take such other action as may be necessary and appropriate to preserve the confidentiality of trade secrets."[35] At the pretrial stage, a protective order will: (1) regulate how discovery occurs; (2) provide for filing documents under seal; (3) require sealing of the records of the action; (4) facilitate in-camera hearings as necessary; and (5) otherwise restrict disclosure of the secret.

Protective orders generally allow the parties to determine the precise level of secrecy accorded to particular documents. For example, a protective order might specify one classification for confidential information that can be shared with the opposing party's employees and attorneys; another classification for information that can only be shared with the opposing party's attorneys (i.e., "Attorneys' Eyes Only"); and still another classification for the most sensitive information, which can only be shared with the opposing party's outside counsel and not, for example, their in-house attorneys (i.e., "Outside Attorneys' Eyes Only").

[C] Temporary Restraining Orders and Preliminary Injunctions

Immediate injunctive relief is an early priority in cases where the defendant is highly likely to disclose or use the trade secret. In most courts, there are two types—a temporary restraining order (TRO) and a preliminary injunction.[36] As discussed

34. UTSA § 5.

35. 18 U.S.C. § 1835(a).

36. *See* Fed. R. Civ. P. 65(a)–(b). One analysis indicated that a trade secret owner was more likely to obtain a TRO or preliminary injunction in a federal suit against a current or former employee

in Chapter 7, the basic four-part test for both forms of relief is the same in all federal courts and many state courts.[37]

A TRO that bars the defendant from disclosing or using the trade secret provides immediate relief for the plaintiff. Further, given the ex parte nature of the proceeding, it also gives the plaintiff an opportunity to frame the case without interference from the defendant. However, these advantages have corresponding downsides. A federal TRO expires within 14 days of its issuance, unless the plaintiff shows good cause or the defendant consents to an extension.[38] Moreover, the extraordinary nature of a TRO requires the plaintiff to show that it needs *immediate* relief.[39] If there is no indication that a defendant will imminently disclose or use the secret, the plaintiff will have difficulty securing a TRO.

The chief benefit of a preliminary injunction, in contrast, is longevity: it continues until a final judgment is rendered in the case.[40] Given the length of time it takes many cases to get to trial, receiving such relief may spur early settlement talks. Moreover, because a preliminary injunction motion requires briefing on an expedited schedule, the process forces the defendant to show its hand at an early stage in the litigation and—if it was not expecting the litigation—with relatively little preparation. The downside is that the preliminary injunction process takes more time than obtaining a TRO since it requires notice, briefing, and a hearing.

Thus, if S believes that its former employee T is scheduled to appear on *60 Minutes* in a week to disclose S's trade secret, seeking the immediate relief provided by a TRO is the best course. But if T is merely in early discussions to sell the secret to S's competitor U—so there is no imminent threat of disclosure—a preliminary injunction may be sufficient. What if T is planning to flee the country with the only copy of S's trade secret in the next 12 hours? Here S might consider filing suit under the DTSA and invoking its special ex parte seizure remedy.[41]

In order to obtain immediate injunctive relief, the plaintiff must quickly assemble a prima facie case showing—among other things—a likelihood of success on the merits at trial. This task is made more difficult by the fact that, because complaints and preliminary injunction motions are often filed nearly simultaneously, the judge reviewing the preliminary injunction motion may have no prior knowledge about the case.

In briefing the motion, the plaintiff should give the court a persuasive narrative that succinctly explains both the urgency of the suit and the value of the secret. The

---

(42% of the time) than against a business partner (23% of the time). David S. Almeling et al., *A Statistical Analysis of Trade Secret Litigation in Federal Courts*, 45 Gonz. L. Rev. 291, 314 (2009).

37. *See* § 7.02[C].

38. Fed. R. Civ. P. 65(b)(2).

39. Fed. R. Civ. P. 65(b)(1)(A).

40. *See, e.g.*, Alabama v. U.S. Army Corps of Engineers, 424 F.3d 1117, 1128 (11th Cir. 2005).

41. *See* 18 U.S.C. § 1836(b)(2)(A)(i) (in "extraordinary circumstances" a court may "issue an order providing for the seizure of property necessary to prevent the propagation or dissemination of the trade secret that is the subject of the action"). *See also* § 7.02[B].

plaintiff must also decide whether to apply for permission to file its motion under seal, which has the benefit of giving the plaintiff greater latitude to provide details about the secret, but complicates the already-short timeline for filing.

At oral argument, the plaintiff must be aware that the court will be inclined to deny injunctive relief where it would have a disruptive effect on the defendant's business. Accordingly, the plaintiff should be prepared to quickly narrow the scope of the requested relief if it appears likely that the motion will be denied. Finally, if the secret involves highly technical information, both the plaintiff and defendant may consider using slides or other demonstrative aids to help explain their positions.

[D] Motions to Dismiss

The defendant in a trade secret case will often file a motion to dismiss.[42] As the Supreme Court established in the landmark *Ashcroft v. Iqbal* decision, to survive a motion to dismiss the plaintiff must allege "sufficient factual matter, accepted as true, to state a claim to relief that is plausible on its face."[43] In other words, a plaintiff cannot merely assert that it has a trade secret and expect to win the motion.[44] As one district court explained, while a complaint need not "identify ... trade secrets with specificity" due to the "sensitive nature of the alleged trade secret information," a complaint "cannot rely on conclusory statements that simply repeat the elements [of] its claim."[45] Rather, "the plaintiff must disclose sufficient information to infer more than a mere possibility of misconduct."[46]

For instance, in *Hot Stuff Foods, LLC v. Dornbach*, the court held that a complaint that merely alleged the defendant downloaded confidential information that "had independent economic value, was not readily ascertainable by others" and was the subject of "reasonable efforts to maintain its secrecy" had not "pleaded facts showing that the identified information contained trade secrets."[47] Similarly, the complaint in *AutoTrakk, LLC v. Automotive Leasing Specialists, Inc.*—which stated that the plaintiff used "trade secrets in marketing strategies, financial information, customer lists, operations processes, computer programs, program information, data sets, and various valuation tables and calculations"—did not state a cognizable claim because it was "unclear from the amended complaint where the universe of trade secrets begins beyond general business practices or public information."[48]

---

42. One study found that the defendant filed such a motion in 16% of the federal cases reviewed and prevailed 39% of the time. Almeling, *supra* note 36, at 316.

43. 556 U.S 662, 678 (2009).

44. *Id.* ("A pleading that offers labels and conclusions or a formulaic recitation of the elements of a cause of action will not do. Nor does a complaint suffice if it tenders naked assertions devoid of further factual enhancement.") (citations and quotation marks omitted).

45. Protégé Biomedical, LLC v. Z-Medica, LLC, 394 F. Supp. 3d 924, 939 (D. Minn. 2019) (citations and quotation marks omitted).

46. *Id.*

47. 726 F. Supp. 2d 1038, 1044 (D. Minn. 2010).

48. 2017 WL 2936730, at *4 (M.D. Pa. July 10, 2017).

[E] Motions for Summary Judgment

It is difficult for the plaintiff in a trade secret case to win a summary judgment motion. The existence of a trade secret is a question of fact; and whether the defendant misappropriated the secret is also a question of fact. For instance, in *Rockwell Graphic Systems, Inc. v. DEV Industries, Inc.*, the Seventh Circuit explained that whether the plaintiff took reasonable precautions to preserve secrecy could be decided on summary judgment only in an "extreme case," because this element "depends on a balancing of costs and benefits that will vary from case to case...."[49]

On the other hand, a defendant can sometimes prevail on such a motion, most commonly by showing that the information at issue is readily ascertainable or already public knowledge.[50] *Self Directed Placement Corp. v. Control Data Corp.* is an example of a case where summary judgment was held to be appropriate.[51] Plaintiff Self Directed provided a training program to help unemployed people find jobs. One of its instructors later went to work for defendant Control Data, where she established a similar program. Plaintiff alleged that the elements of its program—which included instructor review of "thank you" notes and conducting dress rehearsals for job interviews—should be protected as trade secrets. The Ninth Circuit upheld summary judgment for the defendant on the basis that no trade secrets existed. It endorsed the district court's conclusion that "[e]ach of these items is either already a matter of common public knowledge or completely disclosed to students taking [the plaintiff's] course."[52]

§ 5.07 Trials

Trade secret plaintiffs who take their cases to trial usually succeed. A multi-year analysis found that plaintiffs prevailed in 66% of cases; defendants won 24% of the time; and the results were mixed in the remaining 10%.[53]

One authority compares the trial of a trade secret case to a "morality play."[54] The plaintiff stresses the defendant's wrongful conduct in acquiring, disclosing, or using the secret, invoking "core values of fair play and honesty."[55] In contrast, the defendant relies on "themes of free enterprise and the American dream" to characterize the plaintiff as "greedy and monopolistic."[56] While this analogy may be overbroad—and

49. 925 F.2d 174, 179 (7th Cir. 1991).

50. One study found that most defendants who sought summary judgment in federal trade secret cases were successful. The defendant who was a current or former employee won 54% of time, while a business partner won 51% of the time. Almeling, *supra* note 36, at 314.

51. 908 F.2d 462 (9th Cir. 1990).

52. *Id.* at 465.

53. Rowe, *supra* note 4, at 182.

54. James Pooley, Trade Secrets § 12.01 (1997).

55. *Id.*

56. *Id.*

certainly does not apply to all trade secret trials—it helps to explain how these trials may differ from the ordinary civil case.

Another key difference from regular trials is the overriding importance of maintaining secrecy during the proceedings. Depending on the particular court, a protective order entered at the beginning of the litigation may not cover the trial phase. In this situation, the plaintiff will use a pretrial conference or motion in limine to seek a protective order from the trial judge. Under both the UTSA and DTSA, such an order may: (1) restrict the defendant's attorneys from sharing information with their client's employees and other attorneys; (2) bar jurors, witnesses, and court personnel from disclosing information; (3) close the courtroom to the public when the secret is discussed; and (4) require that transcripts, evidence, and other records in the case be sealed.[57]

The trade secret at issue may involve complex technology, such as a laser system design or a sophisticated computer algorithm. In such cases, the plaintiff's attorney must explain complicated issues—such as the nature and scope of the secret—in layman's language so that the judge and jury understand the case, without sacrificing accuracy. The defendant's attorney may face the same challenge, especially if she plans to rely on expert testimony to demonstrate, for instance, that the information was readily ascertainable or that the plaintiff did not take reasonable precautions.

§ 5.08 Appeals

Over the years, hundreds of UTSA cases have been appealed, creating a substantial body of case law. One study of trade secret appeals found that state courts affirmed the trial court decision 68% of the time.[58] Interestingly, alleged misappropriators prevailed more often than trade secret owners, winning 57% of appeals.[59]

In contrast, the process of developing DTSA case law is in its initial stages.[60] It seems likely that early decisions interpreting the DTSA will address its innovations in detail in order to provide guidance for parties and courts.

A significant benefit to bringing a trade secret claim in federal court is the opportunity to seek an early appeal. Under the final judgment rule, a party must normally wait until litigation is complete before requesting appellate court review.[61] However, federal law grants the right to immediately appeal the denial or grant of a preliminary injunction, which—as discussed above—is a common form of relief sought in trade

---

57. *See* § 5.06[B].

58. David S. Almeling et al., *A Statistical Analysis of Trade Secret Litigation in State Courts*, 46 Gonz. L. Rev. 57, 60 (2010).

59. *Id.*

60. *See* Gregory Lantier & Thomas Sprankling, *The Where, When and What of DTSA Appeals*, Law360 (June 22, 2018 and Oct. 4, 2018).

61. *See* 28 U.S.C. § 1291 (courts of appeals have jurisdiction to review "final decisions of the district courts"); *see also* Mohawk Industries, Inc. v. Carpenter, 558 U.S. 100, 103, 106 (2009) (discussing the basic rule).

secret litigation.[62] Since one of the key elements considered at the preliminary injunction stage is the merits of the underlying claims, the ability to seek a quick review can allow both parties to get a preview of the relative strengths of their arguments at an early stage—perhaps opening the door to settlement.

62. *See* 28 U.S.C. § 1292(a) ("[T]he courts of appeals shall have jurisdiction of appeals from ... [i]nterlocutory orders of the district courts of the United States ... granting, continuing, modifying, refusing or dissolving injunctions....").

Chapter 6

Trade Secret Defenses

§ 6.01 Introduction

As a rule, trade secrets receive less protection than patents or copyrights. It is therefore unsurprising that there are more potential defenses to an action for trade secret misappropriation than an action for patent or copyright infringement. These defenses range from reverse engineering to the special whistleblower immunity created by the Defend Trade Secrets Act.

However, rather than trying to prove an affirmative defense, the defendant in a misappropriation action usually focuses on challenging the plaintiff's prima facie case. For example, the defendant may seek to prove that the information at issue was readily ascertainable, and thus not a trade secret. Alternatively, the defendant might try to show that misappropriation did not occur because the plaintiff consented to use of the information. Some authorities loosely refer to readily ascertainable information, consent, or similar issues as "defenses," though in reality they are merely the flip side of the elements the plaintiff is required to prove.

§ 6.02 Loss of Secrecy

[A] Overview

A trade secret may end if the secret is disclosed. As the Supreme Court observed in *Ruckelshaus v. Monsanto Co.*, "[i]f an individual discloses his trade secret to others who are under no obligation to protect the confidentiality of the information, or otherwise publicly discloses the secret, his property right is extinguished."[1] For example, a comment to the Uniform Trade Secrets Act explains that a person who discovers a trade secret in "public use or on public display" or in "published literature" is not liable for trade secret misappropriation.[2] Thus, if chef A holds a trade secret in his meatloaf recipe, the secret ends when he includes it in a cookbook that is sold to the public.

The owner's disclosure of secret information is relevant to *both* (1) whether a trade secret ever existed[3] and (2) if it did, whether it has ended. This section examines the second situation—where the defendant in a misappropriation action relies on disclosure as a defense.

[B] Voluntary Disclosure by Owner

An owner might voluntarily disclose the trade secret to the public. She could disclose it in advertising, at a trade show, or in a published article. Or she might disclose it in a patent application.

Suppose scientist B develops a new process for freezing cells that he keeps secret for years; he puts the information into a patent application that is later published. All courts would hold that including the information was a public disclosure, and refuse to protect the technique as a trade secret.[4] As a result, an inventor like B cannot simultaneously protect his process under both patent law and trade secret law.

1. 467 U.S. 986, 1002 (1984).
2. UTSA § 1 cmt.
3. *See* §§ 2.04, 2.05.
4. *See, e.g.*, Tewari De-Ox Sys., Inc. v. Mountain States/Rosen, LLC, 637 F.3d 604, 611–12 (5th Cir. 2011).

As the Sixth Circuit explained in *Scharmer v. Carrollton Manufacturing Co.*:

> The property right in a trade secret ceases to exist after the secret has become public property through general disclosure. If a trade secret is patented there is no further right to secrecy. The patent is a legal disclosure with the right to a limited, temporary monopoly granted as the reward for disclosure....
>
> When the patent was granted ... Scharmer's property right in the trade secret ceased prospectively. Thus, he had no right of action for misuse of a trade secret subsequent to that date.[5]

A comment to the UTSA notes that "controlled disclosure to employees and licensees is consistent with the requirement of relative secrecy."[6] But uncontrolled disclosure can be a problem. For example, if C, the owner of a steel mill, gives his customer list to good friend and rival mill owner D, without requiring D to sign a nondisclosure agreement or otherwise limiting use of the list, C has arguably consented to its use by D.

But it is easy to create a more difficult scenario. For example, if C provided the customer list to D as part of a negotiation to sell C's business, some courts would hold that this limited disclosure to further C's economic interests does not preclude trade secret protection.[7]

A closer question is whether C could be deemed to consent to D's use of the list if D were required to sign a nondisclosure agreement, but D used the list only after the agreement expired. Interestingly, several courts considering the question have said that the answer is "yes," on the basis that the express agreement "supplanted" any duty of confidentiality that might otherwise apply.[8]

[C] Distribution of Product by Owner

Information that can be readily ascertained from a product on public sale or display does not qualify for trade secret protection. As a UTSA comment states, "[o]ften, the nature of a product lends itself to being readily copied as soon as it is available on the market."[9] The public sale of a product that embodies a trade secret does *not* necessarily destroy the secret. Protection is lost only if the secret (1) is apparent from the product or (2) could be "readily ascertained." Whether it is readily ascertainable turns on the extent of time, effort, and expense that would be required to reverse engineer the information.[10]

---

5. 525 F.2d 95, 99 (6th Cir. 1975).

6. UTSA § 1 cmt.; *see also* ClearOne Comm'ns, Inc. v. Bowers, 643 F.3d 735, 772–73 (10th Cir. 2011).

7. *See, e.g.*, Wellogix, Inc. v. Accenture, LLP, 788 F. Supp. 2d 523, 540 (S.D. Tex. 2011). *See* § 4.02[D][2][c].

8. *See, e.g.*, Union Pac. R.R. v. Mower, 219 F.3d 1069, 1076 (9th Cir. 2000) ("We hold, as a matter of law, that the Resignation Agreement supplanted—rather than supplemented—Mower's implied duty of confidentiality.").

9. UTSA § 1 cmt.

10. *See* § 2.04[C][2].

Suppose E markets a product containing a secret that is not readily ascertainable. F buys one of the products, spends two years trying to reverse engineer the information, and finally succeeds. On these facts, E's sale of the product did not end the trade secret. F's discovery of the secret also did not end it; although it is now known to F, it is not "generally known" to other persons who can obtain value from it.[11]

[D] Accidental or Mistaken Disclosure by Owner

Trade secrets are sometimes disclosed by accident or mistake. For example, in *B.C. Ziegler & Co. v. Ehren*, the owner's employee carelessly neglected to shred documents showing the addresses of its customers and gave them to a waste paper dealer; one of the owner's competitors then purchased the documents from the dealer.[12]

As a rule, accidental or mistaken disclosure does not necessarily end trade secret protection. Unless the disclosure resulted from the owner's "failure to take reasonable precautions to maintain the secrecy of the information," the Restatement (Third) of Unfair Competition allows the owner to sue the recipient who discloses or uses the information, under certain circumstances.[13] The same result would seemingly follow under the UTSA and DTSA, both of which implicitly recognize that trade secret protection continues, because they allow the owner of accidentally disclosed information to sue the recipient for misappropriation in some situations.[14]

[E] Disclosure by Third Party

A trade secret may also end when a third party discloses it. One common situation involves a person who legally obtained the secret through independent development or reverse engineering. Suppose G sells a product that embodies her trade secret; H spends two years to reverse engineer the product and learns the secret. At this point, H can do whatever he wants with the information, regardless of G's wishes. If H discloses the information publicly, then it will become "generally known" and lose trade secret protection.

Another scenario is disclosure by a government entity. Federal and state governments legally collect a vast array of information that qualifies for trade secret protection. For example, a company that needs Food and Drug Administration approval to market a new drug must submit confidential test data and related information. The extent to which government agencies are required to maintain the secrecy of

---

11. *See* § 2.04[B].

12. 414 N.W.2d 48 (Wis. App. 1987).

13. Restatement (Third) of Unfair Competition § 40(b)(4). *See, e.g.*, Williams v. Curtiss-Wright Corp., 681 F.2d 161 (3d Cir. 1982) (defendant liable for misappropriation by use of information disclosed by mistake).

14. UTSA § 1(2)(ii)(C); 18 U.S.C. § 1839(5)(B)(iii).

such information varies widely. As a general principle, most information held by agencies is subject to public disclosure, particularly under the Freedom of Information Act[15] or similar laws. Again, however, disclosure will not end trade secret protection unless the information becomes generally known.[16]

What if the secret is disclosed by someone who acquired it illegally—by misappropriation? Suppose J steals K's trade secret and emails the information to all of K's competitors. It is well settled that the manner by which the discloser obtained the secret is irrelevant. Here the information is now "generally known" by others who can obtain economic value from its use and, accordingly, it is no longer a trade secret. Reflecting upon this situation, one court lamented that an "anonymous (or judgment proof) defendant can permanently destroy valuable trade secrets, leaving no one to hold liable for the misappropriation."[17] Once this occurs, anyone is free to use the information.[18]

[F] Special Issue: Internet Postings

One challenging issue is whether a secret becomes "readily ascertainable" or "generally known" simply because it was posted on the internet. In *Religious Technology Center v. Netcom On-Line Communication Services, Inc.*, someone anonymously posted secret religious documents from the Church of Scientology in an internet forum devoted to the discussion of Scientology issues; more than 25 million people could have accessed the documents.[19] The court reasoned that this disclosure terminated any trade secrets in the information:

> While the Internet has not reached the status where a temporary posting on a newsgroup is akin to publication in a major newspaper or on a television network, those with an interest in using the Church's trade secrets to compete with the Church are likely to look to the newsgroup. Thus, posting works to the Internet makes them "generally known" to the relevant people—the potential "competitors" of the Church.[20]

On the other hand, the court in *DVD Copy Control Association, Inc. v. Bunner* cautioned that an internet posting "does not necessarily destroy the secret if the publication is sufficiently obscure or transient or otherwise limited so that it does not become

---

15. 5 U.S.C. §552.

16. *See, e.g.*, Myers v. Williams, 819 F. Supp. 919 (D. Or. 1993) (FDA's mistaken disclosure of trade secret formula to prison inmate pursuant to FOIA did not terminate secret).

17. Religious Tech. Center v. Netcom On-Line Communication Serv., Inc., 923 F. Supp. 1231, 1256 (N.D. Cal. 1995).

18. Religious Tech. Center v. Lerma, 908 F. Supp. 1362, 1368 (E.D. Va. 1995) (a "party who merely downloads Internet information cannot be liable for misappropriation because there is no misconduct involved in interacting with the Internet").

19. 923 F. Supp. 1231 (N.D. Cal. 1995).

20. *Id.* at 1256.

generally known to … potential competitors or other persons to whom the information would have some economic value."[21] This statement implies that if the post is "obscure or transient or otherwise limited" the information is not "readily ascertainable" or "generally known."

Relying on the *DVD Copy Control* approach, the court in *Silicon Image, Inc. v. Analogix Semiconductor, Inc.* concluded that obscure internet postings did not destroy the trade secret embodied in plaintiff's source code.[22] It noted that the code was posted only to (1) a members-only website that charged a fee for access and (2) a Chinese language website. There was no evidence that the defendant or "any other competitor was aware of or able to use the source code that was posted…."[23]

§ 6.03 Independent Development

The information protected by trade secret law may not always be the exclusive property of the original developer. As the Supreme Court explained in *Kewanee Oil Co. v. Bicron Corp.*, "trade secret law … does not offer protection against discovery by fair and honest means, such as by independent invention…."[24] Thus, a person who independently develops information that is identical to another person's trade secret is not liable for misappropriation.

Both the UTSA and DTSA recognize the independent development defense. A comment to the UTSA explains that "[d]iscovery by independent invention" is a proper method for obtaining a trade secret.[25] The DTSA takes a more forceful approach, codifying the rule that acquiring trade secret material by "independent derivation" is not an actionable offense.[26]

This defense arises only when the defendant has *actually* obtained the secret by independent development. The fact that the defendant could have learned the secret by its own research is irrelevant.[27]

Moreover, the defendant's development of the information must be entirely independent. In *Affiliated Hospital Products, Inc. v. Baldwin*, the court rejected the defense because defendant's employees had previously seen the plaintiff's trade secret drawings—and accordingly knew to avoid certain pitfalls in their research.[28]

---

21. 10 Cal. Rptr. 3d 185, 192 (App. 2004).
22. 2008 WL 166950 (N.D. Cal. Jan. 17, 2008).
23. *Id.* at *16.
24. 416 U.S. 470, 476 (1974).
25. UTSA § 1 cmt.
26. 18 U.S.C. § 1839(6)(B).
27. Of course, if the information is "readily ascertainable" it does not qualify for trade secret protection. *See* § 2.04[C].
28. 373 N.E.2d 1000, 1006 (Ill. App. 1978).

§ 6.04 Reverse Engineering

Reverse engineering is also a defense to misappropriation. The *Kewanee Oil* Court observed that "trade secret law ... does not offer protection against discovery by fair and honest means, such as ... by so-called reverse engineering...."[29]

The UTSA and DTSA both recognize the reverse engineering defense. A comment to the UTSA provides that "proper means" for acquiring a trade secret include:

> Discovery by "reverse engineering," that is, by starting with the known product and working backward to find the method by which it was developed. The acquisition of the known product must, of course, also be by a fair and honest means, such as purchase of the item on the open market for reverse engineering to be lawful.[30]

The DTSA states that the term "improper means" "does not include reverse engineering...."[31] As a result, acquisition of a trade secret by reverse engineering is not a misappropriation.

A potential distinction between the UTSA and DTSA conceptions of this defense is the UTSA comment requiring that an underlying product be acquired "by a fair and honest means." The DTSA has no such qualifier, although perhaps one could be inferred, using the *noscitur a sociis* canon,[32] from the provision that "improper means" does not include "any other lawful means of acquisition."[33] Barring such a softening interpretation, it appears that under the DTSA, a person who steals a prototype of a new invention and uses that device to reverse engineer protected trade secrets might have a complete defense.[34] Under the UTSA, at least, the case law is clear that such behavior would not allow an infringer to avoid liability.[35]

Suppose that L sues M for misappropriation, and M tries to rely on the reverse engineering defense, arguing that he could have easily reverse engineered the secret. M's defense will fail. It only arises when the defendant *actually* obtained the secret

---

29. Kewanee Oil Co. v. Bicron Corp., 416 U.S. 470, 476 (1974).

30. UTSA § 1 cmt.

31. 18 U.S.C. § 1839(6)(B).

32. The *noscitur a sociis* canon provides that "the meaning of an unclear word or phrase, esp[ecially] one in a list, should be determined by the words immediately surrounding it." Black's Law Dictionary 1274 (Bryan A. Garner ed., 11th ed. 2019).

33. *Id.*

34. *But see, e.g.*, NEXT Payment Solutions, Inc. v. CLEAResult Consulting, Inc., 2018 WL 3637356, at *13 (N.D. Ill, July 31, 2018) (relying on UTSA case law to hold that allegation that "Defendant directed its employees without login credentials to log into the Next System Back End without authorization and reverse-engineer Plaintiff's software for Defendant's benefit" stated a claim for purposes of a motion to dismiss).

35. *See, e.g.*, Telerate Sys., Inc. v. Caro, 689 F. Supp. 221, 233 (S.D.N.Y. 1988) ("[T]he term 'reverse engineering' is not a talisman that may immunize the theft of trade secrets. The relevant inquiry remains whether the means used to obtain the alleged trade secret, including reverse engineering, were proper.").

by reverse engineering. Of course, if M can prove that the information was "readily ascertainable," it does not qualify for trade secret protection at all.

§ 6.05 Privilege or Justification to Disclose

[A] Overview

Under narrow circumstances, a defendant accused of disclosing a trade secret may assert a defense based on privilege or justification. Courts have recognized such a general defense as a matter of common law for decades, though it is rarely asserted.

Two specific justifications are also recognized. The First Amendment provides a defense to trade secret misappropriation in some cases. In addition, the DTSA contains a whistleblower immunity provision that shields persons who disclose trade secrets under certain circumstances.

[B] Common Law

The traditional approach to the privilege defense is summarized in the Restatement (Third) of Unfair Competition. A comment explains that in some situations "the disclosure of another's trade secret for purposes other than commercial exploitation may implicate the interest in freedom of expression or advance another significant public interest."[36] It indicates that a "privilege is likely to be recognized, for example, in connection with the disclosure of information that is relevant to public health or safety, or to the commission of a crime or tort, or to other matters of substantial public concern."[37] Two Supreme Court Justices have echoed this sentiment, citing the Restatement for the proposition that "[w]here publication of private information constitutes a wrongful act, the law recognizes a privilege allowing the reporting of threats to public safety."[38]

Whether the common law defense applies requires a case-by-case determination. The Restatement lays out several relevant factors, such as (1) "the nature of the information," (2) "the purpose of the disclosure," and (3) the "means by which the actor acquired the information."[39]

For example, if chef N tries to protect the public by telling the police that the secret sauce at her employer O's fast food restaurant includes rat poison, the privilege doctrine would provide N with a strong defense against liability. On the other hand, if chef N learned the rat poison secret by hacking into O's computer files and informed the police in the hopes that O's woes would give her an opening to start her own,

36. Restatement (Third) of Unfair Competition § 40 cmt. c; *see also* UTSA § 2 cmt. (recognizing that an injunction may be denied based on "the existence of an overriding public interest which requires the denial of a prohibitory injunction against future damaging use").

37. Restatement (Third) of Unfair Competition § 40 cmt c.

38. Bartnicki v. Vopper, 532 U.S. 514, 539 (2001) (Breyer, O'Connor, JJ., concurring).

39. Restatement (Third) of Unfair Competition § 40 cmt. c.

competing business, N would have a more difficult argument even though the effect of her disclosure on O's business would be the same.

[C] First Amendment

The First Amendment may also bar liability for trade secret disclosure under some circumstances. The House Report on the DTSA reflects the sentiment that the act's "protections against the misappropriation of trade secrets—and the remedies it provides against such misappropriation—are not intended to displace or restrict protections for members of the press recognized under the First Amendment."[40] The report quotes the Supreme Court decision in *Bartnicki v. Vopper*[41] for the principle that " 'if a newspaper lawfully obtains truthful information about a matter of public significance then state officials may not constitutionally punish publication of the information, absent a need ... of the highest order.' "[42]

For example, the defense was successfully asserted in *Democratic National Committee v. Russian Federation.*[43] The case arose when the Russian Federation stole material—including trade secrets—from the plaintiff's computers as part of its effort to interfere with the 2016 presidential election; defendant WikiLeaks subsequently disseminated this information to the public. Citing *Bartnicki*, the district court held that the plaintiff's "privacy interest in the alleged trade secrets is insufficient to overcome the strong public interest in the publication of matters of paramount public concern."[44] It stressed that the "information is plainly of the type entitled to the strongest protection that the First Amendment offers."[45]

[D] Whistleblower Immunity

Among its innovations, the DTSA added a powerful protection for those who disclose trade secrets to government officials or in certain court filings. 18 U.S.C. § 1833(b)(1) provides that "[a]n individual shall not be held criminally or civilly liable under any Federal or State trade secret law for the disclosure of a trade secret" under two specific circumstances. Under the first formulation, subpart (A), the disclosure must be made "(i) in confidence to a Federal, State, or local government official, either directly or indirectly, or to an attorney; *and* (ii) solely for the purpose of reporting or investigating a suspected violation of law."[46] Alternatively, under subpart (B) immunity lies if the disclosure "is made in a complaint or other document filed in a lawsuit or other proceeding, if such filing is made under seal."[47]

---

40. H.R. Rep. No. 114-529, at 10 n.11 (2016).
41. 532 U.S. 514, 528 (2001) (quoting Smith v. Daily Mail Publ'g Co., 443 U.S. 97, 109 (1979)).
42. H.R. Rep. No. 114-529, at 11 n. 11 (2016).
43. 392 F. Supp. 3d 410 (S.D.N.Y 2019).
44. *Id.* at 437.
45. *Id.*
46. 18 U.S.C. § 1833(b)(1)(A) (emphasis added).
47. *Id.* § 1833(b)(1)(B).

It is significant that § 1833(b)(1) offers immunity from suit, as opposed to a mere defense from liability. It may be invoked at an early stage in the proceeding, thereby allowing a defendant to avoid discovery and other burdens of litigation.[48] As one scholar who helped to draft the provision explains, it is intended to prevent corporations from "deter[ing] potential whistleblowers through the threat of costly trade secret litigation" by placing the "burden of proof on the trade secret owner seeking to impose liability on a potential whistleblower ... to come forward with concrete evidence" that immunity is not appropriate.[49]

The DTSA also includes a complementary provision in § 1833(b)(2) that permits the use of a trade secret in anti-retaliation lawsuits. It states that "[a]n individual who files a lawsuit for retaliation by an employer for reporting a suspected violation of law may disclose the trade secret to the attorney of the individual and use the trade secret information in the court proceeding, if the individual—(A) files any document containing the trade secret under seal; and (B) does not disclose the trade secret, except pursuant to court order."[50]

At first blush, the anti-retaliation lawsuit rule seems similar to the § 1833(b)(1)(B) protection, but it is perhaps best thought of as a sword rather than a shield. The latter protects an employee from being drawn into costly trade secret litigation, while the former gives an employee an affirmative right to use a trade secret to prove a point in his own case so long as he follows certain guidelines. Thus employee P who discloses a trade secret to the government—or to a court in a sealed declaration—could avoid being sued by employer Q by resort to § 1833(b)(1)(A)–(B). If Q then fired P in retaliation for blowing the whistle on Q's practices, P could use the trade secret as part of his lawsuit against the company under § 1833(b)(2).

The § 1833(b) immunity and use provisions are both subject to an important statutory caveat: they cannot be construed to "authorize, or limit liability for, an act that is otherwise prohibited by law, such as the unlawful access of material by unauthorized means."[51] While this provision has not yet been interpreted, it presumably limits the scope of protection to individuals who learn the trade secret by proper means. For example, if employee R is in charge of manufacturing frozen pizza for company S and learns the secret recipe includes arsenic, he could disclose that information to the government and rely on the immunity provision. However, if T, a company janitor, learns about the arsenic only by cracking a company safe after hours, he would not receive immunity.

One interesting question raised by the passage of the DTSA is how the whistleblower immunity interacts with the common law privilege. While the DTSA expressly does not preempt any state law "remedies,"[52] none of its provisions indicates whether it

48. *See* Peter S. Menell, *The DTSA Whistleblower Immunity Provision: A Legislative History*, 1 Bus., Entrepreneurship & Tax L. Rev. 398, 425–26 (2017).

49. *Id.*

50. 18 U.S.C. § 1833(b)(2).

51. 18 U.S.C. § 1833(b)(5).

52. *See* § 6.07[B].

preempts defenses. There may be an argument that the whistleblower immunity laid out in the DTSA precludes future use of the common law privilege.

§ 6.06 Statute of Limitations

The UTSA and DTSA both follow the same basic statute of limitations rule. Suit must be filed within three years after the misappropriation is discovered "or by the exercise of reasonable diligence should have been discovered."[53] In other words, both laws apply a reasonable person standard for the start of the limitations period.[54] The justification given for this rule is that "some acts may be difficult for a plaintiff to detect or comprehend."[55] Notably, courts interpreting the UTSA have concluded that something more than the mere suspicion of misappropriation is required to trigger the rule.[56]

Some states have modified the length of the limitations period listed in the UTSA. Notably, in early drafts of the DTSA, the statute of limitations was five years; it was reduced to three years to mirror the UTSA.[57]

The UTSA resolved a split of authority on when the limitations period began to run. Before its enactment, courts were divided on whether the period started running (1) when the misappropriation started or (2) only when the misappropriation ended.[58] The act provides that a "continuing misappropriation constitutes a single claim"— i.e., that the initial misappropriation triggers the statute of limitations period.[59] This rule is based on finality concerns. The commentary accompanying the act explains that "[i]f objectively reasonable notice of misappropriation exists, three years is sufficient time to vindicate one's legal rights."[60] The DTSA follows the same approach.[61]

This "single claim" approach, as some courts have called it, is a significant departure from how other intellectual property statutes operate. As the Sixth Circuit has explained, copyright and patent law apply a "continuing wrong" approach, meaning that when an infringer "commits successive violations ... each infringing act starts a new limitations period."[62] In contrast, under the trade secret statutes, the claim "arises

53. 18 U.S.C. § 1836(d); UTSA § 6.

54. *See, e.g.*, Weinreich v. Lube, 46 F. App'x 462, 462–463 (9th Cir. 2002) ("The district court properly dismissed Weinreich's UTSA ... claim[] as untimely because his pleadings reveal that through the exercise of diligence he should have discovered his claims in 1995 yet he did not file his initial complaint until March 9, 1999.").

55. Thermech Eng'g Corp. v. Abbot Lab., 2003 WL 23018553, at *4 (Dec. 22, 2003 Cal. App. Ct.).

56. *See, e.g.*, Sokol Crystal Prod., Inc. v. DSC Communications Corp., 15 F.3d 1427, 1430 (7th Cir. 1994).

57. Sen. Rep. No. 114-220, at 9–10 (2016).

58. UTSA § 6 cmt.

59. UTSA § 6.

60. *Id.* cmt.

61. 18 U.S.C. § 1836(d).

62. Allied Erecting & Dismantling Co., Inc. v. Genesis Equip. & Mfg., Inc., 805 F.3d 701, 704 (6th Cir. 2015) (citations and quotation marks omitted).

for a given plaintiff against a given defendant only once, at the time of the initial misappropriation, subject" of course, "to the discovery rule."[63]

In summary, assume that U improperly acquired company V's secret recipe for barbecue sauce in 2015 without V's knowledge. Under both the DTSA and UTSA, V's lawsuit would unquestionably be within the statute of limitations if it were filed in 2017. But if V does not sue until 2020, its suit will be barred unless it can prove that it could not have reasonably discovered the misappropriation sooner.

§ 6.07 Preemption or Displacement

[A] Overview

Preemption is sometimes available as a defense in trade secret cases. It is well settled that patent law does not preempt state trade secret law,[64] though copyright law does preempt in certain situations.[65] The DTSA does not preempt state trade secret remedies, except in one narrow situation. But the state versions of the UTSA do displace various common law causes of action.[66]

[B] Preemption by DTSA

The DTSA does not preempt state trade secret law, except for whistleblower protection. Section 1838 states that the DTSA "shall not be construed to preempt or displace any other remedies, whether civil or criminal, provided by United States Federal, State, commonwealth, possession, or territory law for the misappropriation of a trade secret," except for section 1833(b).[67] As discussed above, that section provides immunity from civil or criminal liability "under any Federal or State trade secret law for the disclosure of a trade secret" for certain whistleblowers and court filings.[68]

[C] Displacement of Common Law by UTSA

The state-adopted versions of the UTSA supersede or "displace" various common law causes of action for trade secret misappropriation. One of the goals of the UTSA was to substitute a uniform approach for "the various property, quasi-contractual,

63. *Id.* at 705.

64. *See* § 3.02[D].

65. *See* § 3.03[D].

66. Sources often refer to this provision as "preempting" common law actions. But this is something of a misnomer. As commonly understood, "preemption" is a term of art for what occurs when a federal law (for example, the Constitution or a statute) supersedes state law pursuant to the Supremacy Clause of the Constitution. *See* U.S. Const. art. VI, § 2.

67. 18 U.S.C. § 1838.

68. *See* § 6.05[D].

and violation of fiduciary relationship theories of noncontractual liability utilized at common law."[69]

The 1985 UTSA expressly "displaces conflicting tort, restitutionary, and other law of this State providing civil remedies for misappropriation of a trade secret," except for (1) contractual remedies, (2) "other civil remedies that are not based upon misappropriation of a trade secret," and (3) criminal remedies.[70] This language is broad enough to displace, for example, causes of action such as breach of fiduciary duty, conversion, fraud, quantum meruit, quasi-contract, restitution, tortious interference, and unfair competition.

However, the extent to which the UTSA displaces common law theories varies widely from state to state. Certain states still use the 1979 UTSA, which has slightly different wording. While most states adopted the 1985 UTSA, some amended its displacement provision in the process. Finally, some state courts interpret the UTSA provision narrowly, while others interpret it broadly.

The UTSA drafters emphasized that it "is not a comprehensive statement of civil remedies."[71] For instance, it does not displace litigation based on a "duty voluntarily assumed through an express or an implied-in-fact contract," such as the breach of an agreement not to disclose trade secrets.[72] Nor does it preclude actions based on duties imposed by law that do not depend on the existence of a trade secret, such as an agent's duty of loyalty.[73]

§ 6.08 Equitable Defenses

[A] Overview

When a plaintiff requests an equitable remedy, such as an injunction, courts have significant discretion to fashion relief based on public policy concerns.[74] Three equitable defenses often crop up in the trade secret context.

[B] Unclean Hands

First, the unclean hands principle—"he who comes into equity must come with clean hands"—can pose a substantial impediment to an unethical plaintiff. As the Supreme Court has explained, this maxim means that equitable relief is not available "to one tainted with inequitableness or bad faith relative to the matter in which he seeks relief."[75] It does not mean that trade secret plaintiffs must have lived "blameless

69. UTSA pref. note.

70. UTSA § 7.

71. *Id.* cmt.

72. *Id.*

73. *Id.*

74. *See generally* 11A Charles Alan Wright & Arthur R. Miller, Federal Practice & Procedure: Federal Rules of Civil Procedure § 2946 (4th ed. 2019 update).

75. *See* Precision Instrument Mfg. Co. v. Auto. Maintenance Mach. Co., 324 U.S. 806, 814 (1945).

lives" to protect their intellectual property, but "it does require that they shall have acted fairly and without fraud or deceit as to the controversy in issue."[76] Imagine, for example, that construction company W seeks an injunction barring company X from using W's special formula for cement, on the basis that X stole the formula. If X can plausibly argue that the theft was in retaliation for W stealing its customer list, X would have a plausible unclean hands defense.[77] On the other hand, if the best argument X can muster is that W has behaved unethically in general (e.g., by misrepresenting the quality of X's work to past customers), the unclean hands defense is unlikely to succeed.[78]

A wrinkle to the unclean hands doctrine is that the defendant must show that he was actually injured by the plaintiff's improper acts. The Fifth Circuit's decision in *Alcatel USA, Inc. v. DGI Technologies, Inc.* is instructive.[79] There, Alcatel, which manufactured telephone systems and accompanying operating system software, sued DGI for trade secret infringement because DGI had improperly acquired Alcatel manuals and used them to build its own rival software and hardware for use with the Alcatel systems. Defendant DGI argued that the trade secret claim was precluded by the unclean hands doctrine because Alcatel had improperly installed a software patch in its products intended to prevent customers from using DGI's product. The Fifth Circuit concluded that the unclean hands doctrine was inapplicable because the software patch did not actually work, and DGI presented no evidence that any of its customers were deterred by Alcatel's use of the patch.

[C] Laches

Another equitable defense sometimes asserted in trade secret actions is laches. Laches "bars the plaintiff whose unreasonable delay in prosecuting a claim or protecting a right has worked a prejudice to the defendant."[80] The Supreme Court explained in *SCA Hygiene Products Aktiebolag v. First Quality Baby Products, LLC* that laches generally "cannot be invoked to bar legal [i.e., monetary] relief" if Congress has enacted an applicable statute of limitations, meaning that the doctrine is almost certainly not available in DTSA actions for monetary relief.[81]

Whether the Court's reasoning will be extended to state law trade secrets claims with their own statutes of limitations remains to be seen. At least one district court

---

76. *Id.* at 814–15 (citation and quotation marks omitted).

77. *Cf.* Future Plastics, Inc. v. Ware Shoals Plastics, Inc. 340 F. Supp. 1376, 1384 (D.S.C. 1972) (unclean hands barred company from obtaining an injunction against defendant employee's use of trade secrets where company had permitted another to engage in the same behavior).

78. *See* Vacco Indus., Inc. v. Van Den Berg, 6 Cal. Rptr. 2d 602, 612 (App. 1992) (holding that the behavior supporting an unclean hands defense must "pertain to the very subject matter involved and affect the equitable relations between the litigants") (citation and quotation marks omitted).

79. 166 F.3d 772 (5th Cir. 1999).

80. SCA Hygiene Prods. Aktiebolag v. First Quality Baby Products, LLC, 137 S. Ct. 954, 960 (2017) (quoting 1 D. Dobbs, Law of Remedies § 2.3(5) (2d ed. 1993)).

81. *Id.*

has taken this approach,[82] but it is notable that *SCA Hygiene*'s rationale relied heavily on federal separation-of-powers principles—a theory that may not have the same force at the state level. For example, in *Williams v. Restaurant Technologies, Inc.* the court applied the laches doctrine to bar all monetary relief where the plaintiff delayed filing suit for over seven years after it was aware of the defendant's improper conduct.[83]

Laches certainly remains an available defense in the injunction context, albeit not a particularly promising one for trade secret defendants. Courts are hesitant to apply it in light of the short three-year statute of limitations used by most states.[84] The laches defense is probably most useful in the rare situation when a plaintiff has exceeded the statute of limitations, but has an excuse that avoids the suit being barred on those grounds.

[D] Acquiescence

A third equitable doctrine, acquiescence, often goes hand-in-hand with laches. In a nutshell, the acquiescence rule can bar relief where the plaintiff was aware its trade secret was being used by others without its consent and did nothing.[85] Thus, for example, if tech company Y is aware that former employee Z is using its secret algorithm without its consent and takes no legal action, Z would have a strong acquiescence argument. Alternatively, if A sends its algorithm to competitor B with no spoken or unspoken understanding that the algorithm will be kept secret, A may be barred from receiving injunctive relief. As a Washington state court summarized: "Where information is transmitted pursuant to contract in circumstances where the originator knows or should know that the recipient has a legitimate business use for the information, the originator must secure confidentiality by express or implied provision of the contract; absent such provision, he is not entitled to equitable relief."[86]

Like some of the defenses discussed above, acquiescence can go directly to the merits of plaintiff's claim. If the plaintiff does not object when others use the trade secret, it may not have made reasonable efforts to maintain secrecy.

82. 2017 WL 6811800 (N.D. Fla. Dec. 8, 2017).

83. Anaconda Co. v. Metric Tool & Die Co., 485 F. Supp. 410, 431 (E.D. Pa. 1980).

84. *See, e.g.*, Sunbelt Rentals, Inc. v. Head & Engquist Equip., LLC, 620 S.E.2d 222, 232 (N.C. App. 2005); Garth v. Staktek Corp., 876 S.W.2d 545, 550–51 (Tex. App. Ct. 1994).

85. *See* Sears, Roebuck & Co. v. L-M Mfg. Co., 256 F.2d 517, 520 (3d Cir. 1958); *cf.* Surgidev Corp. v. Eye Tech., Inc., 828 F.2d 452, 457 (8th Cir. 1987) (rejecting defense because "nothing in the record suggests that Surgidev acquiesced to use by past employees of its trade secrets or that any of these employees unlawfully misappropriated Surgidev trade secrets").

86. Pacific Title, Inc. v. Pioneer Nat'l Title Ins. Co. Inc., 658 P.2d 684, 688 (Wash. App. 1983).

Chapter 7

Trade Secret Remedies

§ 7.01 Introduction

In general, the successful plaintiff in a trade secret case may obtain two main remedies: an injunction to prevent future misappropriation and damages to compensate for past misappropriation.

Both remedies were available under common law and state statutes before the Uniform Trade Secrets Act was adopted, but their parameters varied widely. As the UTSA drafters noted: "Under technological and economic pressures, industry continues to rely on trade secret protection despite the doubtful and confused status of both common law and statutory remedies."[1] The UTSA was drafted, in part, to address the "undue uncertainty concerning ... the appropriate remedies for misappropriation of a trade secret."[2] The drafters explain that it "codifies the results of the better reasoned cases concerning the remedies for trade secret misappropriation."[3]

The UTSA provides that the court may issue an injunction against actual or threatened misappropriation. In exceptional circumstances, the court may allow the defendant to use the trade secret in the future, conditioned upon payment of a reasonable royalty. The Defend Trade Secrets Act section on injunctive relief is largely similar to the UTSA provision.

Further, the UTSA allows the plaintiff to recover damages, which can include both its actual loss and the unjust enrichment caused by misappropriation. Alternatively, the court may measure damages by the amount of a reasonable royalty. Punitive damages and attorney's fees are also available under some circumstances. The counterpart DTSA sections are almost identical to the UTSA provisions.

An empirical study of trade secret cases tried to judgment over a fifteen-year period—ending just before enactment of the DTSA—revealed interesting data.[4] In 81% of the cases where a permanent injunction was issued, the trade secret owner also received damages.[5] Damages were awarded to the owner in 36% of the cases where a permanent injunction was not obtained.[6]

§ 7.02 Pretrial Remedies

[A] Overview

In many cases, there is an imminent danger that the defendant will disclose or use the trade secret in a manner that irreparably harms its owner. A secondary concern is that the defendant may destroy evidence. Three pretrial remedies address these concerns: an ex parte civil seizure order; a temporary restraining order; and a preliminary injunction.

The DTSA provides a novel pretrial remedy in narrow circumstances: an ex parte order that allows seizure of computers and other property as necessary to prevent further dissemination of the secret. However, this procedure is cumbersome and rarely used.[7]

---

1. UTSA pref. note (quoting Comment, *Theft of Trade Secrets: The Need for a Statutory Solution*, 120 U. Pa. L. Rev. 378, 380–81 (1971)).

2. UTSA pref. note.

3. *Id.*

4. Elizabeth A. Rowe, *Unpacking Trade Secret Damages*, 55 Hous. L. Rev. 155 (2017).

5. *Id.* at 196.

6. *Id.*

7. In the first year after passage of the DTSA, a motion for ex parte seizure was made in only 2% of cases. David S. Levine & Christopher B. Seaman, *The DTSA at One: An Empirical Study of the First Year of Litigation under the Defend Trade Secrets Act*, 53 Wake Forest L. Rev. 105, 150 (2018).

The traditional pretrial remedy against future misappropriation is a preliminary injunction that bars the defendants from disclosing or using the information during the pendency of the lawsuit; this is often preceded by a temporary restraining order. This remedy can also be used to protect evidence from destruction. One study found that plaintiffs sought a preliminary injunction in 45% of the early cases brought under the DTSA.[8]

[B] Ex Parte Civil Seizure

The most innovative—and controversial—feature of the DTSA is the ex parte civil seizure provision. It states that in "extraordinary circumstances" the court may issue an order providing for the "seizure of property necessary to prevent the propagation or dissemination of the trade secret that is the subject of the action," without advance notice to the defendant.[9] The UTSA does not provide an analogous remedy.[10]

The DTSA legislative history states that this provision "is an important remedy for trade secret owners because it 'enable[s] a trade secret owner under limited, controlled conditions, to proactively contain a theft before it progresses and the trade secret is lost.'"[11] Congress anticipated that it would be used "in instances in which a defendant is seeking to flee the country or planning to disclose the trade secret to a third party immediately or is otherwise not amenable to the enforcement of the court's orders."[12]

Suppose that A steals B's trade secret and is about to email the information to C, a foreign company that competes with B. B could apply for a temporary restraining order to prevent such disclosure, but there is a clear risk that this would prompt A to email the secret to C before the hearing occurs.[13] On these facts, A could apply for an order authorizing seizure of B's computers or other electronic devices that contain the information, without any need to notify B in advance.

The court may issue a seizure order only if eight criteria are satisfied: (1) a temporary restraining order or similar relief would be inadequate; (2) immediate and irreparable injury will occur if the seizure is not ordered; (3) the harm to the applicant from denying the application outweighs the harm to the defendant and third parties; (4) the applicant is likely to succeed on the merits of its misappropriation lawsuit against the person against whom seizure is sought; (5) the person has actual possession

8. *Id.*

9. 18 U.S.C. § 1836(b)(2)(A)(i). Under some circumstances, a temporary restraining order may also be issued without prior notice to the defendant. *See, e.g.*, Fed. R. Civ. P. 65(b)(1).

10. However, a court would presumably have the inherent equitable power to order such a seizure to protect a plaintiff from irreparable injury.

11. Sen. Rep. No. 114-220, at 3 (2016) (citation omitted).

12. *Id.* at 6.

13. Of course, such an application can be made on an ex parte basis. The DTSA authorizes the special civil seizure remedy only where, inter alia, a temporary restraining order or similar equitable relief would be inadequate because "the party to which the order would be issued would evade, avoid, or otherwise not comply with such an order." 18 U.S.C. § 1836(b)(2)(A)(ii)(I).

of the secret and any property to be seized;[14] (6) the application adequately describes the matter to be seized and its location; (7) the person would "destroy, move, hide, or otherwise make such matter inaccessible to the court" if the applicant were to provide notice; and (8) the applicant has not publicized the requested seizure.[15]

Ex parte seizure is controversial because it may cause irreparable harm to the business of an innocent party who has no opportunity to contest the order. The DTSA provides safeguards against such abuse. First, a person subject to the seizure order may "move the court at any time to dissolve or modify the order."[16] Second, the applicant must post security "for the payment of the damages that any person may be entitled to recover as a result of a wrongful or excessive seizure,"[17] and anyone damaged by such a seizure may sue for damages.[18]

The legislative history underlying this remedy suggests that it may also be used "where necessary to preserve evidence."[19] In practice, ex parte seizure orders are rarely issued and mainly used to prevent destruction of evidence.[20]

[C] Temporary Restraining Orders and Preliminary Injunctions

[1] Generally

As a rule, in order to obtain a preliminary injunction the plaintiff must establish that: (a) she is likely to succeed on the merits; (b) she is likely to suffer irreparable harm if the injunction is denied; (c) the balance of equities tips in her favor; and (d) an injunction is in the public interest.[21] The purpose of a temporary restraining order (TRO) is to preserve the status quo until a preliminary injunction motion may be

---

14. This element protects most third parties against seizure. Thus, "the operator of a server on which another party has stored a misappropriated trade secret, or an online intermediary such as an Internet service provider, would not be subject to seizure because their servers, and the data stored upon them, would not be in the actual possession of the defendant against whom seizure was ordered." H.R. Rep. No. 114-220, at 10 (2016).

15. 18 U.S.C. § 1836(b)(2)(A)(ii).

16. *Id.* (b)(2)(F)(iii).

17. *Id.* (b)(2)(B)(vi).

18. *Id.* (b)(2)(G).

19. Sen. Rep. No. 114-220, at 3 (2016).

20. *See, e.g.*, Axis Steel Detailing, Inc. v. Prilex Detailing LLC, 2017 WL 8947964 (D. Utah June 29, 2017); Solar Connect, LLC v. Endicott, 2018 WL 2386066 (D. Utah Apr. 6, 2018).

21. Winter v. Natural Res. Defense Council, Inc., 555 U.S. 7, 20 (2008). *Winter* did not expressly address the "sliding scale" approach that some circuits had applied to these factors, and accordingly it appears to survive. For example, in the Ninth Circuit a preliminary injunction will issue "where the likelihood of success is such that 'serious questions going to the merits' were raised and the balance of hardships 'tips sharply toward the plaintiff,' provided that the plaintiff can also demonstrate the other two *Winter* factors." California v. U.S. Dept. of Health & Human Services, 941 F.3d 410, 424 (9th Cir. 2019). *See also* § 5.06[C].

heard by the court; a TRO application is evaluated under the same factors that govern the issuance of a preliminary injunction.[22]

Likelihood of success: The first element is straightforward. The plaintiff must show it is more likely than not that the defendant misappropriated the trade secret.[23]

Irreparable harm: The law governing this element is clear under the UTSA, but somewhat murky under the DTSA.

For the purposes of injunctive relief, most state courts presume that misappropriation of a trade secret would cause irreparable harm. In *InnoSys, Inc. v. Mercer*, the Utah Supreme Court observed that "[a] trade secret is a right of property" and "[s]uch rights are protected by a legal presumption of harm."[24] It explained that the basis for this presumption is "the difficulty of measuring the extent of actual economic injury."[25] Public disclosure destroys a trade secret; and it is often difficult to compute the damages caused by its destruction. As a Texas appellate court noted while upholding a preliminary injunction, "[t]he threatened disclosure of trade secrets constitutes irreparable injury as a matter of law."[26]

Federal courts traditionally followed the same approach. However, in *eBay, Inc. v MercExchange, LLC*, the Supreme Court held that irreparable injury may not be presumed from patent infringement, but instead must be proven.[27] Does the *eBay* logic apply equally to a trade secret misappropriation action under the DTSA? While the Supreme Court has not addressed the issue, an argument can be made that *eBay* should not apply to trade secrets, which are fundamentally different from patents.[28] A core theme underlying patent law is that disclosure of the invention allows it to serve as raw material for others to develop new products and processes. Thus, public disclosure is essential for a patent. But it is fatal to a trade secret.

Assuming that proof of irreparable injury is required, a plaintiff in a trade secret case can satisfy this element by showing that damages would be difficult or impossible to calculate. This standard is met where the plaintiff would have difficulty quantifying its lost profits, its loss of prospective customers, the injury to its goodwill, or the value of the trade secret.[29] For instance, in *WHIC LLC v. NextGen Laboratories, Inc.*,

---

22. *See, e.g.*, H.Q. Milton, Inc. v. Webster, 2017 WL 5625929 (N.D. Cal. Nov. 22, 2017) (granting application for TRO to prevent defendants from further disclosure or use of plaintiff's claimed trade secrets).

23. *See* Chapter 4.

24. 364 P.3d 1013, 1020 (2015).

25. *Id.*

26. IAC, Ltd. v. Bell Helicopter Textron, Inc., 160 S.W.3d 191, 200 (Tex. App. 2005).

27. 547 U.S. 388 (2006).

28. *Compare* First Western Capital Mgmt. Co. v. Malamed, 874 F.3d 1136, 1143 (10th Cir. 2017) (stating that irreparable harm cannot be presumed in trade secret cases) *with* Vendavo, Inc. v. Long, 397 F. Supp. 3d 1115, 1143 n. 21 (N.D. Ill. 2019) (observing that the presumption of irreparable harm in trade secret cases remains "intact" in the Seventh Circuit).

29. *See, e.g.*, Henry Schein, Inc. v. Cook, 191 F. Supp. 3d 1072, 1077 (N.D. Cal. 2016) (threatened loss of customers was irreparable injury).

the district court found that irreparable harm was likely where the defendant's use of a confidential customer list would cause the plaintiff to "lose goodwill in the eyes of customers."[30]

Balance of equities: In applying this element, the court determines whether the impact on the defendant if the injunction is granted would be more severe than the injury to the plaintiff if it were denied. In most cases, this element strongly favors protecting the plaintiff's trade secret against misappropriation. However, where an injunction against disclosure or use of the secret would seriously damage the defendant's business, this element may favor the defendant. Thus, in *Litton Systems, Inc. v. Sundstrand*, the Federal Circuit agreed that the defendant would suffer a greater hardship because the injunction would "result in breach of existing sale contracts and loss of $12,000,000 of investment, would directly impact 350 jobs, and would cause the loss of over $60,000,000 in projected sales over the next five years."[31]

Public interest: Many courts recognize a public policy in favor of preventing the unauthorized disclosure of trade secrets.[32] The district court in *Henry Schein, Inc. v. Cook* explained: "[T]he public interest is ... served by enabling the protection of trade secrets."[33] Thus, in most trade secret cases, the public interest favors injunctive relief.

[2] Inevitable Disclosure Doctrine

Suppose that D's former employee E is about to start a new job with D's competitor F, where E will almost certainly disclose some of D's trade secrets. Can D obtain a preliminary injunction that bars E from working for F?

This hypothetical introduces one of the most controversial concepts in trade secret law—the inevitable disclosure doctrine.[34] In jurisdictions that follow this doctrine, a court may enjoin a former employee from working for his employer's competitor if this will inevitably lead to the disclosure or use of trade secrets. As the UTSA provides, a court is empowered to enjoin "threatened misappropriation."[35] The inevitable disclosure doctrine is a specialized application of this principle; a court issuing such an injunction has presumably concluded that future misappropriation is highly likely. On the other hand, some states reject the doctrine because it restricts employee mobility, and therefore impairs free competition.

The Seventh Circuit applied the doctrine in the well-known case of *PepsiCo, Inc. v. Redmond*.[36] Redmond, a former general manager for PepsiCo, accepted an offer to become the chief operating officer for Gatorade and Snapple. PepsiCo obtained a

30. 341 F. Supp. 3d 1147, 1165 (D. Haw. 2018).

31. 750 F.2d 952, 960 (Fed. Cir. 1984).

32. *See, e.g.*, Norand Corp. v. Parkin, 785 F. Supp. 1353, 1356 (N.D. Iowa 1990).

33. *Henry Schein, Inc.*, 191 F. Supp. 3d at 1078.

34. The doctrine is rarely used. An empirical study revealed that plaintiffs relied on it in less than 1% of the cases studied. Rowe, *supra* note 4, at 187.

35. UTSA § 2(a).

36. 54 F.3d 1262 (7th Cir. 1995).

preliminary injunction to prevent this employment on the basis that it would inevitably lead him to use PepsiCo's secret information about how it planned to "price, distribute, and market its sports drinks and new age drinks."[37] Upholding the injunction, the Seventh Circuit noted the district court's conclusion that "unless Redmond possessed an uncanny ability to compartmentalize information, he would necessarily be making decisions about Gatorade and Snapple by relying on his knowledge of [PepsiCo's] trade secrets."[38]

Does the DTSA reject the doctrine? After authorizing courts to enjoin "threatened misappropriation," the act states that an injunction may not "prevent a person from entering into an employment relationship...."[39] On its face, this language appears to bar a court from using the doctrine. Moreover, the section further provides that any "conditions placed on such employment" must be based on "evidence of threatened misappropriation and not merely on the information the person knows."[40] This language seems to imply that an injunction must be based on something more than the former employee's knowledge. However, some federal courts appear to apply the doctrine in DTSA cases, with little textual analysis.[41]

§ 7.03 Permanent Injunctions

[A] Overview

The traditional remedy against future misappropriation is a permanent injunction. After trial, the successful plaintiff may obtain a judgment that prohibits the defendant from disclosing or using the trade secret. In trade secret cases, such an injunction usually lasts only as long as required to eliminate the commercial advantage the defendant obtained by misappropriation. Thus, although it is labelled a "permanent" injunction—to distinguish it from a preliminary injunction—it is far from permanent.

In exceptional circumstances, the court may award a royalty injunction—essentially an injunction that allows the defendant to continue using the trade secret, but requires that it pay a reasonable royalty to the plaintiff.

Finally, the court may issue injunctions that require the defendant to take affirmative acts, such as returning documents or other items to the trade secret owner.

---

37. *Id.* at 1270.

38. *Id.* at 1269. *See also* Bimbo Bakeries USA, Inc. v. Botticella, 613 F.3d 102 (3d Cir. 2010) (affirming injunction that barred one of seven employees who knew the secret recipe for Thomas' English Muffins from working for a competitor).

39. 18 U.S.C. § 1836(b)(3)(A)(I). The DTSA's legislative history indicates that this limitation was included "to protect employee mobility." H.R. Rep. No. 114-220, at 12 (2016).

40. 18 U.S.C. § 1836(b)(3)(A)(I).

41. *See, e.g.*, Mickey's Linen v. Fischer, 2017 WL 3970593 (N.D. Ill. Sept. 8, 2017); Molon Motor & Coil Corp. v. Nidec Motor Corp., 2017 WL 1954531 (N.D. Ill. May 11, 2017).

[B] Injunctions against Disclosure or Use

[1] Generally

The UTSA provides that "[a]ctual or threatened misappropriation may be enjoined."[42] Similarly, the DTSA states that "a court may ... grant an injunction ... to prevent any actual or threatened misappropriation...."[43]

The elements required for a permanent injunction are the same as those for a preliminary injunction, except that the plaintiff has already succeeded on the merits. Thus, the plaintiff must establish three elements: (a) she is likely to suffer irreparable harm if the injunction is denied; (b) the balance of equities tips in her favor; and (c) an injunction is in the public interest. The earlier discussion of these elements in the section on preliminary injunctions applies equally here.[44]

It is important to remember that an injunction is a discretionary remedy. The UTSA and DTSA merely indicate that the court "may" grant an injunction. The plaintiff who wins at trial is not automatically entitled to an injunction.

[2] Duration

An injunction in a trade secret case lasts only for a specified duration. This is called a "lead-time" or "head-start" injunction. As the UTSA drafters explain, "an injunction should last for as long as is necessary, but no longer than is necessary, to eliminate the commercial advantage or 'lead time' with respect to good faith competitors that a person has obtained through misappropriation."[45] It would be anti-competitive to bar a defendant from using such information in perpetuity.

Suppose that G steals H's secret doughnut recipe, but the evidence shows that G could have reverse engineered the formula in a year. On these facts, the court will enjoin G from using the formula only for one year. This period is long enough to eliminate the lead-time advantage that G's theft would have provided.

Winston Research Corp. v. Minnesota Mining & Manufacturing Corp. provides a real-world example of a "permanent" injunction with an expiration date.[46] In that case, defendant Winston misappropriated trade secrets that the plaintiff had used in creating a new tape recorder; it utilized this information to develop a competing machine. Although the plaintiff requested a perpetual injunction, the court concluded that the secrets "would shortly be fully disclosed" when it began selling its tape recorders to the public.[47] Accordingly, it enjoined the defendants from using the information only for two years—"for the approximate period it would require a legit-

42. UTSA § 2(a).

43. 18 U.S.C. § 1836(b)(3)(A)(i). The DTSA also authorizes the U.S. Attorney General to bring a civil action to obtain "appropriate injunctive relief." 18 U.S.C. § 1836(a).

44. *See* § 7.02[C][1].

45. UTSA § 2 cmt.

46. 350 F.2d 134 (9th Cir. 1965).

47. *Id.* at 141.

imate ... competitor to develop a successful machine after public disclosure of the secret information."[48]

Notably, the UTSA provides that "an injunction shall be terminated when the trade secret has ceased to exist."[49] This is consistent with the traditional rule that a court has continuing jurisdiction to dissolve or modify an injunction in light of changed circumstances. By definition, once trade secret protection ends—for example, by publication of a patent application that discloses the secret—continued injunctive relief is not necessary to protect the plaintiff from any harm caused by the defendant's misappropriation.

The DTSA does not expressly address how long an injunction should last. However, it provides that an injunction shall be granted "on such terms as the court deems reasonable."[50] Since the DTSA is largely based on the UTSA, it seems likely that federal courts will follow the UTSA approach on duration.[51]

[C] Royalty Injunctions

The UTSA states that in "exceptional circumstances" an injunction may "condition future use [of the trade secret] upon payment of a reasonable royalty."[52] In this situation, the court denies the plaintiff's request for an injunction that prohibits future use of the secret, and instead permits the defendant to continue its use by paying a royalty.[53] The DTSA contains a similar provision.[54]

The court has broad discretion to determine if exceptional circumstances exist. Such circumstances could include (1) "the existence of an overriding public interest which requires the denial of a prohibitory injunction" and (2) "a person's reasonable reliance upon acquisition of a misappropriated trade secret in good faith and without reason to know of its prior misappropriation that would be prejudiced by a prohibitory injunction."[55]

Skycam, LLC v. Bennett illustrates this principle.[56] Both parties manufactured aerial camera systems used to broadcast sporting events. After the jury concluded that the defendant had developed its system by stealing the plaintiff's trade secrets, the court issued a royalty injunction. It explained: "A prohibitory injunction would eliminate competition and technological innovation in the aerial camera market—which has relatively few competitors—in derogation of the public interest."[57]

---

48. *Id.* at 142.
49. UTSA § 2(a).
50. 18 U.S.C. § 1836(b)(3)(A)(i).
51. *See, e.g.*, Par Pharm., Inc. v. QuVa Pharma, Inc., 764 F. App'x 273 (3d Cir. 2019) (using lead-time approach in action brought under both the DTSA and New Jersey's version of the UTSA).
52. UTSA § 2(b).
53. *Id.* But the UTSA drafters noted that in "some situations" where exceptional circumstances exist, the court may conclude that no royalty need be paid. UTSA § 2 cmt.
54. 18 U.S.C. § 1836(b)(3)(A)(iii).
55. UTSA § 2 cmt.
56. 2012 WL 4483610 (N.D. Okla. Sept. 27, 2012).
57. *Id.* at *3.

Where the court issues a royalty injunction, the defendant may be obligated to pay royalties "for no longer than the period of time for which use could have been prohibited."[58] This reflects the same concept that underlies the lead-time injunction. For example, if the trade secret could have been reversed engineered in two years, the defendant need only pay royalties for two years.

[D] Other Injunctive Relief

Finally, the UTSA states that "[i]n appropriate circumstances, affirmative acts to protect a trade secret may be compelled by court order."[59] The DTSA contains a similar provision authorizing mandatory injunctions.[60] Such an injunction might require the defendant to return stolen documents, surreptitious photos, or other objects embodying the trade secret to the owner.[61] Similarly, where the defendant has secured a patent on the trade secret or an invention based on the secret, an injunction could compel the defendant to assign the patent to the plaintiff.[62]

§ 7.04 Compensatory Damages

[A] Overview

The successful plaintiff in a trade secret case may obtain both an injunction that prevents future misappropriation and damages to compensate it for past misappropriation. As a practical matter, damages are available only when the defendant has either disclosed or used the secret; the defendant's mere acquisition of the information ordinarily causes no monetary harm.[63]

The UTSA and DTSA use the same two standards for measuring compensatory damages. Under the basic standard, the plaintiff recovers its actual loss plus the benefit received by the defendant. Alternatively, damages may be based on the amount of a reasonable royalty. The basic standard is used in the vast majority of cases, while the royalty approach is rare.[64]

---

58. UTSA § 2(b). *See also* 18 U.S.C. § 1836(b)(3)(A)(iii).

59. UTSA § 2(c).

60. 18 U.S.C. § 1836(b)(3)A)(ii).

61. UTSA § 2 cmt.

62. Restatement (Third) of Unfair Competition § 44 cmt. e.

63. *See, e.g.*, News America Mktg. In-Store, Inc. v. Marquis, 862 A.2d 837 (Conn. App. 2004) (upholding trial court decision to award no damages where defendant wrongfully acquired secrets but never disclosed, used, or benefited from them). *But see* Food Servs. of Am., Inc. v. Carrington, 2013 WL 4507593 (D. Ariz. Aug. 23, 2013) (suggesting that plaintiff could recover damages for the time its employees spent in reviewing the misappropriated documents).

64. One study found that over a fifteen-year period compensatory damages comprised 85% of all damage awards, while the reasonable royalty standard accounted for only 4.73% of such awards. Rowe, *supra* note 4, at 175.

A UTSA comment explains that an award of compensatory damages—like an injunction—is limited to the "period in which information is entitled to protection as a trade secret, plus the additional period, if any, in which a misappropriator retains an advantage over good faith competitors because of misappropriation."[65] For example, if J wrongfully used K's secret for three years, but could have obtained the information through reverse engineering in one year, K can recover damages for only one year of use.

[B] Basic Standard

[1] Generally

The UTSA states that a plaintiff may recover "both the actual loss caused by misappropriation and the unjust enrichment caused by misappropriation that is not taken into account in computing actual loss."[66] In other words, the basic measure of damages is the amount of the plaintiff's *loss* plus the amount of the defendant's *gain*, as long as there is no double counting.[67] The DTSA uses the same standard, though it is phrased somewhat differently.[68]

Why should the plaintiff recover under both approaches, rather than being required to choose one? First, in a trade secret case it is often difficult for the plaintiff to meet the normal standard of proving damages with reasonable certainty. As the Sixth Circuit opined in a pre-UTSA trade secret dispute, "[o]ur review of the case law leads us to the conclusion that every case requires a flexible and imaginative approach to the problem of damages."[69] Second, the defendant in a misappropriation case is viewed as a wrongdoer who improperly acquired, disclosed, or used the secret and, accordingly, was unjustly enriched. Yet, as the Restatement (Third) of Unfair Competition explains, "in many circumstances the loss to the plaintiff and the gain to the defendant do not fully overlap."[70] As a result, the flexible UTSA/DTSA standard seeks to both compensate the plaintiff and recover the benefit unjustly obtained by the defendant.

[2] Lost Profits

The common scenario where the plaintiff loses profits because of the defendant's misappropriation illustrates the relationship between actual loss and unjust enrichment.

As the Restatement (Third) of Unfair Competition observes, "[a] frequent element of loss resulting from the appropriation of a trade secret is the lost profit that the

---

65. UTSA § 3 cmt.

66. *Id.* § 3(a).

67. However, the UTSA also provides that damages may not be awarded if a defendant's "material and prejudicial change of position prior to acquiring knowledge or reason to know of misappropriation renders a monetary recovery inequitable." UTSA § 3(a).

68. 18 U.S.C. § 1836(b)(3)(B). The legislative history of the DTSA indicates that this standard was "drawn directly" from the UTSA. H.R. Rep. No. 114-220, at 13 (2016).

69. Univ. Computing Co. v. Lykes-Youngstown Corp., 504 F.2d 518, 538 (6th Cir. 1974).

70. Restatement (Third) of Unfair Competition § 45 cmt. c.

plaintiff would have earned in the absence of the use by the defendant."[71] Suppose that L is able to manufacture a unique product because it uses a secret process; for each additional unit L sells, it earns $20 in profit. M steals the secret, uses it, and sells 10,000 units of the same product. On these simple facts—only two competitors selling the identical product—L can prove that it would have sold those 10,000 units but for M's theft. Thus, L's actual loss is $200,000 ($20 per unit times 10,000 units).[72]

Similarly, the defendant's unjust enrichment might be measured by the profits it made from the misappropriation. In this situation, a plaintiff like L is only required to prove the amount of the defendant's sales; the defendant then has the burden of "establishing any portion of the sales not attributable to the trade secret and any expenses to be deducted in determining net profits."[73] Assume that M was able to earn $25 in profit for each unit it sold, for a total of $250,000 in profits.

On these facts, L cannot recover both its actual loss ($200,000) and M's profits ($250,000) because this would be double counting. L receives only $250,000, the larger amount. The Restatement explains that: "Both compensatory and restitutionary objectives are ordinarily satisfied ... if the plaintiff is permitted to recover only the greater of the two measures."[74]

[3] Other Actual Losses

The plaintiff may also recover for other losses caused by the defendant's use of the information. One example is price erosion. If the plaintiff reduced its prices to compete with the defendant, it may recover this loss. Similarly, the plaintiff is entitled to compensation for the advertising and promotional costs it incurred to recapture customers lost due to the misappropriation. More broadly, where the misappropriation disrupted the growth of the plaintiff's business or caused it to lose other market opportunities such as royalties, damages for these losses may also be awarded.[75]

The most severe loss occurs where the defendant publicly discloses the information, since this destroys the secret. In this situation, the plaintiff is entitled to recover the fair market value of the information at the time of disclosure.[76] Suppose that N wrongfully obtains O's secret process and applies for a patent; once the application is published, the trade secret ends and N is liable for its value. If the trade secret was the principal asset of O's business, O may also be entitled to compensation for the resulting loss in the value of the business, as long as this is not a double recovery.

---

71. *Id.* cmt. e.

72. L may also be able to recover lost profits on "sales of spare parts, service, supplies, or other items normally purchased from the original seller." *Id.*

73. *Id.* cmt. f.

74. *Id.* cmt. c.

75. *See, e.g.*, Wellogix, Inc. v. Accenture, LLP, 716 F.3d 867 (5th Cir. 2013) (upholding $26 million award where misappropriation lowered value of plaintiff's business).

76. *See, e.g.*, Precision Plating & Metal Finishing Inc. v. Martin-Marietta Corp., 435 F.2d 1262, 1263–64 (5th Cir. 1970).

[4] Unjust Enrichment

The unjust enrichment approach is useful in a wide variety of situations beyond the simple situation where two competitors sell the same product.

For instance, the trade secret owner may not be able to prove any actual loss even where it directly competes with the defendant. As the Restatement comments, "[t]he nature of a competitive marketplace ... often makes it difficult for a plaintiff to prove lost sales or other losses attributable to the appropriation of a trade secret."[77] In this situation, the plaintiff can recover unjust enrichment damages measured by the defendant's profits.

This standard is particularly important where the parties do not compete with each other. Suppose that P and Q sell different products. P has its employee R get a job with Q, where she learns one of Q's secret manufacturing techniques. P then uses the technique to improve its product. On these facts, Q has no actual loss, while P was unjustly enriched. Q is entitled to an award of damages to the extent that P benefited from the secret.

Unjust enrichment is also a helpful tool when the defendant used the trade secret to save research and development costs, but did not ultimately market a product. This approach determines the defendant's gain by "comparing the defendant's actual costs with the costs that the defendant would have incurred to achieve the same result without the use of the appropriated trade secret."[78] For example, in *Telex Corp. v. International Business Machines Corp.*, Telex misappropriated trade secrets that were central to a new IBM product that took six years and $30 million to create.[79] This allowed Telex to develop an equivalent product in only 18 months, with a saving of $10 million in research costs; but Telex never actually marketed the product. On these facts, the Tenth Circuit agreed that Telex was unjustly enriched by $10 million.

[C] Alternative Standard: Reasonable Royalty

In the alternative, the plaintiff "can request that damages be based upon a demonstrably reasonable royalty," an approach borrowed from patent law.[80] The UTSA states that:

> In lieu of damages measured by any other methods, the damages caused by misappropriation may be measured by imposition of liability for a reasonable royalty for a misappropriator's unauthorized disclosure or use of a trade secret.[81]

---

77. Restatement (Third) of Unfair Competition § 45 cmt. c.

78. *Id.* cmt. f.

79. 510 F.2d 894 (10th Cir. 1975). *See also* GlobeRanger Corp. v. Software AG United States of America, Inc., 836 F.3d 477 (5th Cir. 2016) (upholding $15 million award where defendant saved development costs).

80. UTSA § 3 cmt.

81. *Id.* § 3(a).

The DTSA contains an almost identical provision.[82]

A reasonable royalty is the theoretical "price that would be agreed upon by a willing buyer and a willing seller for the use made of the trade secret by the defendant."[83] This approach tries to determine the hypothetical amount that the parties would have accepted if they had actually negotiated in good faith at the time of misappropriation.

The royalty standard is useful where it is difficult to prove both the plaintiff's actual loss and the defendant's unjust gain. For example, it may be appropriate where the loss to the plaintiff cannot be adequately proven, and (1) the defendant's gain "apparently exceeds the plaintiff's loss" but is hard to measure or (2) the defendant's "inefficiency results in little or no profit" from its use of the secret.[84] *Mid-Michigan Computer Systems, Inc. v. Marc Glassman, Inc.* illustrates the point.[85] There the defendant copied the plaintiff's trade secret software in order to upgrade its computer system, but the amount of its gain could not be determined; the Sixth Circuit upheld a $2 million award based on the royalty standard.

It is important to distinguish the royalty damages standard from the royalty injunction; they serve quite different purposes. As a UTSA comment succinctly summarizes: "[d]amages are awarded for a misappropriator's past conduct and ... a royalty order injunction regulates a misappropriator's future conduct...."[86]

§ 7.05 Punitive Damages

Under the UTSA, the court may award punitive damages in an amount up to twice the compensatory damages for "willful and malicious misappropriation."[87] The UTSA drafters comment that this section "follows federal patent law in leaving discretionary trebling to the judge even though there may be a jury."[88] The DTSA contains a nearly identical provision.[89]

The UTSA and DTSA do not define "willful" or "malicious." As a result, courts vary somewhat in interpreting their meaning. Most courts would broadly agree with the approach taken in *Contour Design, Inc. v. Chance Mold Steel Co., Ltd.*: "A finding of 'willful and malicious misappropriation' under New Hampshire's version of the Uniform Trade Secrets Act ... requires a finding that the defendant engaged in the

82. 18 U.S.C. § 1836(b)(3)(B)(ii). However, its legislative history indicates that Congress preferred the basic standard for compensatory damages and did not want to "encourage the use of reasonable royalties to resolve trade secret misappropriation." H.R. Rep. No. 114-220, at 13 (2016).

83. Restatement (Third) of Unfair Competition § 45 cmt. d.

84. *Id.* cmt. g.

85. 416 F.3d 505 (6th Cir. 2005). *See also* StorageCraft Tech. Corp. v. Kirby, 744 F.3d 1183 (10th Cir. 2014) (affirming $2.92 million award based on royalty standard where defendant disclosed plaintiff's source code to a competitor).

86. UTSA § 3 cmt.

87. *Id.* § 3(b). A number of UTSA states either modified or omitted this section.

88. *Id.* cmt.

89. 18 U.S.C. § 1836(b)(3)(C).

acts of misappropriation with the intent to bring about their likely results and with ill will, hatred, hostility, or evil motive."[90] However, some courts interpret "malice" to include conscious disregard of the rights of another, rather than requiring ill will, hostility, or evil motive.[91]

For example, the UTSA punitive damages standard was applied in *Mattel, Inc. v. MGA Entertainment, Inc.*[92] Based on a jury finding that Mattel willfully and maliciously misappropriated MGA's trade secrets, the court awarded $85 million in punitive damages. It described Mattel's conduct as follows:

> For years, the company's senior management encouraged employees to use false pretenses to access competitors' private displays at international toy fairs and improperly acquire competitive information, including price lists, advertising plans, and unreleased product attributes. Mattel disseminated the improperly acquired information through internal memoranda ... and company-wide presentations ...; praised the employees that committed the wrongdoing ...; [and] used MGA's trade secret information to preempt MGA's unreleased products.... These "market intelligence" tactics were intentional, pervasive, long-standing and egregious.... Faced with competition and innovation ... Mattel resorted to nefarious tactics in an attempt to cling to its market position.[93]

§ 7.06 Attorney's Fees

The UTSA provides that a court may award attorney's fees to the prevailing party in three situations: (1) "a claim of misappropriation is made in bad faith"; (2) "a motion to terminate an injunction is made or resisted in bad faith"; or (3) "willful and malicious misappropriation occurs."[94] Again, the DTSA contains an almost-identical provision.[95]

Many courts interpret the phrase "bad faith" as used in the UTSA formulation to require both "objective speciousness of the plaintiff's claim ... and its subjective bad faith in bringing or maintaining the claim."[96] The other key phrase—"willful and malicious"—also appears in the section governing punitive damages; its meaning is discussed above.[97]

---

90. 2011 WL 6300622, at *12 (D.N.H. Dec. 16, 2011).

91. *See, e.g.*, Mangren Research & Dev. Corp. v. Nat'l Chemical Co., Inc., 87 F.3d 937, 946 (7th Cir. 1996).

92. 801 F. Supp. 2d 950 (C.D. Cal. 2011).

93. *Id.* at 954–55.

94. UTSA § 4.

95. 18 U.S.C. § 1836(3)(D). The DTSA legislative history indicates that this section was "modeled" on the parallel UTSA provision. H.R. Rep. No. 114-529, at 13 (2016).

96. *See, e.g.*, Gemini Aluminum Corp. v. Cal. Custom Shapes, Inc., 116 Cal. Rptr. 2d 358, 368 (App. 2002).

97. *See* § 7.05.

Chapter 8

Trade Secrets and Employment

§8.01 Introduction

Most trade secret disputes arise out of employment relationships. By definition, a corporation or other business entity can only function through its employees. Employees are thus both the main *source* of an employer's trade secrets and the biggest *threat* to the security of those secrets. Two main issues arise:

- Who owns the trade secret—the employer or the employee?
- How can the employer protect its trade secrets from misappropriation by employees?

The majority of trade secrets are developed by people who are employed by someone else. As a result, ownership disputes often arise. Suppose that A hires B to write computer programs, and B does so in the regular course of his job duties in A's office;

in this situation, A clearly owns the trade secrets embodied in the programs. The question becomes more complex, however, if B was not hired to write programs or if he writes programs at home in his spare time.

Current or former employees are also responsible for most trade secret misappropriation. In the ordinary course of business, employers must disclose such secrets to employees in order to benefit from them. Two modern trends exacerbate the risk of misappropriation. First, employees are increasingly mobile. Rather than remaining with one company, workers today are more likely to have a series of jobs. Second, technology has made it much easier to steal trade secrets. Instead of trying to smuggle secret documents through a guarded exit, an employee might take a picture of them on his personal phone and send the picture to a private email account. Or if C's employee D is unhappy with his current salary, he might email himself a list of C's customers and hope to profit from the list when he takes a similar job with a new employer.

Well-established bodies of law govern the ownership and misappropriation of trade secrets. However, employers increasingly rely on employment contracts or free-standing nondisclosure agreements to supplement or supplant these rules. The widespread use of these contracts requires courts to balance broad public policy concerns: protecting the employee's right to choose her job, preventing misappropriation, encouraging innovation, and promoting free competition.

§ 8.02 Who Owns the Trade Secret?

[A] Overview

Suppose that E is employed by company F. If E develops a valuable new chemical process, who owns the trade secret? Absent an agreement, common law principles govern the answer to this question. Depending on the circumstances, either E or F may be the owner.

Of course, these principles can be changed by contract. Today many employees—particularly those working for large corporations—are required to execute agreements by which they assign their trade secrets to the employer. Courts closely scrutinize these assignment agreements, and statutes in some states impose restrictions on their scope. In the hypothetical above, E is probably bound by such an agreement and, F therefore owns the secret.

The ownership issue is vital because corporations and other business entities can only function through employees. This means that most trade secrets are developed by employees—who in turn might have ownership claims. It is estimated that up to 90% of inventions are created by employees.[1]

1. Ingersoll-Rand Co. v. Ciavatta, 542 A.2d 879, 886 (N.J. 1988) ("The contractual allocation of invention rights between employers and employees is especially critical given the fact that 80% to 90% of all inventions in the United States are made by employed inventors.").

[B] Common Law Approach

Over time, a series of patent ownership cases developed rules for determining who owns an "invention" created by an employee. It was logical for courts to apply this approach to unpatented inventions, which were protected by trade secret law. Later courts extended this approach to trade secrets other than inventions. As the Restatement (Third) of Unfair Competition observes: "Although the rules governing ownership of valuable information created during an employment relationship are most frequently applied to inventions, the rules are also applicable to information such as customer lists, marketing ideas, and other valuable business information."[2]

Under the common law approach, the employee's status determines who owns the inventions or other trade secrets that he develops. There are three categories: (1) the employee who is "hired to invent"; (2) the employee who is not "hired to invent" but uses employer resources to invent; and (3) the employee who invents on her own time without using employer resources.

First, the employer owns a trade secret developed by an employee within the scope of her job duties. The Restatement explains that "valuable information that is the product of an employee's assigned duties is owned by the employer...."[3] The justification for this result is straightforward—the employee's salary fully compensates for her inventive work. Accordingly, in the E-F hypothetical above, employer F owns the process so long as developing it was within the scope of E's duties.

Litigation sometimes arises about the scope of the employee's job duties. An example is *Northern Electric Co., Inc. v. Torma*, where defendant Torma was assigned to repair servo motors for various customers.[4] While on the job, he entered readings, settings, and other repair data in a notebook, along with information from manufacturer's manuals and internet sites. Torma later claimed that he owned the data because he was not "specifically assigned" to collect it by the employer.[5] But the court held that the compilation "clearly arose out of his assigned duties."[6]

Second, the employee owns a trade secret that she created outside the scope of her assigned duties, but with use of the employer's resources. In this situation, the employer is usually entitled to what is termed a shop right—i.e., "an irrevocable, nonexclusive, royalty-free license to use the innovation."[7] The Supreme Court explained the basis for this principle in *United States v. Dubilier Condenser Corp.*:

> [W]here a servant, during his hours of employment, working with his master's materials and appliances, conceives and perfects an invention for which

---

2. Restatement (Third) of Unfair Competition §42 cmt. e.
3. *Id.*
4. 819 N.E.2d 417 (Ind. App. 2005).
5. *Id.* at 424.
6. *Id.* at 425.
7. Restatement (Third) of Unfair Competition §42 cmt. e. But a shop right will not arise where the employee's use of employer resources was minimal. *See, e.g.*, Aero Bolt & Screw Co. v. Iaia, 5 Cal. Rptr. 53 (App. 1960).

> he obtains a patent, he must accord his master a nonexclusive right to practice the invention.... This is an application of equitable principles. Since the servant uses his master's time, facilities, and materials to attain a concrete result, the latter is in equity entitled to use that which embodies his own property and to duplicate it as often as he may find occasion to employ similar appliances in his business.[8]

Because the shop right is based in equity, courts vary somewhat on when it will be recognized.[9]

Suppose now that F hired E as a personnel manager, rather than an inventor. For several months, E uses his office computer to research chemical processes over his lunch hour and after work. On these facts, E owns the new process he developed because the work was not within his job duties, but F will likely hold a shop right in that process.

Finally, the employee owns a trade secret that she developed on her own time without using employer resources. This follows from the general rule that "the law ordinarily assigns ownership of an invention or idea to the person who conceives it."[10] Thus, if E developed the new process outside of working hours by using only his own resources, E owns the process—regardless of whether such research was within his assigned duties—and F has no right to use it.

[C] Assignment Agreements

[1] Basics

It is easy to understand why employers use assignment agreements. From the employer's standpoint, the common law doctrines are vague, often require fact-intensive litigation, and—most importantly—do not provide enough protection. The employer's interests are better served by requiring each new employee to execute a contract that assigns all future inventions and other secrets to the employer.

Given the disparity in bargaining power in the employer-employee relationship, it is unsurprising that assignment agreements heavily favor the employer. In the typical agreement, the employee assigns all the trade secrets that she creates to the employer, regardless of the circumstances under which they were created—thus ignoring the common law distinctions. This includes trade secrets that the employee developed on her own time, without the use of any employer resources.

A simple assignment agreement for a new employee might provide as follows:

> I hereby irrevocably assign to the Corporation all inventions, patents, copyrights, trade secrets, and other intellectual property that I develop during the period of my employment with the Corporation or within two years after such employment ends.

8. 289 U.S. 178, 188–89 (1933).
9. McElmurry v. Arkansas Power & Light Co., 995 F.2d 1576, 1580–82 (Fed. Cir. 1993).
10. Restatement (Third) of Unfair Competition §42 cmt. e.

Many companies require each new employee to sign a comprehensive employment agreement, which includes an assignment clause, a nondisclosure clause, and related provisions.

The law governing these assignments distinguishes between (1) contracts for assignment of trade secrets developed *during* employment and (2) contracts that also require assignment of secrets developed *after* employment ends.

[2] Secrets Developed During Employment

Contracts for assignment of trade secrets that are developed during employment are usually enforceable.[11] However, courts will strictly construe them against the employer. An example is *Mattel, Inc. v. MGA Entertainment, Inc.*, which was a dispute about who owned the idea for a new line of dolls, as reflected in sketches and a prototype doll body.[12] The employee who developed the idea had entered into an agreement that assigned all inventions and other information created "at any time during my employment by the Company" to Mattel.[13] Mattel argued that this language encompassed all inventions developed by the employee during this time period; indeed, on its face the language is clear. In an echo of the common law approach, however, MGA insisted that it only covered inventions that were *also* within the scope of the employee's assigned duties. The district court granted the plaintiff's motion for summary judgment on the issue. However, construing the language narrowly, the Ninth Circuit held that it was ambiguous and reversed the decision.[14]

Statutes in a handful of states restrict assignment agreements in order to protect employees. California Labor Code § 2870 is a typical "inventor's rights" statute. Under this provision, an assignment of an "invention that the employee developed entirely on his or her own time without using the employer's equipment, supplies, facilities, or trade secret information" is unenforceable as against public policy. However, inventions that (a) relate to the employer's business or (b) result from work performed by the employee for the employer are exempt from the statute. In effect, this statute partly codifies the common law rule that an employee who invents on her own time without using employer resources owns the invention.

[3] Secrets Developed After Employment

It is often difficult to know exactly when an invention or other trade secret is developed. For example, the process of "invention" may have many stages—a glimmer of insight, a tentative approach, an experimental process, a firm concept, a prototype, and a finished product. Further, an employee who is about to leave the job may have

11. Restatement (Third) of Unfair Competition § 42 cmt. g ("[A]greements relating to the ownership of inventions and discoveries made by employees during the term of the employment are generally enforceable according to their terms.").

12. 616 F.3d 904 (9th Cir. 2009).

13. *Id.* at 912.

14. *Id.* at 912–13.

an incentive not to tell the employer about trade secrets that she has created. In order to deal with these concerns, assignment agreements often include a *holdover clause* (sometimes called a trailer clause), by which the employee agrees to assign all inventions and other trade secrets that she develops for a period of time after employment ends. Such clauses "prevent an employee from appropriating to his own use or to the use of a subsequent employer inventions relating to and stemming from work done for a former employer."[15]

Holdover clauses are often overbroad, encompassing trade secrets that have no relationship at all to the employer. Further, since they make it harder for employees to obtain new jobs, these clauses tend to restrict competition and constrain employee mobility. As one court observed: "The law does not look favorably upon covenants which place 'a mortgage on a man's brain, to bind all its future products.'"[16]

Courts closely scrutinize holdover clauses to ensure that they are reasonable in both duration and subject matter. As the court summarized in *Dorr-Oliver, Inc. v. United States*:

> Hold-over clauses in employment contracts are enforceable only if they constitute a reasonable and justifiable restriction on the right of employees to work in their profession for subsequent employers.... In construing and applying hold-over clauses, the courts have held that they must be limited to reasonable times ... and to subject matter which an employee worked on or had knowledge of during his employment.... Unless expressly agreed otherwise, an employer has no right under a hold-over clause to inventions made outside the scope of the employee's former activities, and made on and with a subsequent employer's time and funds.[17]

In that case, the defendant's new invention—a trailer for carrying cargo on pallets—had no relation to his prior work for the plaintiff on missile and space vehicles. As a result, the court held that the clause was unenforceable.

The case law on duration varies widely. Courts generally seem to enforce holdover clauses with a duration of a year or less.[18] Beyond this point, the longer the duration, the more likely it is that the clause will be invalidated. An example is *GTI Corp. v. Calhoon*, where the court refused to enforce a clause with a duration of five years, noting that it "unreasonably restricts Calhoon's right to utilize his general skill and knowledge in subsequent employment" and accordingly was against public policy.[19]

15. Dorr-Oliver, Inc. v. United States, 432 F.2d 447, 452 (Ct. Cl. 1970).

16. New Britain Mach. Co. v. Yeo, 358 F.2d 397, 405 (6th Cir. 1966) (quoting DeLong Corp. v. Lucas, 178 F. Supp. 104 (S.D.N.Y. 1959)).

17. *Dorr-Oliver*, 432 F.2d at 452.

18. *See, e.g.*, Milliken & Co. v. Morin, 731 S.E.2d 288 (S.C. 2012).

19. GTI Corp. v. Calhoon, 309 F. Supp. 762, 774 (S.D. Ohio 1969).

§ 8.03 Protection for Employer Trade Secrets

[A] Overview

Employees pose the biggest danger to trade secrets. One study of state trade secret litigation found that current or former employees were the alleged misappropriators in 77% of cases.[20] Yet companies must disclose their trade secrets to employees as a matter of course in order to operate. As one scholar noted, treating "employees simultaneously as valued members of the corporate family and as threats to the company's trade secrets can be a delicate balancing act."[21]

In the most common scenario, employee G learns certain trade secrets owned by her employer H in the regular course of her work. G eventually leaves this job and takes a new position with J, a business that competes with H. G then discloses the secrets to J's employees. At this point, H has two possible causes of action against G. First, it can sue G for *misappropriation.* Second, if G signed a nondisclosure agreement, H can also sue for *breach of contract.*[22]

Yet, as the Restatement (Third) of Unfair Competition observes, "[a]pplication of the rules protecting trade secrets in cases involving competition by former employees requires a careful balancing of interests."[23] In particular, the employer's interest in protecting its trade secrets is limited by the public interest in preserving the freedom of employees to obtain new jobs where they can better use their talents, and thereby promoting free competition.

[B] Misappropriation Liability

In the G-H hypothetical above, G is now probably liable to H for misappropriation of trade secrets under the Uniform Trade Secrets Act and Defend Trade Secrets Act. Although G acquired the information legally, she disclosed it wrongfully—in violation of the duty to maintain secrecy that probably arises from her status as an employee, whether or not reflected in a contract.[24] In most situations, the employee's common law duty of loyalty "includes a duty not to disclose the employer's confidential information to others."[25]

---

20. David S. Almeling et al., *A Statistical Analysis of Trade Secret Litigation in State Courts,* 46 Gonz. L. Rev. 57, 69 (2010).

21. Elizabeth A. Rowe, *Information Security and Trade Secrets, in* Harboring Data: Information Security, Law, and the Corporation 92, 98 (Andrea M. Matwyshyn ed., 2009).

22. Of course, if J's employees knew or should have known that G was improperly disclosing H's trade secrets, H may be able to sue J as well.

23. Restatement (Third) of Unfair Competition § 42 cmt. b.

24. *See* § 4.02[D][2][b].

25. Restatement (Third) of Unfair Competition § 42 cmt. b.

[C] Nondisclosure Agreements

[1] Basics

H might also be able to sue G for breach of contract. Businesses increasingly require new employees to sign nondisclosure agreements as a matter of course, either as part of a comprehensive employment contract or as a stand-alone agreement. Under such an agreement, the employee typically promises not to disclose or use the employer's trade secrets that he learns in the course of his employment; the agreement often specifies categories of secrets that it covers.[26] In addition, the agreement may encompass a broad range of non-secret information.

Nondisclosure agreements are typically complex and lengthy. Here is an unusually short sample:

> I agree not to disclose or use at any time, whether during my employment with the Corporation or after such employment ends, any trade secret or confidential information of the Corporation that I learn during my employment, unless the Corporation gives its advance written consent for such disclosure or use.

Although employees with access to trade secrets usually have a duty of confidentiality as a matter of agency law, nondisclosure agreements offer several advantages to the employer: (a) clarifying the scope of the protected information; (b) reminding employees about their duty; (c) establishing ownership of the information; and (d) evidencing the employer's reasonable efforts to maintain secrecy. As the Restatement notes, "[a]n agreement between the parties that characterizes specific information as a 'trade secret' can be an important although not necessarily conclusive factor in determining whether the information qualifies for protection as a trade secret...."[27]

Most importantly, a nondisclosure agreement gives the employer a separate cause of action when a current or former employee discloses or uses a trade secret. The employer may sue for breach of contract either in lieu of or together with a claim for misappropriation.

Nondisclosure agreements are noncontroversial when they duplicate the confidentiality obligations that employees already have at common law. Accordingly, courts routinely enforce these agreements. The Restatement explains that "a contract prohibiting [the] use or disclosure [of a trade secret] is generally enforceable according to its terms."[28] In contrast, courts scrutinize certain other employer-employee contracts, such as invention assignment agreements[29] and noncompetition agreements.[30]

---

26. A duty not to disclose trade secrets may also arise from an implied contract. *See, e.g.*, Winston Research Corp. v. Minnesota Mining & Manufacturing Co., 350 F.2d 134, 140 (9th Cir. 1965) ("In the present case, an agreement not to disclose might be implied from [the employer's] elaborate efforts to maintain the secrecy of its development program, and the employees' knowledge of these efforts and participation in them.").

27. Restatement (Third) of Unfair Competition §39 cmt. d.

28. *Id.* §41 cmt. d.

29. *See* §8.02[C].

30. *See* §8.03[D].

The DTSA requires the employer to ensure that any nondisclosure agreement or other agreement with an employee governing "the use of a trade secret or other confidential information" properly notifies the employee about the whistleblower immunity arising under the act.[31] An employer who fails to comply cannot recover punitive damages or attorney's fees in later litigation against the employee.[32]

[2] Protected Information

Can a nondisclosure agreement protect information that is *not* a trade secret? Suppose, for example, that company K uses a special mining technique. None of K's competitors know about the technique, but K makes no particular effort to preserve its secrecy. As a result, the technique does not qualify for trade secret protection. K's employee L discloses the technique to K's competitors in violation of the nondisclosure agreement she signed. Is L liable for breach of contract?

The majority view is that an employer may use a nondisclosure agreement to safeguard confidential information that does not qualify for trade secret protection.[33] The UTSA provides that it does not displace "contractual remedies, whether or not based upon misappropriation of a trade secret."[34] Thus, the New Hampshire Supreme Court explained in *Mortgage Specialists, Inc. v. Davey* that its state version of the UTSA "continues to permit individuals and corporate entities to protect their valuable commercial information *contractually*, regardless of whether such information meets the statutory definition of [a] 'trade secret'...."[35] Similarly, in interpreting Virginia's version of the UTSA, the Fourth Circuit observed in *Decision Insights, Inc. v. Sentia Group, Inc.* that the breach of contract claims in the case:

> do not require a finding that the materials at issue qualify as a trade secret, because the respective nondisclosure clauses apply to "any confidential or proprietary information ... owned or used by" [the plaintiff]. This contractual language is broader than the definition of a "trade secret" under the Act and, thus, the nondisclosure language may apply to the software code and other proprietary materials at issue even if those materials are not covered by the Act.[36]

The fact that contract law can provide broader protection than trade secret law raises serious policy concerns. The widespread use of nondisclosure agreements that

31. 18 U.S.C. § 1833(b)(3)(A). *See* § 6.04[D]. In this context, "employee" includes "any individual performing work as a contractor or consultant for an employer." 18 U.S.C. § 1833(b)(4).

32. 18 U.S.C. § 1833(b)(3)(C).

33. See Restatement of Employment Law § 8.06 cmt. d ("[N]ondisclosure agreements that cover confidential information not rising to the level of trade secret may provide the employer additional protection not available under the UTSA.").

34. UTSA § 7(b)(1). A comment to this section notes: "The enforceability of covenants not to disclose trade secrets and covenants not to compete that are intended to protect trade secrets ... is governed by other law."

35. 904 A.2d 652, 664 (N.H. 2006) (emphasis in original).

36. 416 F. App'x 324, 331–32 (4th Cir. 2011).

encompass non-secret information may discourage innovation, restrict free competition, and impair employee mobility.[37]

At the same time, public policy somewhat limits the extent to which non-secret information can be shielded by contract. The Restatement cautions that an agreement which covers information that is "generally known or in which the promisee has no protectable interest, such as a former employee's promise not to use information that is part of the employee's general skill and training … may be unenforceable as an unreasonable restraint of trade."[38] Moreover, even if a nondisclosure agreement covers non-secret information, it ends once the information enters the public domain. There is no justification for protecting the confidentiality of information that is no longer confidential.

[3] Enforcement

A nondisclosure agreement can provide the employer with various advantages if a breach occurs. If the agreement contains an arbitration clause, the employer can benefit from the greater secrecy, lower cost, and faster resolution that arbitration provides, as compared to ordinary litigation. And if litigation is appropriate, the employer will ensure that the case is decided according to the favorable law that it designated in the agreement's choice-of-law clause.

Further, it is easier to litigate a breach of contract case than a trade secret misappropriation case. The plaintiff need only prove four elements: (a) the existence of the contract; (b) the plaintiff's performance or excuse for nonperformance; (c) the defendant's breach; and (d) damages resulting from the breach. However, the defenses available in a breach of contract action vary to some extent from those available in a misappropriation action. For example, the statute of limitations may be shorter or longer, depending on the jurisdiction.

The biggest difference between the two theories is the available remedies. For example, compensatory damages for misappropriation are likely to be larger; they can include both (a) the actual loss suffered by the plaintiff (usually measured by lost profits) *and* (b) "the unjust enrichment caused by misappropriation that is not taken into account in computing actual loss."[39] In contrast, compensatory damages for breach of contract are limited to the actual detriment caused by the defendant's breach.[40] Similarly, punitive damages may be available in a misappropriation case, but not on a contract theory.[41]

On the other hand, the existence of a nondisclosure agreement makes it more likely that the court will enjoin a former employee from working at a competing company where there is serious risk he will disclose the former employer's trade

---

37. *See* § 1.03.
38. Restatement (Third) of Unfair Competition § 41 cmt. d.
39. UTSA § 3(a). *See* § 7.04[B].
40. Restatement (Second) of Contracts § 347.
41. UTSA § 3(b). *See* § 7.05.

secrets, under the inevitable disclosure doctrine.[42] One commentator asserts that "the single most advantageous use of [a nondisclosure] agreement might be to establish an express basis for enjoining competitive employment which would jeopardize the employer's trade secrets...."[43]

[D] Noncompetition Agreements

[1] Basics

On its face, a noncompetition agreement merely bars an employee from leaving his job to work for a company that competes with the former employer. But in practice this type of agreement—or a noncompetition clause in a comprehensive employment agreement—is routinely used as a shield against the disclosure of trade secrets.

For instance, if M's employee N executes a valid noncompetition agreement, she is prohibited from performing similar work for M's competitors for a period after her employment ends. As a result, N is effectively barred from disclosing M's secrets to any competitor, simply because she cannot work for any competitors.

Use of a noncompetition agreement avoids the proof difficulties that an employer like M might face in litigating a misappropriation action. As the Fourth Circuit observed in *Comprehensive Technologies International, Inc. v. Software Artisans, Inc.*, a decision enforcing a noncompetition agreement: "It will often be difficult, if not impossible, to prove that a competing employee has misappropriated trade secret information belonging to his former employer."[44]

The scope of such an agreement may extend well beyond trade secrets to include non-secret information. The Restatement recognizes that "[b]y means of a reasonable covenant not to compete, an employer may achieve protection against the competitive use by a former employee of information not technically protectable as a trade secret."[45]

A basic noncompetition agreement might look like this:

> I agree that for two years after termination of my employment with the Corporation I will not accept employment with any other employer in any subject area of the Corporation's business where I have had substantial involvement during my employment with the Corporation if that employer competes with the Corporation in that subject area and is located in the United States.

Noncompetition agreements are increasingly common—and controversial. Society has a strong interest in encouraging employee mobility and the innovation

---

42. *See* § 7.02[C][2].

43. 1 Roger M. Milgrim & Eric B. Bensen, Milgrim on Trade Secrets § 4.02[1][d][i] (2019).

44. 3 F.3d 730, 739 (4th Cir. 1993).

45. Restatement (Third) of Unfair Competition § 42 cmt. g.

that it facilitates.[46] Moreover, given the disparity of bargaining power in the employer-employee relationship, there is clear risk that such an agreement will be overbroad, insulating the employer from fair competition. The Restatement of Employment Law explains that such agreements "inhibit the freedom of employees to leave their employers and move to other employment where the employees may be more productive; and they frustrate the public interest in promoting competition."[47] As a result, the widespread use of noncompetition agreements to protect non-secret information imperils the policy balance that underlies trade secret law.[48]

[2] Enforcement

Noncompetition agreements are disfavored in most states. As a result, they are strictly construed. Beyond this point, state laws governing their enforceability vary widely. The most common approach is to uphold such an agreement if it is tailored to protect a legitimate interest of the employer—most commonly the protection of trade secrets—and is reasonable in duration, geography, and scope of covered activities.[49] However, noncompetition agreements are invalid in some states.[50]

The duration element is straightforward. In most situations, courts reason that a duration of between one and two years is reasonable, although in certain fast-paced industries this may be too long.[51]

The second element—geographic coverage—is in transition. Traditionally, this was defined by the region in which the former employee physically worked. In the internet era, however, such limits do not adequately protect employers who compete on a global scale. In *Hekimian Laboratories, Inc. v. Domain Systems, Inc.*, for instance, the court upheld a noncompetition agreement with no geographical restrictions in the industry of remote access testing for telecommunications; it explained that the handful of companies in this industry competed on a worldwide basis: "[T]he business of remote access testing is such that the whole world is its stage."[52]

The final element requires a reasonable relationship between the former employee's job duties and the scope of prohibited employment. For example, the agreement in

---

46. For example, the DTSA provides that a court may not issue an injunction (a) to "prevent a person from entering into an employment relationship" or (b) that conflicts "with an applicable State law prohibiting restraints on the practice of a lawful profession, trade, or business." 18 U.S.C. § 1836(b)(3)(A)(i). *See also* § 7.02[C][2].

47. Restatement of Employment Law § 8.06 cmt. a.

48. *See* § 1.03.

49. Restatement of Employment Law §§ 8.06, 8.07; Restatement (Third) of Unfair Competition. § 41 cmt. d.

50. For example, noncompetition agreements are invalid in California unless a special exception applies. Cal. Bus. & Prof. Code § 16600; Edwards v. Arthur Anderson LLP, 81 Cal. Rptr. 3d 282, 288–89 (Cal. 2008). Some decisions suggest that the statute does not bar such agreements if they are used to prevent disclosure of trade secrets, but this view is probably incorrect. *See* The Retirement Group v. Galante, 98 Cal. Rptr. 3d 585 (App. 2009).

51. *See, e.g.*, EarthWeb, Inc. v. Schlack, 71 F. Supp. 2d 299, 313 (S.D.N.Y 1999) (one-year period too long where former employee worked for on-line company).

52. 664 F. Supp. 493, 498 (S.D. Fla. 1987).

Nortec Communications, Inc. v. Lee-Llacer provided that the former employee could not "become employed by or provide services for any existing customer or client of the Company for whom Employee has performed services while employed by the Company ... if such employment or services relates to the products or services offered by the Company."[53] Noting that under Virginia law the agreement may be no broader than necessary to protect the employer, the court found it to be invalid: "There is no regard for whether his employment with a current Nortec client in any way relates to his prior employment with Nortec and involves the use of any skills or knowledge acquired by Mr. Lee-Llacer in his former position."[54]

[E] Nonsolicitation Agreements

[1] Basics

Another technique for reducing the risk of misappropriation is to have the employee enter into a nonsolicitation agreement or agree to a nonsolicitation clause as part of a comprehensive employment agreement. Such an agreement will prevent a former employee from seeking business from the employer's customers, asking other employees to join her, or both. As a practical matter, then, a nonsolicitation agreement is a specialized type of noncompetition agreement.

The business solicitation bar can be a targeted method to protect the employer's customer information, which may be protected as a trade secret. And the employee solicitation bar has the same impact as a covenant not to compete, but on a larger scale—it precludes other employees from taking new jobs where they might disclose trade secrets.

Here is a simple nonsolicitation agreement:

> I agree that for one year after termination of my employment with the Corporation, I will not render services, directly or indirectly, to any person or entity in connection with the sale, marketing, or promotion of any product to any customer of the Corporation who I had any contact with at any time during the two years prior to termination of my employment with the Corporation.

[2] Enforcement

Some authorities, such as the Restatement of Employment Law, assert that a nonsolicitation agreement is enforceable only if it meets the same test as a noncompetition agreement—it must be reasonable in duration, geography, and scope of activity.[55] However, in most states it is easier to enforce a nonsolicitation agreement because it has less effect on competition. Rather than barring all competition by a former em-

53. 548 F. Supp. 2d 226, 228 (E.D. Va. 2008).

54. *Id.* at 231.

55. Restatement of Employment Law § 8.06 cmt. b. *See also, e.g.*, Manitowoc Co., Inc. v. Lanning, 885 N.W.2d 798 (Wis. App. 2016).

ployee, it merely restricts certain activities. For example, in *McFarland v. Schneider* the court upheld the nonsolicitation covenant in a contract, but invalidated the non-competition covenant.[56] Stressing that the noncompetition covenant "would have a significant impact" on the former employee's ability to earn a living, it explained:

> Although a three-year ban on all competition is not unrelated to protection of [the former employer's] legitimate interests, a ban of that breadth is not essential.... Given a strong public policy favoring competition and the adverse consequences to [the former employee] flowing from enforcement of the total ban, I am of the opinion that it should not be enforced....[57]

---

56. 1998 WL 136133 (Mass. Super. Ct. Feb. 17, 1988).

57. *Id.* at *42.

Chapter 9

Trade Secrets and Criminal Law

§ 9.01 Introduction

Trade secret theft can be prosecuted as a criminal offense under a number of federal and state statutes. Since a trade secret is a form of property, traditional property crimes such as burglary, embezzlement, and larceny could apply, depending on the particular facts. Moreover, most states have adopted specialized laws that criminalize trade secret theft.

The Uniform Trade Secrets Act covers only civil liability, not criminal law. The act provides that it does not affect "criminal remedies, whether or not based on misappropriation of a trade secret."[1] Accordingly, any state may prosecute trade secret theft under its domestic law.

The most important development in this area was the adoption of the Economic Espionage Act, which imposes federal criminal liability for trade secret theft. Federal prosecutors have brought a number of high-profile cases under the EEA, many dealing with foreign espionage. Taken together, the Defend Trade Secrets Act and EEA provide national standards for both civil and criminal liability.

1. UTSA § 7(b)(3).

§ 9.02 Economic Espionage Act

[A] Overview

The federal government took a major step toward combating trade secret theft with the enactment of the EEA in 1996.[2] Before its passage, trade secrets were protected exclusively by state laws, which proved to be ineffective in addressing the growing threat of industrial espionage by foreign countries and domestic actors, particularly in cyberspace. As the EEA's legislative history reflects, federal efforts to prosecute such thefts were hampered because there was "no federal statute directly addressing economic espionage or which otherwise protects proprietary information in a thorough, systematic manner."[3]

The EEA criminalizes two types of trade secret misappropriation: "economic espionage" and "theft of trade secrets." It imposes criminal penalties for the wrongful acquisition, use, disclosure, receipt, destruction, or possession of a trade secret:

- for the benefit of "any foreign government, foreign instrumentality, or foreign agent;"[4] or
- "related to a product or service used in or intended for use in interstate commerce, to the economic benefit of anyone other than the owner."[5]

The name of the act is misleading. The reference to "espionage" implies that it covers only the intentional theft of trade secrets by agents acting for foreign countries. As the House Report on the act notes: "Espionage is typically an organized effort by one country's government to obtain the vital national security secrets of another country."[6] In fact, the act criminalizes many other forms of trade secret theft.

The EEA applies to conduct occurring outside of the United States under some circumstances: where the defendant is a U.S. citizen or entity or where "an act in furtherance of the offense was committed in the United States."[7]

The act states that it does not "preempt or displace any other remedies, whether civil or criminal" provided under federal or state law.[8] Accordingly, while it authorizes the U.S. Attorney General to bring a civil action to obtain an injunction against economic espionage or trade secret theft,[9] it does not bar private persons or others from suing under federal or state law for damages or injunctive relief.

The 2016 DTSA was structured as an amendment to the EEA. Accordingly, case law developed under the DTSA is helpful in interpreting the EEA. This is important

---

2. 18 U.S.C. §§ 1831–1839.
3. H.R. Rep. No. 104-788, at 6 (1996). *See* § 9.03.
4. 18 U.S.C. § 1831(a).
5. *Id.* § 1832(a).
6. H.R. Rep. No. 104-788, at 5 (1996).
7. 18 U.S.C. § 1837. *See* § 10.05.
8. 18 U.S.C. § 1838.
9. *Id.* § 1836(a).

because to date comparatively few appellate decisions have interpreted the EEA, while it appears likely that the DTSA will generate a large body of case law.

In practice, criminal prosecutions under the EEA are rare. Over the last two decades, federal prosecutors have brought less than ten cases per year on average. Most of these cases involved (1) a conspiracy to steal trade secrets, (2) foreign nationals or entities, and/or (3) theft of national security secrets.

[B] Prohibited Conduct

[1] Illegal Actions

The two EEA liability sections are 18 U.S.C. § 1831, dealing with economic espionage, and § 1832, covering various offenses that relate to the theft of trade secrets more generally. Both sections encompass the same basic conduct. A person commits an illegal action if he:

> (1) steals, or without authorization appropriates, takes, carries away, or conceals, or by fraud, artifice, or deception obtains a trade secret;
>
> (2) without authorization copies, duplicates, sketches, draws, photographs, downloads, uploads, alters, destroys, photocopies, replicates, transmits, delivers, sends, mails, communicates, or conveys a trade secret;
>
> (3) receives, buys, or possesses a trade secret, knowing the same to have been stolen or appropriated, obtained, or converted without authorization;
>
> (4) attempts to commit any offense described in any of paragraphs (1) through (3); or
>
> (5) conspires with one or more other persons to commit any offense described in any of paragraphs (1) through (3), and one or more of such persons do any act to effect the object of the conspiracy....[10]

This list of criminal conduct is broader than the forms of misappropriation that give rise to civil liability under the UTSA or DTSA.[11] Although the conduct in subpart (1) seems similar to misappropriation, the other subparts encompass a much wider range of activity. For example, copying, altering, destroying, and even possessing a trade secret are all offenses.

---

10. 18 U.S.C. §§ 1831(a), 1832(a). The text of 18 U.S.C. § 1832 refers to "information" rather than "trade secret" in its description of each covered act; otherwise, both sections use identical language to describe the illegal conduct. Sections 1831(b) and 1832(b) similarly impose liability on any organization that commits such an offense.

11. *See* Chapter 4.

[2] Economic Espionage

18 U.S.C. § 1831 imposes liability when a person takes one of the illegal actions listed above "intending or knowing that the offense will benefit any foreign government, foreign instrumentality, or foreign agent...."

In order to establish a violation of this section, the government must prove beyond a reasonable doubt: (1) the information at issue was a trade secret; (2) the defendant "knew" it was a trade secret; (3) the defendant committed one of the listed actions; and (4) the defendant intended or knew that the offense would benefit a foreign government or actor.

The first liability element—that the information was a trade secret—is clear. The EEA and DTSA use the same definition of the key term "trade secret."[12] The discussion of the term in Chapter 2 applies equally to EEA cases.

The second element—the *mens rea* for trade secret "knowledge"—is controversial. Some defendants have argued that it requires the government to prove that they knew that the information met the *legal definition* of a trade secret. Courts generally reject this claim, holding instead more generalized knowledge is sufficient. For instance, in *United States v. Hanjuan Jin* the court reasoned that this element was met if the government proved "the defendant was aware that the information had the general attributes of a trade secret—that it was valuable to its owner because it was not generally known and that the owner had taken measures to protect it."[13]

The third element is straightforward. A well-established body of federal criminal law may be used to interpret its provisions if ambiguity arises.

The type of "benefit" required for the final element could be economic, reputational, strategic, or tactical in nature.[14] The court in *United States v. Chung* found that this element was satisfied where the defendant misappropriated over 300,000 pages of "sensitive and proprietary documents" belonging to Boeing, including information relating to the Space Shuttle, the Chinook helicopter, and other aerospace and military projects, under the direction and control of Chinese officials.[15] It concluded that "Mr. Chung did so because he was a spy."[16]

Consider this example of how the section functions. Suppose that A works at company B, which is developing a new laser system. B's plant has security guards at all office entrances; they check the identity badges of all employees who enter and search the employees when they leave. A, who has signed a nondisclosure agreement, has access to documents concerning the system that are stamped "Confidential—Do Not Remove From Premises." A owns shares in C, a company whose majority shareholder is the government of France. A conceals confidential drawings of the system under

---

12. 18 U.S.C. § 1839(3).

13. 833 F. Supp. 2d 977, 1014 (N.D. Ill. 2012). *See also* United States v. Chung, 633 F. Supp. 2d 1134, 1145–46 (C.D. Cal. 2009) (using similar standard).

14. H.R. Rep. No. 104-788, at 11 (1996).

15. *Chung*, 633 F. Supp. 2d at 1137.

16. *Id.* at 1143.

his clothes and smuggles them out of the office, with the hope that C will benefit from the information.

On these facts, A is liable for economic espionage under § 1831. First, the information is a trade secret. Next, even if A did not know the technical definition of a trade secret, he was aware that the drawings had its "general attributes": B's reasonable security measures put A on notice that the information was valuable and not generally known. Third, A knowingly "stole" the drawings. Finally, A did so in order to benefit C, which is a "foreign instrumentality" because it is "substantially owned" by a foreign government.[17]

[3] Other Thefts of Trade Secrets

More broadly, 18 U.S.C. § 1832 imposes liability for offenses related to the theft of trade secrets that is *not* intended to benefit a foreign government or actor. It provides:

> Whoever, with intent to convert a trade secret, that is related to a product or service used in or intended for use in interstate or foreign commerce, to the economic benefit of anyone other than the owner thereof, and intending or knowing that the offense will, injure any owner of that trade secret, knowingly— [*this language is followed by the list of illegal actions quoted above in [B][1]*]

In order to establish a violation of this section, the government must prove beyond a reasonable doubt three of the *same* elements that apply to § 1831 plus three *additional* elements. The three shared elements are: (1) the information at issue was a trade secret; (2) the defendant "knew" it was a trade secret; and (3) the defendant took one of the illegal actions. These elements are discussed earlier in this chapter.

The additional elements are: (4) the defendant intended to convert the trade secret to the economic benefit of someone other than the owner; (5) the defendant intended or knew that the offense would injure the owner; and (6) the trade secret is related to a product or service used or intended for use in interstate or foreign commerce.

The fourth element—intent to convert for the economic benefit of another—is oddly phrased. The term "convert" usually connotes a wrongful taking of tangible personal property. For example, under this approach stealing a document that embodied a trade secret would be covered, but not memorizing the information in the document. However, courts interpret this term broadly, without suggesting that the section applies only to tangible property.[18] The EEA's legislative history similarly supports this position. The House Report explains that the act would cover both "taking physical possession of the medium" on which the information is stored and situations where the information is "copied, duplicated, photographed, drawn, or otherwise reproduced in some form from the original...."[19]

---

17. 18 U.S.C. § 1839(1).

18. *See, e.g.*, United States v. Howley, 707 F.3d 575 (6th Cir. 2013) (finding a violation of the section where the defendants photographed a secret machine).

19. H.R. Rep. No. 104-788, at 7–8 (1996).

It is not necessary to prove that another party actually received an economic benefit. Rather, the issue is the defendant's intent to confer a benefit on such a party. Thus, in *United States v. Hanjuan Jin*, this element was met because the defendant "took the trade secrets to help her prepare for her future employment."[20]

The defendant's intent or knowledge that the conduct would injure the trade secret owner—the fifth element—is usually proven by circumstantial evidence. For instance, in *United States v. Howley*, the Sixth Circuit reasoned that the defendants had this knowledge where they photographed secret Goodyear machines in order to "help a Goodyear competitor."[21] Conduct designed to help one competitor necessarily reflects an intent to harm another competitor. As the legislative history to the EEA reflects, this element "does not require the government to prove malice or evil intent, but merely that the actor knew or was aware to a practical certainty that his conduct would cause some disadvantage to the rightful owner."[22]

The text of the final element—linkage to interstate or foreign commerce—is identical to the DTSA jurisdictional requirement in 18 U.S.C. § 1836(b)(1) already discussed in Chapter 4.[23]

Consider again A's theft of laser technology from company B, this time as an example of liability for trade secret theft under § 1832. The first three elements of this offense are discussed above. A's intent to convert the secret for the economic benefit of another is satisfied by his hope that C, B's competitor, will benefit from the information. Because C will benefit, A knows that B will be harmed by the theft. Finally, the laser system is a "product" that is presumably intended for future use in interstate and foreign commerce. Accordingly, A is liable under this section.

[C] Defenses

[1] Generally

Three of the defenses to civil liability under the DTSA are also defenses to criminal liability under the EEA: reverse engineering, independent development, and whistleblower immunity. These defenses are discussed in Chapter 6.

The statute of limitations for bringing a criminal prosecution under the EEA is five years from the time the offense was committed.[24] The DTSA limitations period is only three years, although it does not begin running until the misappropriation is discovered or reasonably should have been discovered.[25] Accordingly, under some circumstances criminal charges may still be filed even though a civil action is barred.

20. 833 F. Supp. 2d 977, 1016 (N.D. Ill. 2012).
21. *Howley*, 707 F.3d at 580.
22. H.R. Rep. No. 104-788, at 11–12 (1996).
23. *See* § 4.04.
24. 18 U.S.C. § 3282(a).
25. *Id.* § 1836(d).

[2] Due Process?

Some defendants have asserted that certain EEA provisions are void for vagueness and that prosecution therefore violates the Due Process Clause.[26] It is well settled that a criminal statute is unconstitutionally vague if it "defines an offense in such a way that ordinary people cannot understand what is prohibited or if it encourages arbitrary or discriminatory enforcement."[27] To date, courts have rejected all of these challenges, but a future challenge might succeed based on the facts of the particular case.[28]

For example, the defendant in *United States v. Krumrei* was convicted under § 1832(a) for transmitting one of his employer's trade secrets to a competitor.[29] On appeal, he claimed that the manner in which the EEA defined the crime was unconstitutionally vague. Specifically, he argued that a key element in the trade secret definition—that the owner take "reasonable measures" to protect secrecy—was so vague that ordinary people could not understand it.[30] This claim was far from frivolous because the reasonableness of the owner's measures to maintain secrecy vary from case to case, depending on a balancing of costs and benefits.[31]

However, the Sixth Circuit stressed that the defendant had the burden of establishing that the statute was "vague as applied to his particular case, not merely that the statute could be construed as vague in some hypothetical situation."[32] Because the defendant admitted that he "knew that the information was proprietary and knew that his actions were illegal," the statute was constitutional *as applied to him.*[33] In effect, the court reasoned that the statute did not require proof that the defendant knew the information met the technical definition of a trade secret, but merely proof that he knew it was confidential information belonging to someone else.

[D] Penalties

The penalties for criminal violations of the EEA fall into four categories: imprisonment; fines; forfeiture; and restitution.

A person convicted of economic espionage under § 1831 can be imprisoned for up to fifteen years, fined up to $5,000,000, or both.[34] In contrast, a convicted organization can be fined up to $10,000,000 or three times the value of the trade secret to the organization.[35]

---

26. This defense overlaps somewhat with the *mens rea* element. *See* § 9.02[B][2].
27. United States v. Avant, 907 F.2d 623, 625 (6th Cir. 1990).
28. *Cf.* United States v. Genovese, 409 F. Supp. 2d 253, 258 (S.D.N.Y. 2005) (rejecting due process argument based on "the facts of this case").
29. 258 F.3d 535 (6th Cir. 2001).
30. *Id.* at 538.
31. *See* § 2.05[B].
32. *Krumrei*, 258 F.3d at 537.
33. *Id.* at 539.
34. 18 U.S.C. § 1831(a).
35. *Id.* § 1831(b).

Under § 1832, a person convicted of trade secret theft can be fined up to $250,000,[36] imprisoned for up to ten years, or both.[37] Again, a convicted organization will be fined a larger amount—the greater of $5,000,000 or three times the value of the trade secret to the organization.[38]

In lieu of these fines, a defendant convicted under either section may be fined up to twice the amount it gained by the crime or twice the amount of the trade secret owner's loss.[39]

The EEA also provides for criminal forfeiture—an approach borrowed from the federal approach to illegal drug trafficking.[40] The scope of this provision is potentially troubling. Imagine that D's employee E takes a new job with company F. While working in F's massive plant, E discloses one of D's trade secrets to F's manager. On these facts, the plant is arguably "property" that was "used" to commit a violation of § 1832(a): receipt of a trade secret knowing that it was stolen. An argument might be made that the entire plant is now subject to forfeiture. However, in *Austin v. United States* the Supreme Court held that the permissible scope of a civil *in rem* forfeiture is limited by the Excessive Fines Clause of the Eighth Amendment if the forfeiture is, at least in part, a punishment for an offense.[41] As a result, though forfeiture of the entire plant is highly unlikely, the precise scope of the forfeiture is difficult to assess.

Finally, restitution is mandatory when a defendant is convicted of certain federal crimes, including economic espionage or trade secret theft.[42] 18 U.S.C. § 3663A(a)(1) provides that the court "shall order … that the defendant make restitution to the victim of the offense…." For an offense resulting in damage to, loss, or destruction of property, the order must require the defendant to either return the property or pay compensation if such return is "impossible, impracticable, or inadequate."[43] The amount of compensation is the value of the property on the date of loss or destruction, or on the date of sentencing, whichever is greater.[44]

In the most common case—where the defendant wrongfully uses a stolen trade secret—restitution may provide limited relief to the owner.[45] Suppose that G steals H's trade secret and uses it to produce a competing product, but does not publicly disclose the secret. Arguably H's property has not suffered damage, loss, or destruction

36. The EEA does not specify the maximum amount of this fine. Presumably the amount would be established by the general section on fines in Title 18, 18 U.S.C. § 3571(b). This section provides that the maximum fine for a felony is $250,000. If not, the Eighth Amendment's prohibition of "excessive fines" would potentially set an upper limit on the amount. *See* U.S. Const. amend. VIII.

37. 18 U.S.C. § 1832(a).

38. *Id.* § 1832(b).

39. *Id.* § 3571(d).

40. 18 U.S.C. § 1834.

41. 509 U.S. 602 (1993). The Eighth Amendment provides: "Excessive bail shall not be required, nor excessive fines imposed, nor cruel and unusual punishments inflicted." U.S. Const. amend. VIII.

42. *See* 18 U.S.C. §§ 1834, 3663A(c)(1)(A)(ii).

43. *Id.* § 3663A(b)(1)(B).

44. *Id.*

45. Of course, this assumes that the defendant is solvent.

because the information is still a protected trade secret.[46] However, the more likely outcome is that H suffered a "loss" of property in the form of lost profits; customers would presumably have purchased H's product but for G's theft. Conversely, if G and H are in different industries—or G used only part of the trade secret (such as one name on a 100-person customer list)—H may have difficulty proving that any compensable loss occurred. Of course, if G publicly disclosed the secret, it has been destroyed, which would entitle H to receive its fair market value.

§ 9.03 Other Federal Laws

Criminal prosecution for trade secret theft is also possible under a variety of other federal statutes, depending on the circumstances. However, none of them is as targeted as the EEA, and they are not commonly used.

The National Stolen Property Act imposes criminal sanctions on anyone who "transports, transmits, or transfers in interstate or foreign commerce any goods, wares, merchandise, securities or money, of the value of $5,000 or more, knowing the same to have been stolen, converted or taken by fraud...."[47] Trade secret theft was sometimes prosecuted under this act before the EEA was adopted. But there is a split of authority on whether the act extends to intangible property. The traditional view is that it only applies to tangible objects. Under this approach, the act applies where a physical object that embodies a trade secret (such as a paper drawing of a secret machine part) is transported in interstate commerce, but not where the same information is transmitted electronically.[48] A number of courts, however, reason that the act applies to electronic transfers. As the Southern District of New York noted in *United States v. Farraj*, the text of the act "makes no distinction between tangible and intangible property, or between electronic and other manner of transfer across state lines."[49]

Another potentially applicable statute is the Computer Fraud and Abuse Act.[50] Under this act, anyone who "intentionally" accesses a "protected computer" without authorization[51] and obtains information from it has committed a federal crime.[52] For purposes of the act, a "protected computer" includes any computer used in interstate

46. However, H would be entitled to an award of restitution to cover the expenses it incurred in investigating the loss. 18 U.S.C. § 3663A(b)(4).

47. 18 U.S.C. § 2314.

48. *See, e.g.*, United States v. Yijia Zhang, 995 F. Supp. 2d 340, 349 (E.D. Pa. 2014) (act did not apply to transfer of electronic files over the internet).

49. 142 F. Supp. 2d 484, 488 (S.D.N.Y 2001).

50. 18 U.S.C. § 1030.

51. Courts disagree about the meaning of "without authorization" where an employee uses the employer's computer to access information. *Compare* Int'l Airport Ctr., v. Citrin, 440 F.3d 418 (7th Cir. 2006) (use of computer to access authorized information to serve interests adverse to employer violates duty of loyalty and hence is illegal) *with* United States v. Nosal, 676 F.3d 854 (9th Cir. 2012) (only use of computer to access unauthorized information is illegal).

52. 18 U.S.C. § 1030(a)(2)(C).

or foreign commerce or communication.[53] As a practical matter, almost all computers are used for interstate communication on occasion. As a result, if J wrongfully accesses K's computer to obtain a trade secret, J has probably violated the act.

The federal statutes governing mail fraud and wire fraud also apply to trade secret theft under some circumstances. Mail fraud includes using the U.S. Postal Service or a private mail company in furtherance of a "scheme" for "obtaining ... property by means of false or fraudulent pretenses, representations or promises."[54] Wire fraud covers essentially the same conduct, but requires some sort of electronic communication, such as using the internet. The statute penalizes anyone with a "scheme" for "obtaining ... property by means of false or fraudulent pretenses, representations, or promises" who "transmits or causes to be transmitted by means of wire, radio, or television communication in interstate or foreign commerce, any writings, signs, signals, pictures, or sounds" in order to implement the scheme.[55] Unlike the National Stolen Property Act, these statutes clearly apply to intangible property such as trade secrets.

The federal government could also bring criminal proceedings under statutes such as the Racketeer Influenced and Corrupt Organizations Act (pattern of trade secret theft)[56] or the Trade Secrets Act (disclosure of private trade secret by federal employee).[57]

§ 9.04 State Laws

Most states have enacted specialized laws that criminalize trade secret theft. However, criminal prosecutions for trade secret theft under state law are relatively rare, presumably because prosecutors have higher priorities and limited resources.

State statutes that govern civil liability are usually quite similar because they are based on the UTSA. In contrast, statutes that impose criminal liability vary widely from state to state. Even within a particular state, the law may define a trade secret more narrowly for purposes of criminal prosecution than for civil liability. Some statutes only encompass the theft of technical secrets, rather than all types of trade secrets. Others cover only the theft of physical objects that embody trade secrets, not trade secrets per se. Still others provide broad protection.

For example, the California statute is roughly parallel to the EEA. It provides that a person commits a theft if he "steals, carries away, or uses" a trade secret without authorization, "appropriates any article representing a trade secret entrusted to him," or wrongfully makes a "copy of any article representing a trade secret."[58] Because the

53. *Id.* § 1030(e)(2)(B).

54. 18 U.S.C. § 1341.

55. *Id.* § 1343.

56. *Id.* § 1961–1968.

57. *Id.* § 1905.

58. Cal. Penal Code § 499c(b).

statute largely mirrors the EEA definition of the term "trade secret," it covers trade secrets that are either intangible or embodied in an article.[59] Similarly, its trade secret definition encompasses virtually any type of information.

In contrast, New Jersey takes a narrower approach. A person is guilty of theft if he "unlawfully takes, or exercises unlawful control over, movable property of another with purpose to deprive him thereof."[60] As used in this provision, "property" includes a "trade secret."[61] Yet the term "trade secret" is defined to cover only secret "scientific or technical information."[62] Accordingly, the statute does not cover other types of secret information such as customer lists, financial data, or marketing strategies.

§ 9.05 Interface between Criminal Prosecution and Civil Litigation

Suppose L steals a trade secret owned by M. At this point, M might file a civil action for misappropriation, encourage the government to pursue criminal charges, or both. If the government brings a criminal prosecution, M may be able to obtain compensation for the theft through restitution. Further, an initial criminal prosecution may make it easier for M to prevail in a later civil action.

Criminal prosecution has potential advantages and drawbacks for the victim of trade secret theft. A victim might choose to delay a civil suit until a criminal prosecution is completed, so that it can benefit from the government's efforts to gather evidence and otherwise prove its case. This may be particularly important for victims such as small businesses with limited financial resources. Criminal prosecutors have certain advantages over the plaintiff's attorney in a civil action such as greater resources for obtaining evidence, including search warrants, electronic surveillance, and plea bargains in exchange for testimony. Where the government proves its case beyond a reasonable doubt in a criminal prosecution, the plaintiff in a later civil action will easily establish liability under the less rigorous preponderance of the evidence test.

On the other hand, it is usually difficult for the victim to persuade overburdened prosecutors to pursue criminal charges. Criminal prosecutions for trade secret theft are rare. And where charges are filed, the victim has no control over the prosecution of the action, and thus no ability to ensure that its trade secret is not disclosed to the public in the course of the proceeding—particularly given the defendant's Sixth Amendment right to a public trial.[63] Finally, the statute of limitations may compel

59. *Id.* § 499c(a)(9).

60. N.J. Stat. Ann. § 2C:20-3(a).

61. *Id.* § 2C:20-1(g).

62. *Id.* § 2C:20-1(i).

63. U.S. Const. amend. VI ("In all criminal prosecutions, the accused shall enjoy the right to a speedy and public trial...."). However, 18 U.S.C. § 1835(a) requires the court to take such action as is necessary to "preserve the confidentiality of trade secrets," subject to other laws. Moreover, subsection (b) precludes the court from authorizing the disclosure of "any information the owner asserts to be

the victim to file its action long before the criminal prosecution is completed, so it may not benefit from the government efforts.

Where the victim of trade secret theft wants to pursue both civil and criminal actions, the best strategy is usually to: (1) file a civil action; (2) obtain a preliminary injunction against further disclosure or use of the secret; (3) begin discovery; and (4) then convince the government to bring criminal charges. The civil case will normally be stayed until the criminal prosecution is completed.

a trade secret" unless it first allows the owner to file a "submission under seal that describes the interest of the owner in keeping the information confidential."

Chapter 10

Trade Secrets and International Law

§ 10.01 Overview

Suppose A, a French citizen, misappropriates trade secrets belonging to B, a United States corporation. How can B obtain relief? This chapter explores how a trade secret owner like B can enforce its rights in the international context. B's best approach will be to sue A in a French court under French law governing trade secrets. However, under narrow circumstances, B might be able to obtain relief by taking action within the United States.

Historically, trade secrets were not protected by international law, unlike other forms of intellectual property such as copyrights and patents. The closest analogue to trade secret protection was article 10bis of the Paris Convention for the Protection of Industrial Property (Paris Convention).[1] It required member nations to offer pro-

1. Paris Convention for the Protection of Industrial Property, Mar. 20, 1883, 21 U.S.T. 1583, 828 U.N.T.S. 305.

tection against "unfair competition," which was defined as "[a]ny act of competition contrary to honest practices in industrial or commercial matters."[2] However, scholars disagreed about the meaning of this vague provision. Some asserted that it only applied to misrepresentations made to consumers, while others maintained that it encompassed other conduct such as misappropriation of secret information. In practice, the provision did not effectively protect trade secrets.

The 1994 Agreement on Trade-Related Aspects of Intellectual Property Rights (TRIPS) signaled the birth of international trade secret law.[3] Its article 39 requires all member nations to adopt national legislation to protect "undisclosed information" from being disclosed, acquired, or used in "a manner contrary to honest commercial practices."

TRIPS members are obligated to translate its provisions into binding law at the national level. As part of this effort, the European Union issued its trade secret Directive (EU Directive) in 2016, which specifies how France and other EU nations must implement the article in their national laws.[4] As a result, B could sue A in a French court under French law adopted in compliance with the Directive.

Treaties adopted at the regional and bilateral levels also facilitate trade secret protection. For example, the 1993 North American Free Trade Agreement (NAFTA),[5] binding the United States, Canada, and Mexico, was the first regional treaty to explicitly protect trade secrets. Its successor, the United States-Mexico-Canada Agreement (USMCA),[6] expands this protection in a manner consistent with TRIPS article 39.

Alternatively, B might try to obtain relief against A by taking action within the United States. First, B may be able to sue A in a United States court. The Defend Trade Secrets Act has limited extraterritorial reach; it applies to trade secret misappropriation that occurred outside of the United States, for example, if an "act in furtherance of the offense was committed in the United States."[7] In addition, B might pursue its claim through the International Trade Commission (ITC), a federal agency that has the power to block the entry into the United States of foreign products that were created as a result of trade secret misappropriation.

This chapter discusses each of these avenues for international trade secret protection—TRIPS, the EU Directive, USMCA, extraterritorial enforcement in U.S. courts, and the ITC—in turn.

2. Paris Convention art. 10bis.

3. Agreement on Trade-Related Aspects of Intellectual Property Rights, Apr. 15, 1994, 1869 U.N.T.S. 299, 33 I.L.M. 1197.

4. Directive (EU) 2016/943 of the European Parliament and of the Council of 8 June 2016 on the protection of undisclosed know-now and business information (trade secrets) against their unlawful acquisition, use and disclosure, 2016 O.J. (L 157).

5. North American Free Trade Agreement, Can.-Mex.-U.S., Dec. 17, 1992, 32 I.L.M. 605.

6. Agreement between the United States of America, the United Mexican States, and Canada, Can.-Mex.-U.S., Dec. 2019.

7. 18 U.S.C. § 1837(2).

§ 10.02 Agreement on Trade-Related Aspects of Intellectual Property Rights

[A] Introduction

TRIPS is part of the World Trade Organization (WTO) treaty structure. Currently 164 nations are WTO members and thus are obligated to comply with TRIPS. They encompass all of the world's largest economies—including China, the European Union, India, Russia, and the United States.

TRIPS article 39 provides in relevant part:

> 1. In the course of ensuring effective protection against unfair competition as provided in Article 10bis of the Paris Convention, Members shall protect undisclosed information in accordance with paragraph 2 below....
>
> 2. Natural and legal persons shall have the possibility of preventing information lawfully within their control from being disclosed to, acquired by, or used by others without their consent in a manner contrary to honest commercial practices so long as such information:
>
> (a) is secret in the sense that it is not, as a body or in the precise configuration and assembly of its components, generally known among or readily accessible to persons within the circles that normally deal with the kind of information in question;
>
> (b) has commercial value because it is secret; and
>
> (c) has been subject to reasonable steps under the circumstances, by the person lawfully in control of the information, to keep it secret.

This article creates the first specific international protection for trade secrets. But the provision was controversial. Broadly speaking, industrialized nations favored its inclusion, while developing countries opposed it. Much of this tension stemmed from concerns of industrialized countries that the transfer of technology to developing nations without international protection would jeopardize their trade secrets. Developing nations, in turn, tended to view trade secret protection as a form of continued economic domination by former colonial powers, which threatened the development of their own domestic industries.

Further, there was a fundamental split about the best method to protect trade secrets in TRIPS. The United States and certain other nations argued for a right-based approach: trade secrets should be viewed as a form of property. In contrast, most nations preferred the unfair competition approach embodied in the Paris Convention, which focuses on prohibiting improper conduct rather than protecting rights.

As a result, article 39 is a compromise. The text of the article closely follows NAFTA article 1711, as the United States advocated and which is discussed in more detail below.[8]

---

8. *See* § 10.04[B], [C].

Yet the European view dominates its overall approach. First, the article protects "undisclosed information" rather than "trade secrets." The term "undisclosed information" was selected because it was not part of any nation's legal tradition and was accordingly neutral. Second, the article reflects the unfair competition approach. Its subparagraph (1) states that member nations shall protect undisclosed information "[i]n the course of ensuring effective protection against unfair competition as provided in Article 10bis of the Paris Convention." And the basic liability provision protects undisclosed information against conduct that is "contrary to honest commercial practices." Even though TRIPS recites that undisclosed information is a type of intellectual property,[9] most commentators agree that article 39 does not utilize a property rights approach.[10]

It is important to understand that article 39 is implemented through national law. It sets global minimum standards for protecting undisclosed information, which each member nation must implement by enacting its own laws. Thus, it seeks to ensure that all members have adopted roughly similar laws for safeguarding trade secrets that can be effectively enforced at the national level. Of course, any nation may choose to provide greater protection for such information.

The drafters of article 39 were not particularly concerned about its theoretical approach. Their goal was to create an international standard to protect valuable information, while simultaneously giving each nation the flexibility to implement the standard in accordance with its own legal tradition. In practice, however, many TRIPS nations have not yet fully complied with article 39—particularly developing nations.

[B] Protected Information

The TRIPS definition of "undisclosed information" in article 39(2) was taken almost verbatim from the definition of "trade secret" in NAFTA, as the United States advocated.[11] The NAFTA definition, in turn, was derived from the definition of "trade secret" in the Uniform Trade Secrets Act.[12] Accordingly, the textual meaning of "undisclosed information" in TRIPS is essentially the same as "trade secret" under the UTSA and, by extension, the DTSA.

The first element in the article 39 definition—information that is not "generally known among or readily accessible" to persons who "normally deal" with such information—parallels the UTSA provision that protected information is not "generally

9. TRIPS art. 1(2). *See also* TRIPS pmbl. 3 (stating "intellectual property rights are private rights").

10. The discussion in this section examines article 39(2), which protects undisclosed information in general. Article 39(3), in contrast, addresses a more specific concern. It ensures protection for "undisclosed test or other data" created with "considerable effort" that is submitted to a government as a condition of marketing "pharmaceutical or ... agricultural chemical products which utilize new chemical entities." Member nations are required to protect such data against unfair commercial use. They must also protect such data against its disclosure in general, unless this is necessary to protect the public.

11. NAFTA art. 1711(1).

12. UTSA § 1(4).

known to, and not ... readily ascertainable by" persons who can "obtain economic value from its disclosure or use."[13] Thus, like the UTSA definition, this article requires only relative secrecy, not absolute secrecy. Similarly, the article and the UTSA definition both hinge on whether the information is known within a particular industry, rather than by the public at large.

Is information "readily accessible" if it can be obtained by reverse engineering? TRIPS does not address this question, and scholars disagree on the outcome. Perhaps the best answer is that it depends on the extent of time, effort, and expense that would be required in the process.

"[C]ommercial value," the second element of the TRIPS definition, has the same core meaning as "independent economic value" under the UTSA.[14] Notably both require that the value stem from the fact that the information is secret. However, the UTSA extends to either "actual or potential" value.[15] Because article 39 only refers to "value," it presumably does not include mere potential value.

Finally, the third element—"reasonable steps under the circumstances ... to keep [the information] secret"—is almost identical to the UTSA formulation: "efforts that are reasonable under the circumstances to maintain its secrecy."[16] Standard industry practices and cost-benefit analysis will be relevant in determining whether reasonable steps were taken.

Although the article 39 definition does not expressly include any other components, the nature of TRIPS indicates that it implicitly contains a fourth element: the information must be related to international trade. As its Preamble states, TRIPS seeks to protect "trade-related intellectual property rights."[17] For instance, the secret and valuable cocktail recipe that C uses at her Chicago nightclub has no link to international trade, and arguably would not be protected under TRIPS.

[C] Liability

Liability arises when undisclosed information is "disclosed to, acquired by, or used by others" without the consent of the holder "in a manner contrary to honest commercial practices."[18] A footnote to article 39 explains that:

> For the purpose of this provision, "a manner contrary to honest commercial practices" shall mean at least practices such as breach of contract, breach of confidence and inducement to breach, and includes the acquisition of undisclosed information by third parties who knew, or were grossly negligent in failing to know, that such practices were involved in the acquisition.[19]

---

13. *Id.*
14. *Id.*
15. *Id.*
16. *Id.*
17. TRIPS pmbl. 1(b).
18. *Id.* art. 39(2).
19. *Id.* art. 39 n. 13.

These provisions were adopted almost verbatim from NAFTA, again reflecting the position that the United States advocated during the TRIPS negotiations.[20]

The UTSA and DTSA call the parallel concept "misappropriation," which occurs when a trade secret is disclosed, acquired, or used without the holder's consent after a third party uses "improper means" to obtain it.[21] In this context, the term "improper means" "includes theft, bribery, misrepresentation, breach or inducement of a breach of a duty to maintain secrecy, or espionage through electronic or other means."[22]

In effect, the TRIPS and UTSA/DTSA formulations are substantially similar. Both provide that a trade secret is infringed when it is obtained through some type of wrongful act. And both offer illustrations of wrongful acts rather than an exclusive list. One potential difference is that the UTSA/DTSA list includes specific tortious and criminal acts, while the TRIPS list does not. Yet presumably the use of theft, bribery, misrepresentation, espionage or similar acts would be contrary to "honest commercial practices" and thus be covered by TRIPS. Finally, both impose liability on third parties who disclose or use protected information if they knew or should have known that it was wrongfully acquired.

[D] Enforcement

Under TRIPS, rights in undisclosed information can be protected at two levels. First, TRIPS requires each member nation to create a legal framework so that private parties can enforce their rights in domestic courts.[23] Second, where a nation violates any of its obligations under TRIPS—such as the obligation to adopt domestic legislation protecting undisclosed information—any other member nation may file a complaint with the WTO Dispute Resolution Body, which is an international tribunal to resolve trade disputes.[24] The discussion below addresses private enforcement.

For example, if B, a United States corporation, believes that A, a French citizen, has improperly acquired B's protected information in France, B's basic remedy under TRIPS is to sue A in a French court under French law.

Article 39 mandates that each nation recognize a private cause of action to protect undisclosed information. It provides that "[m]embers shall protect undisclosed information in accordance with paragraph 2 below."[25] Paragraph 2, in turn, requires that private parties "shall have the possibility of preventing information lawfully within their control from being disclosed to, acquired by, or used by others without their consent" under certain conditions.[26] But TRIPS does not specify the particular cause of action that must be used. Accordingly, nations can implement this require-

20. NAFTA arts. 1711, 1721(2).
21. UTSA § 1(2); 18 U.S.C. § 1839(5). *See* §§ 4.02, 4.03.
22. UTSA § 1(1); 18 U.S.C. § 1839(6)(A). *See* § 4.02[D].
23. TRIPS arts. 41–49.
24. *Id.* art. 64.
25. *Id.* art. 39(1).
26. *Id.* art. 39(2).

ment by protecting undisclosed information as property, by imposing tort liability, by using unfair competition law, or through other methods.

More broadly, all member nations must "ensure that enforcement procedures ... are available under their national laws so as to permit effective action against any act of infringement of intellectual property rights covered by this Agreement,"[27] including undisclosed information. Thus, nations must "make available to right holders civil judicial procedures concerning the enforcement" of the rights arising under TRIPS.[28] The judicial authorities in each nation must have the power to prevent infringement from occurring and to award adequate compensatory damages if it does occur.[29]

Thus, in the A-B example above, TRIPS requires that France (1) enact national laws that provide basic protections for undisclosed information and (2) adopt enforcement procedures so that a private party like B can sue for damages and injunctive relief if protected information is wrongfully acquired, disclosed, or used.

§ 10.03 European Union Trade Secret Directive

[A] Introduction

Trade secret protection within the European Union is governed by the lengthy EU Directive "on the protection of undisclosed know-how and business information (trade secrets) against their unlawful acquisition, use and disclosure."[30] The Directive is intended to implement the requirements of TRIPS article 39. All EU members are required to adopt domestic laws that comply with the minimum standards for trade secret protection as set forth in the Directive. Consistent with the principles underlying TRIPS, any EU member may elect to provide greater protection than the Directive mandates.

[B] Protected Information

The EU Directive uses the key term "trade secret" instead of "undisclosed information."[31] Despite this terminology, the Directive rejects the property approach, making it clear that a trade secret is not an intellectual property right.[32] Other than this semantic difference, its definition of "trade secret" is identical to the definition of "undisclosed information" in TRIPS article 39.[33]

Beyond this point, the Directive is far more detailed than article 39, and in some respects reflects United States law. For example, the Preamble indicates that infor-

---

27. *Id.* art. 41(1).
28. *Id.* art. 42.
29. *Id.* arts. 44, 45(1), 50(1)(a).
30. The Directive is 24 pages long; in contrast, the UTSA is 3 pages long.
31. *Id.*
32. Directive pmbl. (1).
33. *Id.* art. 2(1).

mation with "potential" value qualifies for protection, like the UTSA and DTSA.[34] Similarly, the Directive states that its provisions cannot be used to limit "employees' use of experience and skills honestly acquired in the normal course of their employment" when they move to new jobs.[35] This too is consistent with U.S. case law that an employee's general knowledge and skill cannot be a trade secret.[36]

[C] Liability

Unlike TRIPS, the EU Directive provides a list of lawful methods to obtain a trade secret, including independent discovery or creation, reverse engineering, and observation of an object that is available to the public.[37] It somewhat resembles the list of lawful methods in the UTSA.[38]

Article 4 of the Directive, which sets forth the standards for liability, adopts the unfair competition approach. But it is more comprehensive than the parallel text in TRIPS article 39. The acquisition of a trade secret is "unlawful" when it is obtained through (1) unauthorized access, appropriation, or copying of information under the lawful control of the trade secret holder or (2) "any other conduct which, under the circumstances, is considered contrary to honest commercial practices."[39] Like article 39, the Directive does not specifically include tortious or criminal acts in its examples of conduct that is "contrary to honest commercial practices"; but such acts are presumably covered.

The disclosure or use of a secret is unlawful when done by a person who acquired the secret unlawfully, breached a duty not to disclose the secret, or breached a duty to limit the use of the secret.[40] Finally, the acquisition, disclosure, or use of a secret is unlawful if the person knew or should have known that he obtained it from someone who acted unlawfully in disclosing or using it.[41]

In one regard, the Directive would expand liability beyond both TRIPS and the UTSA/DTSA, which only encompass the wrongful acquisition, disclosure, or use of a trade secret. Under the Directive, the production, marketing, export, and import of "infringing goods" are also deemed unlawful if the actor knew or should have known that a trade secret was used unlawfully in creating or marketing the goods.[42] An infringing good is one whose design, production, or marketing "significantly benefits" from the unlawful acquisition, disclosure, or use of a trade secret.[43]

Finally, the Directive goes well beyond both TRIPS and the UTSA/DTSA by expressly authorizing a person to acquire, disclose, or use a trade secret without the

34. *Id.* pmbl. 14.
35. *Id.* art. 1(3)(b).
36. *See* § 2.02[C].
37. Directive art. 3.
38. UTSA § 1 cmt.
39. Directive art. 4(2).
40. *Id.* art 4(3).
41. *Id.* art. 4(4).
42. *Id.* art. 4(5).
43. *Id.* art 2(4).

holder's consent in certain situations. For example, this is permitted when "exercising the right to freedom of expression and information" and for the purpose of protecting "a legitimate interest recognised by Union or national law."[44]

[D] Enforcement

The enforcement provisions of the EU Directive are similar to those in TRIPS. Article 6 broadly provides that EU members must provide "the measures, procedures and remedies necessary to ensure the availability of civil redress against the unlawful acquisition, use, and disclosure of trade secrets."[45] The judicial authorities in each member nation must have the power to prevent infringement of an intellectual property right from occurring, to stop on-going infringement, and to award adequate compensatory damages.[46]

§ 10.04 United States-Mexico-Canada Agreement

[A] Introduction

NAFTA created special trade secret protections relating to trade among Canada, Mexico, and the United States. In turn, these provisions served as the template for TRIPS article 39. In 2019, Canada, Mexico, and the United States entered into the USMCA to replace NAFTA. The USMCA secures somewhat more protection for trade secrets than NAFTA provides.

[B] Protected Information

NAFTA and USMCA both expressly protect "trade secrets." Both also define "trade secret" in virtually the same language. Thus, NAFTA requires each member nation to protect information in so far as:

> (a) the information is secret in the sense that it is not, as a body or in the precise configuration and assembly of its components, generally known among or readily accessible to persons that normally deal with the kind of information in question;
>
> (b) the information has actual or potential commercial value because it is secret;
>
> (c) the person lawfully in control of the information has taken reasonable steps under the circumstances to keep it secret.[47]

44. *Id.* art. 5.
45. *Id.* art. 6(1).
46. *Id.* arts. 10(1), 12(1), 14(1).
47. NAFTA art. 1711(1); USMCA art. 20.72.

This provision is the source of the TRIPS definition of "undisclosed information." A key difference is that the NAFTA/USMCA formulation covers information with either "actual or potential commercial value"—like the UTSA and DTSA[48]—while TRIPS only protects information having "commercial value."

[C] Liability

NAFTA article 1711(1), which was adopted almost verbatim into TRIPS, requires each nation to provide legal means for any person to "prevent trade secrets from being disclosed to, acquired by, or used by others without the consent of the person lawfully in control of the information in a manner contrary to honest commercial practices." The phrase "in a manner contrary to honest commercial practices" is defined exactly as in TRIPS, to include:

> at least practices such as breach of contract, breach of confidence and inducement to breach, and includes the acquisition of undisclosed information by other persons who knew, or were grossly negligent in failing to know, that such practices were involved in the acquisition.[49]

The USMCA essentially incorporates these NAFTA provisions, with slight wording variations, in article 20.72. But it relabels the prohibited conduct as "misappropriation," which better aligns with the UTSA and DTSA. Article 20.72 defines "misappropriation" as:

> the acquisition, use, or disclosure of a trade secret in a manner contrary to honest commercial practices, including the acquisition, use, or disclosure of a trade secret by a third party that knew, or had reason to know, that the trade secret was acquired in a manner contrary to honest commercial practices.

It then clarifies that "misappropriation" does not include situations where a person:

> (a) reverse engineered an item lawfully obtained;
>
> (b) independently discovered information claimed as a trade secret; or
>
> (c) acquired the subject information from another person in a legitimate manner without an obligation of confidentiality or knowledge that the information was a trade secret.

[D] Enforcement

NAFTA requires each nation to provide civil remedies in its domestic courts for trade secrets misappropriation—including provisional remedies, damages, and injunctive relief—in language that is sometimes vague. The USMCA builds on this foundation by describing the remedies in more detail.[50]

48. *See* § 2.03.

49. NAFTA art. 1721.

50. USMCA arts. 20.69, 20.70, 20.71, 20.74, 20.75.

The major enforcement change under the USMCA is in the area of criminal sanctions. NAFTA does not mandate criminal liability for trade secret infringement. However, USMCA article 20.71 requires each nation to provide criminal penalties for the "unauthorized and willful misappropriation" of a trade secret.

§ 10.05 Extraterritorial Enforcement of U.S. Law

The original EEA—which only imposes *criminal* penalties for trade secret misappropriation—clearly has an extraterritorial reach. 18 U.S.C. § 1837 provides:

> This chapter also applies to conduct occurring outside the United States if—
>
> (1) the offender is a natural person who is a citizen or permanent resident alien of the United States, or an organization organized under the laws of the United States or a State or political subdivision thereof; or
>
> (2) an act in furtherance of the offense was committed in the United States.[51]

Congress later adopted the DTSA, which amended the EEA by adding a private *civil* remedy for the misappropriation of trade secrets in § 1836(b). As a result, the extraterritorial reach of § 1837 should logically apply to *both* private civil actions and criminal prosecutions.

The relevant case law—while sparse—follows this interpretation. For example, in *T & S Brass and Bronze Works, Inc. v. Slanina* the plaintiffs brought a federal civil action for trade secret infringement based on acts that primarily occurred in England.[52] In granting plaintiffs' motion for a preliminary injunction, the court observed: "The DTSA applies to conduct occurring outside the United States where, as here, the defendants are citizens of the United States or 'an act in furtherance of the offense was committed in the United States.'"[53]

Under this approach, C, a U.S. corporation, could sue D, an Austrian national, in federal court for trade secret misappropriation that occurred in Austria if at least one relevant act—perhaps as minor as an email or a phone call—occurred in the United States. This would permit C to enjoy the protection of familiar U.S. substantive law and procedure, rather than litigating in a foreign forum.

Yet § 1837 is a double-edged sword. If a U.S. company misappropriates a trade secret abroad, the foreign owner might choose to sue in this country rather than its own nation. One reason would be the scope of pretrial discovery, which is far broader in the United States than in most countries. Similarly, larger damage awards may be available under U.S. law.

---

51. 18 U.S.C. § 1837.
52. 2016 WL 11201768 (D.S.C. Dec. 20, 2016).
53. *Id.* at *6.

§ 10.06 International Trade Commission

The ITC, a quasi-judicial federal agency, has the authority to bar the import of goods that were produced abroad through the misappropriation of trade secrets.[54] Under 19 U.S.C. § 1337, "[u]nfair methods of competition and unfair acts in the importation of articles ... into the United States ... the threat or effect of which is ... to destroy or substantially injure an industry in the United States" or "to restrain ... trade and commerce in the United States" are unlawful.[55] In *TianRui Group Co. Ltd. v. International Trade Commission*, the Federal Circuit interpreted this language to include imported products that were manufactured through the illegal use of trade secrets.[56]

In a sense, one might view this as a sort of extraterritorial application of United States law, since it encompasses trade secret misappropriation that occurs entirely outside of the country. However, as the *TianRui Group* court observed, "the foreign 'unfair' activity at issue in this case is relevant only to the extent that it results in the importation of goods into this country causing domestic injury."[57]

The ITC process begins when a trade secret owner files a complaint. If a preliminary investigation supports the complaint, a formal evidentiary hearing is held before an administrative law judge. The owner and the accused misappropriator are both entitled to participate in the hearing. The judge will issue an "initial determination" on the merits of the complaint, which is forwarded to the Commission for review. If the Commission finds for the owner, it can issue an order that bars importation of infringing articles.

The main advantage of the ITC approach is speed. The complaint process can usually be completed in about 15 months, which is usually faster than DTSA litigation in federal courts. However, the only available remedy is an exclusion order. The Commission is not authorized to award damages or injunctive relief.

---

54. 19 U.S.C. § 1337(d).

55. *Id.* § 1337(a)(1)(A).

56. 661 F.3d 1322 (Fed. Cir. 2011).

57. *Id.* at 1329.

Chapter 11

The Future of Trade Secret Law

§ 11.01 Introduction

Trade secret statutes are short and often vague, providing core concepts but little detail. In one standard compendium, for example, the Uniform Trade Secrets Act occupies 3 pages, while the Defend Trade Secrets Act spans 11 pages.[1] By contrast, the statutes that govern other forms of intellectual property are extensive and complex. The Patent Act is 146 pages long; the Copyright Act is even longer, at 351 pages; and the Lanham Act (the federal trademark statute) occupies 56 pages.[2]

The relative underdevelopment of trade secret statues is problematic. This law will be more important in the future, as the information age unfolds. Technological, commercial, and social changes will inevitably result in the creation of new types of trade secrets that we cannot imagine. At the same time, new technologies may make it easier to steal trade secrets, to protect them, or both. Trade secret law will inevitably evolve in response to these developments.

No field of law remains static, but trade secret law in particular seems to be moving into an era of transition. In order to understand the existing doctrine, it is important to have a sense for the direction that the field is heading. Over time, it seems likely that the trade secret statutes will be refined and expanded to provide greater guidance

1. Peter S. Menell et al., Intellectual Property Statutes (2019).
2. *Id.*

for judges, attorneys, and owners. This will allow businesses, entrepreneurs, and inventors to better protect their secrets and produce more predictable outcomes when disputes arise. Yet the road to doctrinal stability will not be a straightforward one. This chapter provides an overview of issues that may arise.

§ 11.02 Constitutionality of the DTSA

[A] Overview

Is the DTSA constitutional? A threshold question for any new federal statute is whether it comports with the Constitution. In particular, given the amount of money at stake in intellectual property cases, defendants have a strong incentive to challenge the constitutionality of any new statute that creates or modifies intellectual property rights.

For example, the Supreme Court recently considered a challenge to the constitutionality of the 2011 America Invents Act—the most significant revision to the Patent Act in over half a century.[3] The Court rejected the argument that a provision which allowed the Patent and Trademark Office to reconsider the validity of an already-issued patent claim was unconstitutional under Article III and the Seventh Amendment. Similarly, various appellate courts rejected early challenges to portions of the Digital Millennium Copyright Act and the Copyright Act of 1976 under the Constitution's Intellectual Property Clause.[4]

To date, there are no published decisions assessing the constitutionality of the DTSA. But a number of potential challenges might be raised. For example, a litigant could argue that the act's definition of a "trade secret" is unconstitutionally vague. Or, more broadly, a litigant might assert that the act violates the "limited Times" provision of the Intellectual Property Clause because it creates rights with a potentially infinite duration.

[B] Unconstitutionally Vague?

A defendant might claim that the DTSA definition of a trade secret—which provides that information must not be "generally known" and must be subject to "reasonable measures to keep such information secret"—is unconstitutionally vague.[5] Several criminal defendants have made such a challenge to the EEA's terms, albeit without much success, on the theory that they could not have reasonably known

3. *See* Oil States Energy Serv., LLC v. Greene's Energy Group, LLC, 138 S. Ct. 1365 (2018).

4. *See, e.g.*, Universal City Studios, Inc. v. Corley, 273 F.3d 429 (2d Cir. 2001); Nat'l Conference of Bar Examiners v. Multistate Legal Studios, Inc., 692 F.2d 478 (7th Cir. 1982).

5. 18 U.S.C. § 1839(3).

that any of the information they disseminated satisfied the statutory definition of a trade secret.[6]

This argument would also be available to civil litigants, although they would have to satisfy a higher hurdle to prevail. As the Supreme Court explained in *Village of Hoffman Estates v. Flipside, Hoffman Estates, Inc.*, "[t]he degree of vagueness that the Constitution tolerates—as well as the importance of fair notice and fair enforcement—depends in part on the nature of the enactment," with "greater tolerance" given to "enactments with civil rather than criminal penalties because the consequences of imprecision are qualitatively less severe."[7]

[C] Unlimited "Times"?

Another potential issue is whether the DTSA—which does not restrict how long a trade secret can exist—conflicts with the Intellectual Property Clause. The Clause empowers Congress to grant "Inventors the exclusive Right to their respective ... Discoveries" only for "limited Times."[8] In *Eldred v. Ashcroft*, the Supreme Court recognized that Congress does not have the authority to create "a regime of perpetual copyrights."[9] Because the DTSA sets no time limit on how long a trade secret lasts, it may be vulnerable to a similar "limited Times" argument.

In *Kewanee Oil Co. v. Bicron Corp.*, the Court held that state trade secret law was not void under the Supremacy Clause, because it did not clash with the objectives of federal patent law.[10] In the process, it recognized that patent law and trade secret law share the common goal of "encouraging invention."[11] But it found little overlap between the two systems because there was only a "remote" possibility that an inventor with a patentable invention would choose to rely on trade secret law rather than patent law.[12] Of course, its ruling focused solely on the limits of *state* authority—i.e., whether state trade secret law "conflict[ed] with the operation of the laws in th[e] area [of patents and copyrights] passed by Congress."[13] Accordingly, the Court had no occasion to consider the limits of *congressional* authority.

Today some inventors with patentable inventions choose to rely on trade secret law rather than patent law, both to avoid public disclosure and to receive potentially infinite

---

6. *See, e.g.*, United States v. Genovese, 409 F. Supp. 2d 253, 256–58 (S.D.N.Y. 2005); United States v. Krumrei, 258 F.3d 535, 539 (6th Cir. 2001); *see generally* Robert Damion Jurrens, *Fool Me Once:* U.S. v. Aleynikov *and the Theft of Trade Secrets Clarification Act of 2012*, 28 Berkeley Tech. L.J. 833 (2013).

7. 455 U.S. 489, 498–99 (1982).

8. U.S. Const. art. I, §8, cl. 8.

9. 537 U.S. 186, 209 (2003).

10. 416 U.S. 470 (1974).

11. *Id.* at 484.

12. *Id.* at 490.

13. *Id.* at 479.

protection. In this sense, trade secret law may be used as a substitute for patent law, contrary to the *Kewanee Oil* Court's assumption. In this light, the DTSA effectively creates a form of patent-like protection that is not restricted to "limited Times."

Defenders of the DTSA would point to the fact that it was enacted under the Commerce Clause rather than the Intellectual Property Clause, and thus is not subject to the "limited Times" constraint.[14] Arguably, however, it would be a strange result if Congress could use the *general* Commerce Clause power to enact legislation that it could not adopt under the more *specific* Intellectual Property Clause.[15] Had the Framers intended for some types of intellectual property to receive protection for an unlimited term, presumably they would have said so.[16]

On the other hand, the Second Circuit rejected an analogous argument in *United States v. Martignon*.[17] The court upheld an anti-bootlegging statute that created copyright-like protection for live musical performances under the Commerce Clause, even though the performances were not "fixed" and, accordingly, could not be protected by copyright law as "Writings" under the Intellectual Property Clause. It reasoned that "in order to demonstrate unconstitutionality, [the plaintiff] must demonstrate that [the statute] is a copyright law and not just that it is copyright-like."[18] *Martignon* thus suggests that even if the DTSA creates patent-like protection for trade secrets, it is not a patent law and, accordingly, that it was properly enacted under the Commerce Clause.[19]

§ 11.03 Interface between State and Federal Law

One important provision of the DTSA—arguably, the *most* important section—is a limitation on the statute's scope. To avoid any implication that the DTSA preempts

---

14. *See* 18 U.S.C. § 1836(b)(1) (authorizing civil action for misappropriation "if the trade secret is related to a product or service used in, or intended for use in, interstate or foreign commerce"); *see also* Conor Tucker, *The DTSA's Federalism Problem: Federal Jurisdiction over Trade Secrets*, 28 Fordham Intell. Prop. Media & Ent. L.J. 1, 23 n.134 (2017) (noting that the DTSA was enacted under the Commerce Clause).

15. *Cf.* Kevin J. Hickey, *The Copyright/Commerce Clause Collision: A Subject Matter Approach*, 82 U. Cin. L. Rev. 1, 56 (2013) (concluding that "[a]cts of Congress that are so similar to traditional forms of intellectual property protection so as to be 'copyright laws' must comport with the requirements of the Copyright Clause—notwithstanding the availability of an alternative enumerated power").

16. *Cf.* State Farm Fire & Casualty Co. v. United States ex rel. Rigsby, 137 S. Ct. 436, 443 (2016) ("It is proper to infer that, had Congress intended to require dismissal for a violation of the seal requirement, it would have said so.").

17. 492 F.3d 140 (2d Cir. 2007). *See also* In re Trade-Mark Cases, 100 U.S. 82 (1879).

18. *Martignon*, 492 F.3d at 150.

19. However, the *Martignon* court relied in part on the rationale that the statute only imposed criminal penalties and did "not create and bestow property rights upon authors or inventors...." *Id.* at 151. This rationale does not apply to the DTSA, which protects trade secrets as intellectual property. *See* § 1:05[C].

the UTSA or other state law protections, Congress included an express statement that the act should "not be construed to preempt or displace any other remedies, whether civil or criminal, provided by United States Federal, State, commonwealth, possession, or territory law for the misappropriation of a trade secret...."[20]

Since the DTSA's enactment in 2016, most trade secret cases brought in federal court have alleged claims under both this act and the particular state's version of the UTSA.[21] This anti-preemption provision creates dilemmas that courts will have to grapple with in the coming years.

First, as noted in prior chapters, the DTSA and UTSA share many identical or near-identical provisions. Because a version of the UTSA was adopted decades ago in most states, the case law interpreting the UTSA is far better developed than that interpreting the DTSA. Should judges rely on existing UTSA doctrine when interpreting overlapping DTSA provisions?

This approach has the benefit of making DTSA rulings more predictable for litigants, who can rely on existing law to determine their likelihood of success. On the other hand, it threatens to fracture the federal DTSA into fifty-plus bodies of state-dependent case law, which eliminates one of the major promised benefits of the DTSA—uniformity. It also requires glossing over the textual differences between the two statutes, such as the definition of a trade secret[22] and the DTSA's suggestion that any "lawful" method of acquiring a trade secret does not constitute improper means.[23]

Second, despite their similarities, differences exist between these two statutory schemes on the scope of remedies. In particular, state law may be more beneficial to plaintiffs in some respects. For example, the DTSA appears to bar use of the inevitable disclosure doctrine, while the UTSA does not;[24] and federal law may require proof of irreparable injury in order to obtain an injunction, which the UTSA does not.[25] These differences logically raise the question: can the plaintiff who sues in federal court obtain the benefit of these state law rules?

Third, state courts traditionally give deference to federal court interpretations of federal law, while federal courts must do their utmost to interpret state law as a state court would. How does this form of mutual respect work when a suit invokes both a UTSA claim and a DTSA claim, premised on the same basic conduct? For example, should a federal court defer to state doctrine on the UTSA claim but chart its own course on the DTSA claim, even if it means that a plaintiff might prevail on the one claim but not the other? While this course might sound appealing in the abstract, it

20. 18 U.S.C. § 1838.

21. One early study found that misappropriation claims based on state law were asserted in 84% of DTSA cases. David S. Levine & Christopher B. Seaman, *The DTSA at One: An Empirical Study of the First Year of Litigation Under the Defend Trade Secrets Act*, 53 Wake Forest L. Rev. 105, 143 (2018).

22. *See* § 2.01[B].

23. *See* § 4.02[D][4][b].

24. See § 7.02[C][2].

25. See § 7.02[C][1].

could mean that *precisely the same statutory language* would be construed two different ways in the same opinion.

§ 11.04 Interface between Civil and Criminal Law

Because the DTSA was appended onto the existing EEA, the two acts share statutory definitions for a number of key terms, including "trade secret," "misappropriation," and "improper means."[26] The federal government has brought very few prosecutions under the EEA—less than ten per year. Yet these cases may have an outsized impact on DTSA case law in the future due to a doctrine that has special force in the criminal context: the rule of lenity.

Under the rule of lenity, any lingering ambiguity in a criminal statute—after all other available methods of statutory interpretation are applied—is construed in favor of the defendant. As former Justice Antonin Scalia and Bryan Garner explained, this rule reflects the basic notion that if a law's commands are "not clear, the consequences should be visited on the party more able to avoid and correct the effects of shoddy legislative drafting—namely, the federal Department of Justice or its state equivalent."[27]

Notably, the rule of lenity applies even in the civil law context when the underlying statute "has both criminal and noncriminal applications," on the theory that a court must "interpret the statute consistently" regardless of the identities of the litigants.[28] Due to the overlap between the EEA and DTSA, even civil defendants sued for misappropriation under the DTSA have a slightly stronger argument that anything unclear in the key definitional terms of the DTSA should be interpreted in their favor.

§ 11.05 Impact of Patent Law

Trade secret law is gradually evolving from a tort-based doctrine dedicated to preserving commercial morality into an intellectual property law doctrine focused on promoting innovation—much like patent law. Because this transition is not complete, the current law may be viewed as a work in progress. How will this continuing transition affect trade secret law in the future? In particular, will we see the partial "patentization" of trade secret law?

Patent law and trade secret law are already close cousins. As the *Kewanee Oil* Court recognized, both doctrines serve the policy of incentivizing innovation.[29] Further, in

26. *See generally* 18 U.S.C. § 1839.
27. Antonin Scalia & Bryan A. Garner, Reading Law: The Interpretation of Legal Texts 299 (2012).
28. Leocal v. Ashcroft, 543 U.S. 1, 11 n. 8 (2004).
29. Kewanee Oil Co. v. Bicron Corp., 416 U.S. 470, 484 (1974).

some situations the inventor of a new product or process could choose to rely on either form of protection—but not both. Within this area of overlap, a trade secret can substitute for a patent. Accordingly, the evolution of trade secret law may be affected by patent law concepts.

For example, should the owner of a trade secret be required to make "reasonable efforts" to maintain secrecy? Obviously, a patentee is not subject to this requirement; public disclosure is a key theme in patent law. The rationale for the reasonable efforts standard is not entirely clear because other elements—such as the prohibition on protection for information that is generally known or readily ascertainable—already ensure that an individual cannot claim a trade secret on public information.

One might argue that the reasonable efforts requirement rebuts any argument that the owner acquiesced in the use of the secret by others: "If the owner fails to attempt to safeguard his or her proprietary information, no one can be rightfully accused of misappropriating it."[30] Alternatively, it might reflect the traditional maxim that "the laws aid the vigilant, not those who sleep."[31] Under this second approach, the owner who fails to reasonably protect his secret is not entitled to invoke the court's aid. Or perhaps the requirement stems from the equitable doctrine of unclean hands: "[T]he employer must come into court with clean hands; the employer cannot complain of the employee's use of information if the employer has never treated the information as secret."[32] Ultimately, one scholar concludes that the requirement serves no real purpose, and is probably a holdover from "traditional tort notions of contributory negligence...."[33]

Second, should there be some sort of "fair use" defense (akin to the copyright doctrine) to trade secret misappropriation—i.e., a defense to liability when the trade secret is used for a limited and transformative purpose?[34] The scope of patent infringement is narrow. A patent is infringed only when the defendant's product or process incorporates all elements of a particular claim. For example, broadly speaking, if the patent claim has ten elements and the defendant's product copies nine of those elements, but adds a new tenth element, the defendant is not liable.[35] The policy rationale for this standard is that it encourages other inventors to use the patent as raw material to create new and improved products. In contrast, the scope of trade secret misappropriation is broad, reflecting its tort-based origin. A defendant is liable for

30. H.R. Rep. No. 104-788, at 7 (1996).

31. The Latin phrase is *vigilantibus et non dormientibus jura subveniunt*, translated as "[t]he laws aid the vigilant, not those who sleep." Black's Law Dictionary 2023 (Bryan A. Garner ed., 11th ed. 2019). As one court summarized, "[t]he law helps those who help themselves, generally aids the vigilant, but rarely the sleeping, and never the acquiescent." Hannan v. Dusch, 153 S.E. 824, 831 (Va. 1930).

32. Electro-Craft Corp. v. Controlled Motion, Inc., 332 N.W.2d 890, 901 (Minn. 1983).

33. Mark A. Lemley, *The Surprising Virtues of Treating Trade Secrets as IP Rights*, 61 Stan. L. Rev. 311, 348 (2008).

34. *See generally* Deepa Varadarajan, *Trade Secret Fair Use*, 83 Fordham L. Rev. 1401 (2014).

35. This assumes that the doctrine of infringement by equivalents does not apply. This doctrine is used only in "exceptional cases." Amgen Inc. v. Sandoz Inc., 923 F.3d 1023, 1029 (Fed. Cir. 2019).

using the secret even with "independently created improvements or modifications if the result is substantially derived from the trade secret."[36] A fair use defense to misappropriation would better align trade secret law with patent law. For instance, such a defense could protect journalists who describe a trade secret in order to critique it (such as a computer algorithm that discriminates against certain classes of people) or competitors who use a fraction of a trade secret as part of a broader innovation.

Finally, should there be a term limit on trade secret protection?[37] The twenty-year patent term reflects a compromise between two competing goals: encouraging innovation and promoting free competition. In contrast, the duration of a trade secret is uncertain. The secret might be destroyed within weeks or months, for example, by public disclosure after reverse engineering; on the other hand, in theory it might endure in perpetuity. Allowing trade secret protection to exist for a lengthy period may impair competition, since it precludes others from using the information. Moreover, as noted above, the lack of a fixed time limit might be unconstitutional in the context of the DTSA.

§ 11.06 Trade Secrets and Contracts

To what extent can non-secret information be protected by contract? Put another way, should the law impose more stringent limits on the ability of parties to contract out of "official" trade secret law?[38]

In practice, disclosure restrictions imposed by contract significantly expand the scope of legally protectable information. One scholar observes that "[t]here is no other area of intellectual property law where the main body of law is supplemented by such a confusing, inconsistent host of alternative possibilities."[39] Nondisclosure and noncompetition agreements, in particular, may be viewed as separate regimes akin to trade secret law in that they both protect information secrecy.

The problem is that these agreements typically seek to protect not only legally defined trade secrets, but also a wide range of *non-trade secret* information.[40] Nondisclosure agreements do this expressly, often by describing the protected information in vague terms that employees and other signatories may not understand. Noncompetition agreements do this implicitly, by preventing the signatories from working for other employers.

Only certain information qualifies for protection as trade secrets. As discussed in Chapter 1, the scope of protectable trade secrets reflects a compromise between com-

---

36. Restatement (Third) of Unfair Competition § 40 cmt. c.

37. *See* Lemley, *supra* note 33, at 352–53.

38. *Id.* at 350–51.

39. Charles Tait Graves, *Trade Secrecy and Common Law Confidentiality: The Problem of Multiple Regimes*, *in* The Law and Theory of Trade Secrecy: A Handbook of Contemporary Research 77 (Rochelle C. Dreyfuss & Katherine J. Strandburg eds., 2011).

40. *See* § 8.03[C][2], [D][1].

peting goals.[41] On the one hand, the law safeguards trade secrets in order to encourage innovation and protect commercial morality. On the other hand, it restricts the strength and scope of this protection in order to promote free competition and ensure employee mobility.

Nondisclosure and noncompetition agreements threaten this policy balance. By insulating non-trade secrets from disclosure, they both restrict competition and impair employee mobility. Consider employee A, who works for company B. A has signed a nondisclosure agreement that bars her from disclosing B's trade secrets and "any other information relating to B's business." A may well be reluctant to take a new job, given the risk that she might inadvertently mention non-trade secret information to her new employer and be sued by B. Further, the prospective new employer will be less able to compete effectively with B, because it does not have access to such non-trade secret information. That said, freedom of contract is a fundamental principle in the U.S. legal system, and courts are hesitant to place substantive limits on the ability of consenting adults to enter into legally binding agreements.[42]

In the future, legislatures and courts will probably revisit the permissible scope of contract protection. In the process, they will confront a variety of questions, such as these. Should there be any limit on the type of non-secret information that the contract may cover? How specifically must such information be defined in the contract? And how long may the contract remain in effect?

§ 11.07 International Trade Secret Law

Trade secret law is well established in the United States and a number of other countries. However, despite the TRIPS mandate that members adopt domestic legislation to protect "undisclosed information," in most nations the legal framework for safeguarding trade secrets is still incomplete.[43] Many developing countries, in particular, appear to have little interest in trade secret protection, which in their eyes predominantly benefits developed countries. As a result, a U.S. entity may not be able to effectively protect its secrets by suing for misappropriation in a foreign country. It remains to be seen whether other countries will adopt adequate domestic laws that foreign parties can use to protect trade secrets. History teaches that the key is reciprocity. A nation is more likely to respect foreign-owned intellectual property when its citizens have created a substantial body of domestic intellectual property and want to ensure that their own rights are protected abroad.

41. *See* § 1.03.

42. *See, e.g.*, David P. Weber, *Restricting the Freedom of Contract: A Fundamental Prohibition*, 16 Yale Hum. Rts. & Dev. L.J. 51, 53 (2013) ("While in some contexts states have successfully limited the right to contract based on status, or capacity, those limitations are an exception to the general rule of the freedom of contract.").

43. *See* § 10.02.

Successful implementation of the TRIPS mandate might reshape U.S. trade secret law. The TRIPS approach is founded on unfair competition law as embodied in the Paris Convention for the Protection of Industrial Property.[44] Modern U.S. law, in contrast, has shifted from the tort approach (which included unfair competition) to the property approach. Certainly, the text of TRIPS article 39 gives each nation substantial flexibility on how to protect undisclosed information. But—in the long run—a body of well-developed international trade secret law oriented toward preventing unfair competition might undercut the U.S. focus on recognizing trade secrets as property in order to promote innovation.[45]

---

44. *Id.*

45. On the other hand, the liability provisions of both NAFTA and the USMCA already reflect the unfair competition approach. *See* § 10.04[C]. To date, this has had no discernable impact on U.S. trade secret law.

Appendix A

Uniform Trade Secrets Act, with 1985 Amendments

PREFATORY NOTE

A valid patent provides a legal monopoly for seventeen years in exchange for public disclosure of an invention. If, however, the courts ultimately decide that the Patent Office improperly issued a patent, an invention will have been disclosed to competitors with no corresponding benefit. In view of the substantial number of patents that are invalidated by the courts, many businesses now elect to protect commercially valuable information through reliance upon the state law of trade secret protection. *Kewanee Oil Co. v. Bicron Corp.*, 416 U.S. 470 (1974), which establishes that neither the Patent Clause of the United States Constitution nor the federal patent laws pre-empt state trade secret protection for patentable or unpatentable information, may well have increased the extent of this reliance.

The recent decision in *Aronson v. Quick Point Pencil Co.*, 99 S.Ct. 1096, 201 USPQ 1 (1979) reaffirmed *Kewanee* and held that federal patent law is not a barrier to a contract in which someone agrees to pay a continuing royalty in exchange for the disclosure of trade secrets concerning a product.

Notwithstanding the commercial importance of state trade secret law to interstate business, this law has not developed satisfactorily. In the first place, its development is uneven. Although there typically are a substantial number of reported decisions in states that are commercial centers, this is not the case in less populous and more agricultural jurisdictions. Secondly, even in states in which there has been significant litigation, there is undue uncertainty concerning the parameters of trade secret protection, and the appropriate remedies for misappropriation of a trade secret. One commentator observed:

> "Under technological and economic pressures, industry continues to rely on trade secret protection despite the doubtful and confused status of both common law and statutory remedies. Clear, uniform trade secret protection is urgently needed. . . ."

Comment, "Theft of Trade Secrets: The Need for a Statutory Solution", 120 U.Pa.L.Rev. 378, 380–81 (1971).

In spite of this need, the most widely accepted rules of trade secret law, § 757 of the Restatement of Torts, were among the sections omitted from the Restatement of Torts, 2d (1978).

The Uniform Act codifies the basic principles of common law trade secret protection, preserving its essential distinctions from patent law. Under both the Act and common law principles, for example, more than one person can be entitled to trade secret protection with respect to the same information, and analysis involving the "reverse engineering" of a lawfully obtained product in order to discover a trade secret is permissible. *Compare* Uniform Act, Section 1(2) (misappropriation means acquisition of a trade secret by means that should be known to be improper and unauthorized disclosure or use of information that one should know is the trade secret of another) *with Miller v. Owens-Illinois, Inc.*, 187 USPQ 47, 48 (D.Md.1975) (alternative holding) (prior, independent discovery a complete defense to liability for misappropriation) *and Wesley-Jessen, Inc., v. Reynolds*, 182 USPQ 135, 144–45, (N.D.Ill.1974) (alternative holding) (unrestricted sale and lease of camera that could be reversed engineered in several days to reveal alleged trade secrets preclude relief for misappropriation).

For liability to exist under this Act, a Section 1(4) trade secret must exist and either a person's acquisition of the trade secret, disclosure of the trade secret to others, or use of the trade secret must be improper under Section 1(2). The mere copying of an unpatented item is not actionable.

Like traditional trade secret law, the Uniform Act contains general concepts. The contribution of the Uniform Act is substitution of unitary definitions of trade secret and trade secret misappropriation, and a single statute of limitations for the various property, quasi-contractual, and violation of fiduciary relationship theories of noncontractual liability utilized at common law. The Uniform Act also codifies the results of the better reasoned cases concerning the remedies for trade secret misappropriation.

SECTION 1. DEFINITIONS. As used in this [Act], unless the context requires otherwise:

(1) "Improper means" includes theft, bribery, misrepresentation, breach or inducement of a breach of a duty to maintain secrecy, or espionage through electronic or other means;

(2) "Misappropriation" means:

(i) acquisition of a trade secret of another by a person who knows or has reason to know that the trade secret was acquired by improper means; or

(ii) disclosure or use of a trade secret of another without express or implied consent by a person who

(A) used improper means to acquire knowledge of the trade secret; or

(B) at the time of disclosure or use, knew or had reason to know that his knowledge of the trade secret was

(I) derived from or through a person who had utilized improper means to acquire it;

(II) acquired under circumstances giving rise to a duty to maintain its secrecy or limit its use; or

(III) derived from or through a person who owed a duty to the person seeking relief to maintain its secrecy or limit its use; or

(C) before a material change of his [or her] position, knew or had reason to know that it was a trade secret and that knowledge of it had been acquired by accident or mistake.

(3) "Person" means a natural person, corporation, business trust, estate, trust, partnership, association, joint venture, government, governmental subdivision or agency, or any other legal or commercial entity.

(4) "Trade secret" means information, including a formula, pattern, compilation, program, device, method, technique, or process, that:

(i) derives independent economic value, actual or potential, from not being generally known to, and not being readily ascertainable by proper means by, other persons who can obtain economic value from its disclosure or use, and

(ii) is the subject of efforts that are reasonable under the circumstances to maintain its secrecy.

COMMENT

One of the broadly stated policies behind trade secret law is "the maintenance of standards of commercial ethics." *Kewanee Oil Co. v. Bicron Corp.*, 416 U.S. 470 (1974). The Restatement of Torts, Section 757, Comment (f), notes: "A complete catalogue of improper means is not possible," but Section 1(1) includes a partial listing.

Proper means include:

1. Discovery by independent invention;

2. Discovery by "reverse engineering", that is, by starting with the known product and working backward to find the method by which it was developed. The acquisition of the known product must, of course, also be by a fair and honest means, such as purchase of the item on the open market for reverse engineering to be lawful;

3. Discovery under a license from the owner of the trade secret;

4. Observation of the item in public use or on public display;

5. Obtaining the trade secret from published literature.

Improper means could include otherwise lawful conduct which is improper under the circumstances; e.g., an airplane overflight used as aerial reconnaissance to determine the competitor's plant layout during construction of the plant. *E. I. du Pont de Nemours & Co., Inc. v. Christopher*, 431 F.2d 1012 (CA5, 1970), cert. den. 400 U.S. 1024 (1970). Because the trade secret can be destroyed through public knowledge, the unauthorized disclosure of a trade secret is also a misappropriation.

The type of accident or mistake that can result in a misappropriation under Section 1(2)(ii)(C) involves conduct by a person seeking relief that does not constitute a failure of efforts that are reasonable under the circumstances to maintain its secrecy under Section 1(4)(ii).

The definition of "trade secret" contains a reasonable departure from the Restatement of Torts (First) definition which required that a trade secret be "continuously used in one's business." The broader definition in the proposed Act extends protection to a plaintiff who has not yet had an opportunity or acquired the means to put a trade secret to use. The definition includes information that has commercial value from a negative viewpoint, for example the results of lengthy and expensive research which proves that a certain process will *not* work could be of great value to a competitor.

Cf. Telex Corp. v. IBM Corp., 510 F.2d 894 (CA10, 1975) per curiam, cert. dismissed 423 U.S. 802 (1975) (liability imposed for developmental cost savings with respect to product not marketed). Because a trade secret need not be exclusive to confer a competitive advantage, different independent developers can acquire rights in the same trade secret.

The words "method, technique" are intended to include the concept of "know-how."

The language "not being generally known to and not being readily ascertainable by proper means by other persons" does not require that information be generally known to the public for trade secret rights to be lost. If the principal persons who can obtain economic benefit from information are aware of it, there is no trade secret. A method of casting metal, for example, may be unknown to the general public but readily known within the foundry industry.

Information is readily ascertainable if it is available in trade journals, reference books, or published materials. Often, the nature of a product lends itself to being readily copied as soon as it is available on the market. On the other hand, if reverse engineering is lengthy and expensive, a person who discovers the trade secret through reverse engineering can have a trade secret in the information obtained from reverse engineering.

Finally, reasonable efforts to maintain secrecy have been held to include advising employees of the existence of a trade secret, limiting access to a trade secret on "need to know basis", and controlling plant access. On the other hand, public disclosure of information through display, trade journal publications, advertising, or other carelessness can preclude protection.

The efforts required to maintain secrecy are those "reasonable under the circumstances." The courts do not require that extreme and unduly expensive procedures be taken to protect trade secrets against flagrant industrial espionage. See *E. I. du Pont de Nemours & Co., Inc. v. Christopher, supra.* It follows that reasonable use of a trade secret including controlled disclosure to employees and licensees is consistent with the requirement of relative secrecy.

SECTION 2. INJUNCTIVE RELIEF.

(a) Actual or threatened misappropriation may be enjoined. Upon application to the court, an injunction shall be terminated when the trade secret has ceased to exist, but the injunction may be continued for an additional reasonable period of time in order to eliminate commercial advantage that otherwise would be derived from the misappropriation.

(b) In exceptional circumstances, an injunction may condition future use upon payment of a reasonable royalty for no longer than the period of time for which use could have been prohibited. Exceptional circumstances include, but are not limited to, a material and prejudicial change of position prior to acquiring knowledge or reason to know of misappropriation that renders a prohibitive injunction inequitable.

(c) In appropriate circumstances, affirmative acts to protect a trade secret may be compelled by court order.

COMMENT

Injunctions restraining future use and disclosure of misappropriated trade secrets frequently are sought. Although punitive perpetual injunctions have been granted, *e.g., Elcor Chemical Corp. v. Agri-Sul, Inc.*, 494 S.W.2d 204 (Tex.Civ.App.1973), Section 2(a) of this Act adopts the position of the trend of authority limiting the duration of injunctive relief to the extent of the temporal advantage over good faith competitors gained by a misappropriator. See, *e.g., K-2 Ski Co. v. Head Ski Co., Inc.*, 506 F.2d 471 (CA9, 1974) (maximum appropriate duration of both temporary and permanent injunctive relief is period of time it would have taken defendant to discover trade secrets lawfully through either independent development or reverse engineering of plaintiff's products).

The general principle of Section 2(a) and (b) is that an injunction should last for as long as is necessary, but no longer than is necessary, to eliminate the commercial advantage or "lead time" with respect to good faith competitors that a person has obtained through misappropriation. Subject to any additional period of restraint necessary to negate lead time, an injunction accordingly should terminate when a former trade secret becomes either generally known to good faith competitors or generally knowable to them because of the lawful availability of products that can be reverse engineered to reveal a trade secret.

For example, assume that A has a valuable trade secret of which B and C, the other industry members, are originally unaware. If B subsequently misappropriates the trade secret and is enjoined from use, but C later lawfully reverse engineers the trade secret, the injunction restraining B is subject to termination as soon as B's lead time has been dissipated. All of the persons who could derive economic value from use of the information are now aware of it, and there is no longer a trade secret under Section 1(4). It would be anti-competitive to continue to restrain B after any lead time that B had derived from misappropriation had been removed.

If a misappropriator either has not taken advantage of lead time or good faith competitors already have caught up with a misappropriator at the time that a case is decided, future disclosure and use of a former trade secret by a misappropriator will not damage a trade secret owner and no injunctive restraint of future disclosure and use is appropriate. See, *e.g., Northern Petrochemical Co. v. Tomlinson*, 484 F.2d 1057 (CA7, 1973) (affirming trial court's denial of preliminary injunction in part because an explosion at its plant prevented an alleged misappropriator from taking advantage of lead time); *Kubik, Inc. v. Hull*, 185 USPQ 391 (Mich.App.1974) (discoverability of trade secret by lawful reverse engineering made by injunctive relief punitive rather than compensatory).

Section 2(b) deals with the special situation in which future use by a misappropriator will damage a trade secret owner but an injunction against future use nevertheless is inappropriate due to exceptional circumstances. Exceptional circumstances include the existence of an overriding public interest which requires the denial of a prohibitory injunction against future damaging use and a person's reasonable reliance upon acquisition of a misappropriated trade secret in good faith and without reason to know of its prior misappropriation that would be prejudiced by a prohibitory injunction against future damaging use. *Republic Aviation Corp. v. Schenk*, 152 USPQ 830 (N.Y.Sup.Ct.1967) illustrates the public interest justification for withholding prohibitory injunctive relief. The court considered that enjoining a misappropriator from supplying the U.S. with an aircraft weapons control system would have endangered military personnel in Viet Nam. The prejudice to a good faith third party justification for withholding prohibitory injunctive relief can arise upon a trade secret owner's notification to a good faith third party that the third party has knowledge of a trade secret as a result of misappropriation by another. This notice suffices to make the third party a misappropriator thereafter under Section 1(2)(ii)(B)(I). In weighing an aggrieved person's interests and the interests of a third party who has relied in good faith upon his or her ability to utilize information, a court may conclude that restraining future use of the information by the third party is unwarranted. With respect to innocent acquirers of misappropriated trade secrets, Section 2(b) is consistent with the principle of 4 Restatement Torts (First) § 758(b) (1939), but rejects the Restatement's literal conferral of absolute immunity upon all third parties who have paid value in good faith for a trade secret misappropriated by another. The position taken by the Uniform Act is supported by *Forest Laboratories, Inc. v. Pillsbury Co.*, 452 F.2d 621 (CA7, 1971) in which a defendant's purchase of assets of a corporation to which a trade secret had been disclosed in confidence was not considered to confer immunity upon the defendant.

When Section 2(b) applies, a court has discretion to substitute an injunction conditioning future use upon payment of a reasonable royalty for an injunction prohibiting future use. Like all injunctive relief for misappropriation, a royalty order injunction is appropriate only if a misappropriator has obtained a competitive advantage through misappropriation and only for the duration of that competitive advantage. In some situations, typically those involving good faith acquirers of trade secrets misappropriated by others, a court may conclude that the same considerations that render a prohibitory injunction against future use inappropriate also render a royalty order injunction inappropriate. See, generally, *Prince Manufacturing, Inc. v. Automatic Partner, Inc.*, 198 USPQ 618 (N.J.Super.Ct.1976) (purchaser of misappropriator's assets from receiver after trade secret disclosed to public through sale of product not subject to liability for misappropriation).

A royalty order injunction under Section 2(b) should be distinguished from a reasonable royalty alternative measure of damages under Section 3(a). See the Comment to Section 3 for discussion of the differences in the remedies.

Section 2(c) authorizes mandatory injunctions requiring that a misappropriator return the fruits of misappropriation to an aggrieved person, *e.g.*, the return of stolen blueprints or the surrender of surreptitious photographs or recordings.

Where more than one person is entitled to trade secret protection with respect to the same information, only that one from whom misappropriation occurred is entitled to a remedy.

SECTION 3. DAMAGES.

(a) Except to the extent that a material and prejudicial change of position prior to acquiring knowledge or reason to know of misappropriation renders a monetary recovery inequitable, a complainant is entitled to recover damages for misappropriation. Damages can include both the actual loss caused by misappropriation and the unjust enrichment caused by misappropriation that is not taken into account in computing actual loss. In lieu of damages measured by any other methods, the damages caused by misappropriation may be measured by imposition of liability for a reasonable royalty for a misappropriator's unauthorized disclosure or use of a trade secret.

(b) If willful and malicious misappropriation exists, the court may award exemplary damages in an amount not exceeding twice any award made under subsection (a).

COMMENT

Like injunctive relief, a monetary recovery for trade secret misappropriation is appropriate only for the period in which information is entitled to protection as a trade secret, plus the additional period, if any, in which a misappropriator retains an advantage over good faith competitors because of misappropriation. Actual damage to a complainant and unjust benefit to a misappropriator are caused by misappropriation during this time alone. See *Conmar Products Corp. v. Universal Slide Fastener Co.*, 172 F.2d 150 (CA2, 1949) (no remedy for period subsequent to disclosure of trade secret by issued patent); *Carboline Co. v. Jarboe*, 454 S.W.2d 540 (Mo.1970) (recoverable monetary relief limited to period that it would have taken misappropriator to discover trade secret without misappropriation). A claim for actual damages and net profits can be combined with a claim for injunctive relief, but, if both claims are granted, the injunctive relief ordinarily will preclude a monetary award for a period in which the injunction is effective.

As long as there is no double counting, Section 3(a) adopts the principle of the recent cases allowing recovery of both a complainant's actual losses and a misappropriator's unjust benefit that are caused by misappropriation. *E.g., Tri-Tron International v. Velto*, 525 F.2d 432 (CA9, 1975) (complainant's loss and misappropriator's benefit can be combined). Because certain cases may have sanctioned double counting in a combined award of losses and unjust benefit, *e.g., Telex Corp. v. IBM Corp.*, 510 F.2d

894 (CA10, 1975) (per curiam), cert. dismissed, 423 U.S. 802 (1975) (IBM recovered rentals lost due to displacement by misappropriator's products without deduction for expenses saved by displacement; as a result of rough approximations adopted by the trial judge, IBM also may have recovered developmental costs saved by misappropriator through misappropriation with respect to the same customers), the Act adopts an express prohibition upon the counting of the same item as both a loss to a complainant and an unjust benefit to a misappropriator.

As an alternative to all other methods of measuring damages caused by a misappropriator's past conduct, a complainant can request that damages be based upon a demonstrably reasonable royalty for a misappropriator's unauthorized disclosure or use of a trade secret. In order to justify this alternative measure of damages, there must be competent evidence of the amount of a reasonable royalty.

The reasonable royalty alternative measure of damages for a misappropriator's past conduct under Section 3(a) is readily distinguishable from a Section 2(b) royalty order injunction, which conditions a misappropriator's future ability to use a trade secret upon payment of a reasonable royalty. A Section 2(b) royalty order injunction is appropriate only in exceptional circumstances; whereas a reasonable royalty measure of damages is a general option. Because Section 3(a) damages are awarded for a misappropriator's past conduct and a Section 2(b) royalty order injunction regulates a misappropriator's future conduct, both remedies cannot be awarded for the same conduct. If a royalty order injunction is appropriate because of a person's material and prejudicial change of position prior to having reason to know that a trade secret has been acquired from a misappropriator, damages, moreover, should not be awarded for past conduct that occurred prior to notice that a misappropriated trade secret has been acquired.

Monetary relief can be appropriate whether or not injunctive relief is granted under Section 2. If a person charged with misappropriation has materially and prejudicially changed position in reliance upon knowledge of a trade secret acquired in good faith and without reason to know of its misappropriation by another, however, the same considerations that can justify denial of all injunctive relief also can justify denial of all monetary relief. See *Conmar Products Corp. v. Universal Slide Fastener Co.*, 172 F.2d 1950 (CA2, 1949) (no relief against new employer of employee subject to contractual obligation not to disclose former employer's trade secrets where new employer innocently had committed $40,000 to develop the trade secrets prior to notice of misappropriation).

If willful and malicious misappropriation is found to exist, Section 3(b) authorizes the court to award a complainant exemplary damages in addition to the actual recovery under Section 3(a) an amount not exceeding twice that recovery. This provision follows federal patent law in leaving discretionary trebling to the judge even though there may be a jury, *compare* 35 U.S.C. Section 284 (1976).

Whenever more than one person is entitled to trade secret protection with respect to the same information, only that one from whom misappropriation occurred is entitled to a remedy.

SECTION 4. ATTORNEY'S FEES. If (i) a claim of misappropriation is made in bad faith, (ii) a motion to terminate an injunction is made or resisted in bad faith, or (iii) willful and malicious misappropriation exists, the court may award reasonable attorney's fees to the prevailing party.

COMMENT

Section 4 allows a court to award reasonable attorney fees to a prevailing party in specified circumstances as a deterrent to specious claims of misappropriation, to specious efforts by a misappropriator to terminate injunctive relief, and to willful and malicious misappropriation. In the latter situation, the court should take into consideration the extent to which a complainant will recover exemplary damages in determining whether additional attorney's fees should be awarded. Again, patent law is followed in allowing the judge to determine whether attorney's fees should be awarded even if there is a jury, *compare* 35 U.S.C. Section 285 (1976).

SECTION 5. PRESERVATION OF SECRECY. In an action under this [Act], a court shall preserve the secrecy of an alleged trade secret by reasonable means, which may include granting protective orders in connection with discovery proceedings, holding in-camera hearings, sealing the records of the action, and ordering any person involved in the litigation not to disclose an alleged trade secret without prior court approval.

COMMENT

If reasonable assurances of maintenance of secrecy could not be given, meritorious trade secret litigation would be chilled. In fashioning safeguards of confidentiality, a court must ensure that a respondent is provided sufficient information to present a defense and a trier of fact sufficient information to resolve the merits. In addition to the illustrative techniques specified in the statute, courts have protected secrecy in these cases by restricting disclosures to a party's counsel and his or her assistants and by appointing a disinterested expert as a special master to hear secret information and report conclusions to the court.

SECTION 6. STATUTE OF LIMITATIONS. An action for misappropriation must be brought within 3 years after the misappropriation is discovered or by the exercise of reasonable diligence should have been discovered. For the purposes of this section, a continuing misappropriation constitutes a single claim.

COMMENT

There presently is a conflict of authority as to whether trade secret misappropriation is a continuing wrong. *Compare Monolith Portland Midwest Co. v. Kaiser Aluminum & Chemical Corp.*, 407 F.2d 288 (CA9, 1969) (not a continuing wrong under California law—limitation period upon all recovery begins upon initial misappropriation) with *Underwater Storage, Inc. v. U. S. Rubber Co.*, 371 F.2d 950 (CADC, 1966), cert. den., 386 U.S. 911 (1967) (continuing wrong under general principles—limitation period with respect to a specific act of misappropriation begins at the time that the act of misappropriation occurs).

This Act rejects a continuing wrong approach to the statute of limitations but delays the commencement of the limitation period until an aggrieved person discovers or reasonably should have discovered the existence of misappropriation. If objectively reasonable notice of misappropriation exists, three years is sufficient time to vindicate one's legal rights.

SECTION 7. EFFECT ON OTHER LAW.

(a) Except as provided in subsection (b), this [Act] displaces conflicting tort, restitutionary, and other law of this State providing civil remedies for misappropriation of a trade secret.

(b) This [Act] does not affect:

(1) contractual remedies, whether or not based upon misappropriation of a trade secret;

(2) other civil remedies that are not based upon misappropriation of a trade secret; or

(3) criminal remedies, whether or not based upon misappropriation of a trade secret.

COMMENT

This Act does not deal with criminal remedies for trade secret misappropriation and is not a comprehensive statement of civil remedies. It applies to a duty to protect competitively significant secret information that is imposed by law. It does not apply to a duty voluntarily assumed through an express or an implied-in-fact contract. The enforceability of covenants not to disclose trade secrets and covenants not to compete that are intended to protect trade secrets, for example, is governed by other law. The Act also does not apply to a duty imposed by law that is not dependent upon the existence of competitively significant secret information, like an agent's duty of loyalty to his or her principal.

SECTION 8. UNIFORMITY OF APPLICATION AND CONSTRUCTION. This [Act] shall be applied and construed to effectuate its general purpose to make uniform the law with respect to the subject of this [Act] among states enacting it.

SECTION 9. SHORT TITLE. This [Act] may be cited as the Uniform Trade Secrets Act.

SECTION 10. SEVERABILITY. If any provision of this [Act] or its application to any person or circumstance is held invalid, the invalidity does not affect other provisions or applications of the [Act] which can be given effect without the invalid provision or application, and to this end the provisions of this [Act] are severable.

SECTION 11. TIME OF TAKING EFFECT. This [Act] takes effect on ______, and does not apply to misappropriation occurring prior to the effective date. With respect to a continuing misappropriation that began prior to the effective date, the [Act] also does not apply to the continuing misappropriation that occurs after the effective date.

COMMENT

The Act applies exclusively to misappropriation that begins after its effective date. Neither misappropriation that began and ended before the effective date nor misappropriation that began before the effective date and continued thereafter is subject to the Act.

SECTION 12. REPEAL. The following Acts and parts of Acts are repealed:

(1)

(2)

(3)

Appendix B

Economic Espionage Act, as Amended by the Defend Trade Secrets Act

18 U.S.C. § 1831: Economic espionage

(a) **In general.** Whoever, intending or knowing that the offense will benefit any foreign government, foreign instrumentality, or foreign agent, knowingly—

(1) steals, or without authorization appropriates, takes, carries away, or conceals, or by fraud, artifice, or deception obtains a trade secret;

(2) without authorization copies, duplicates, sketches, draws, photographs, downloads, uploads, alters, destroys, photocopies, replicates, transmits, delivers, sends, mails, communicates, or conveys a trade secret;

(3) receives, buys, or possesses a trade secret, knowing the same to have been stolen or appropriated, obtained, or converted without authorization;

(4) attempts to commit any offense described in any of paragraphs (1) through (3); or

(5) conspires with one or more other persons to commit any offense described in any of paragraphs (1) through (3), and one or more of such persons do any act to effect the object of the conspiracy,

shall, except as provided in subsection (b), be fined not more than $5,000,000 or imprisoned not more than 15 years, or both.

(b) **Organizations.** Any organization that commits any offense described in subsection (a) shall be fined not more than the greater of $10,000,000 or 3 times the value of the stolen trade secret to the organization, including expenses for research and design and other costs of reproducing the trade secret that the organization has thereby avoided.

18 U.S.C. § 1832: Theft of trade secrets

(a) Whoever, with intent to convert a trade secret, that is related to a product or service used in or intended for use in interstate or foreign commerce, to the economic benefit of anyone other than the owner thereof, and intending or knowing that the offense will, injure any owner of that trade secret, knowingly—

(1) steals, or without authorization appropriates, takes, carries away, or conceals, or by fraud, artifice, or deception obtains such information;

(2) without authorization copies, duplicates, sketches, draws, photographs, downloads, uploads, alters, destroys, photocopies, replicates, transmits, delivers, sends, mails, communicates, or conveys such information;

(3) receives, buys, or possesses such information, knowing the same to have been stolen or appropriated, obtained, or converted without authorization;

(4) attempts to commit any offense described in paragraphs (1) through (3); or

(5) conspires with one or more other persons to commit any offense described in paragraphs (1) through (3), and one or more of such persons do any act to effect the object of the conspiracy,

shall, except as provided in subsection (b), be fined under this title or imprisoned not more than 10 years, or both.

(b) Any organization that commits any offense described in subsection (a) shall be fined not more than the greater of $5,000,000 or 3 times the value of the stolen trade secret to the organization, including expenses for research and design and other costs of reproducing the trade secret that the organization has thereby avoided.

18 U.S.C. § 1833: Exceptions to prohibitions

(a) **In general.** This chapter does not prohibit or create a private right of action for—

(1) any otherwise lawful activity conducted by a governmental entity of the United States, a State, or a political subdivision of a State; or

(2) the disclosure of a trade secret in accordance with subsection (b).

(b) **Immunity from liability for confidential disclosure of a trade secret to the Government or in a court filing.**

(1) **Immunity.** An individual shall not be held criminally or civilly liable under any Federal or State trade secret law for the disclosure of a trade secret that—

(A) is made—

(i) in confidence to a Federal, State, or local government official, either directly or indirectly, or to an attorney; and

(ii) solely for the purpose of reporting or investigating a suspected violation of law; or

(B) is made in a complaint or other document filed in a lawsuit or other proceeding, if such filing is made under seal.

(2) **Use of trade secret information in anti-retaliation lawsuit.** An individual who files a lawsuit for retaliation by an employer for reporting a suspected violation of law may disclose the trade secret to the attorney of the individual and use the trade secret information in the court proceeding, if the individual—

(A) files any document containing the trade secret under seal; and

(B) does not disclose the trade secret, except pursuant to court order.

(3) **Notice.**

(A) **In general.** An employer shall provide notice of the immunity set forth in this subsection in any contract or agreement with an employee that governs the use of a trade secret or other confidential information.

(B) **Policy document.** An employer shall be considered to be in compliance with the notice requirement in subparagraph (A) if the employer provides a cross-reference to a policy document provided to the employee that sets forth the employer's reporting policy for a suspected violation of law.

(C) **Non-compliance.** If an employer does not comply with the notice requirement in subparagraph (A), the employer may not be awarded exemplary damages or attorney fees under subparagraph (C) or (D) of section 1836(b)(3) in an action against an employee to whom notice was not provided.

(D) **Applicability.** This paragraph shall apply to contracts and agreements that are entered into or updated after the date of enactment of this subsection.

(4) **Employee defined.** For purposes of this subsection, the term "employee" includes any individual performing work as a contractor or consultant for an employer.

(5) **Rule of construction.** Except as expressly provided for under this subsection, nothing in this subsection shall be construed to authorize, or limit liability for, an act that is otherwise prohibited by law, such as the unlawful access of material by unauthorized means.

18 U.S.C. § 1834: Criminal forfeiture

Forfeiture, destruction, and restitution relating to this chapter shall be subject to section 2323, to the extent provided in that section, in addition to any other similar remedies provided by law.

18 U.S.C. § 1835: Orders to preserve confidentiality

(a) **In general.** In any prosecution or other proceeding under this chapter, the court shall enter such orders and take such other action as may be necessary and appropriate to preserve the confidentiality of trade secrets, consistent with the requirements of the Federal Rules of Criminal and Civil Procedure, the Federal Rules of Evidence, and all other applicable laws. An interlocutory appeal by the United States shall lie from a decision or order of a district court authorizing or directing the disclosure of any trade secret.

(b) **Rights of trade secret owners.** The court may not authorize or direct the disclosure of any information the owner asserts to be a trade secret unless the court allows the owner the opportunity to file a submission under seal that describes the interest of the owner in keeping the information confidential. No submission under seal made under this subsection may be used in a prosecution under this chapter for any purpose other than those set forth in this section, or otherwise required by law. The provision of information relating to a trade secret to the United States or the court in connection with a prosecution under this chapter shall not constitute a waiver of trade secret protection, and the disclosure of information relating to a trade secret in connection with a prosecution under this chapter shall not constitute a waiver of trade secret protection unless the trade secret owner expressly consents to such waiver.

18 U.S.C. § 1836: Civil proceedings

(a) The Attorney General may, in a civil action, obtain appropriate injunctive relief against any violation of this chapter.

(b) **Private civil actions.**

(1) **In general.** An owner of a trade secret that is misappropriated may bring a civil action under this subsection if the trade secret is related to a product or service used in, or intended for use in, interstate or foreign commerce.

(2) **Civil seizure.**

(A) **In general.**

(i) **Application.** Based on an affidavit or verified complaint satisfying the requirements of this paragraph, the court may, upon ex parte application but only in extraordinary circumstances, issue an order providing for the seizure of property necessary to prevent the propagation or dissemination of the trade secret that is the subject of the action.

(ii) **Requirements for issuing order.** The court may not grant an application under clause (i) unless the court finds that it clearly appears from specific facts that—

(I) an order issued pursuant to Rule 65 of the Federal Rules of Civil Procedure or another form of equitable relief would be inadequate to achieve the purpose of this paragraph because the party to which the order would be issued would evade, avoid, or otherwise not comply with such an order;

(II) an immediate and irreparable injury will occur if such seizure is not ordered;

(III) the harm to the applicant of denying the application outweighs the harm to the legitimate interests of the person against whom seizure would be ordered of granting the application and substantially outweighs the harm to any third parties who may be harmed by such seizure;

(IV) the applicant is likely to succeed in showing that—

(aa) the information is a trade secret; and

(bb) the person against whom seizure would be ordered—

(AA) misappropriated the trade secret of the applicant by improper means; or

(BB) conspired to use improper means to misappropriate the trade secret of the applicant;

(V) the person against whom seizure would be ordered has actual possession of—

(aa) the trade secret; and

(**bb**) any property to be seized;

(**VI**) the application describes with reasonable particularity the matter to be seized and, to the extent reasonable under the circumstances, identifies the location where the matter is to be seized;

(**VII**) the person against whom seizure would be ordered, or persons acting in concert with such person, would destroy, move, hide, or otherwise make such matter inaccessible to the court, if the applicant were to proceed on notice to such person; and

(**VIII**) the applicant has not publicized the requested seizure.

(**B**) **Elements of order.** If an order is issued under subparagraph (A), it shall—

(**i**) set forth findings of fact and conclusions of law required for the order;

(**ii**) provide for the narrowest seizure of property necessary to achieve the purpose of this paragraph and direct that the seizure be conducted in a manner that minimizes any interruption of the business operations of third parties and, to the extent possible, does not interrupt the legitimate business operations of the person accused of misappropriating the trade secret;

(**iii**)

(**I**) be accompanied by an order protecting the seized property from disclosure by prohibiting access by the applicant or the person against whom the order is directed, and prohibiting any copies, in whole or in part, of the seized property, to prevent undue damage to the party against whom the order has issued or others, until such parties have an opportunity to be heard in court; and

(**II**) provide that if access is granted by the court to the applicant or the person against whom the order is directed, the access shall be consistent with subparagraph (D);

(**iv**) provide guidance to the law enforcement officials executing the seizure that clearly delineates the scope of the authority of the officials, including—

(**I**) the hours during which the seizure may be executed; and

(**II**) whether force may be used to access locked areas;

(**v**) set a date for a hearing described in subparagraph (F) at the earliest possible time, and not later than 7 days after the order has issued, unless the party against whom the order is directed and others harmed by the order consent to another date for the hearing, except that a party against whom the order has issued or any person harmed by the order may move the court at any time to dissolve or modify the order after giving notice to the applicant who obtained the order; and

(**vi**) require the person obtaining the order to provide the security determined adequate by the court for the payment of the damages that any person may be entitled to recover as a result of a wrongful or excessive seizure or wrongful or excessive attempted seizure under this paragraph.

(C) **Protection from publicity.** The court shall take appropriate action to protect the person against whom an order under this paragraph is directed from publicity, by or at the behest of the person obtaining the order, about such order and any seizure under such order.

(D) **Materials in custody of court.**

(i) **In general.** Any materials seized under this paragraph shall be taken into the custody of the court. The court shall secure the seized material from physical and electronic access during the seizure and while in the custody of the court.

(ii) **Storage medium.** If the seized material includes a storage medium, or if the seized material is stored on a storage medium, the court shall prohibit the medium from being connected to a network or the Internet without the consent of both parties, until the hearing required under subparagraph (B)(v) and described in subparagraph (F).

(iii) **Protection of confidentiality.** The court shall take appropriate measures to protect the confidentiality of seized materials that are unrelated to the trade secret information ordered seized pursuant to this paragraph unless the person against whom the order is entered consents to disclosure of the material.

(iv) **Appointment of special master.** The court may appoint a special master to locate and isolate all misappropriated trade secret information and to facilitate the return of unrelated property and data to the person from whom the property was seized. The special master appointed by the court shall agree to be bound by a non-disclosure agreement approved by the court.

(E) **Service of order.** The court shall order that service of a copy of the order under this paragraph, and the submissions of the applicant to obtain the order, shall be made by a Federal law enforcement officer who, upon making service, shall carry out the seizure under the order. The court may allow State or local law enforcement officials to participate, but may not permit the applicant or any agent of the applicant to participate in the seizure. At the request of law enforcement officials, the court may allow a technical expert who is unaffiliated with the applicant and who is bound by a court-approved non-disclosure agreement to participate in the seizure if the court determines that the participation of the expert will aid the efficient execution of and minimize the burden of the seizure.

(F) **Seizure hearing.**

(i) **Date.** A court that issues a seizure order shall hold a hearing on the date set by the court under subparagraph (B)(v).

(ii) **Burden of proof.** At a hearing held under this subparagraph, the party who obtained the order under subparagraph (A) shall have the burden to prove the facts supporting the findings of fact and conclusions of law necessary to support the order. If the party fails to meet that burden, the seizure order shall be dissolved or modified appropriately.

(iii) **Dissolution or modification of order.** A party against whom the order has been issued or any person harmed by the order may move the court at any time to dissolve or modify the order after giving notice to the party who obtained the order.

(iv) **Discovery time limits.** The court may make such orders modifying the time limits for discovery under the Federal Rules of Civil Procedure as may be necessary to prevent the frustration of the purposes of a hearing under this subparagraph.

(G) **Action for damage caused by wrongful seizure.** A person who suffers damage by reason of a wrongful or excessive seizure under this paragraph has a cause of action against the applicant for the order under which such seizure was made, and shall be entitled to the same relief as is provided under section 34(d)(11) of the Trademark Act of 1946 (15 U.S.C. 1116(d)(11)). The security posted with the court under subparagraph (B)(vi) shall not limit the recovery of third parties for damages.

(H) **Motion for encryption.** A party or a person who claims to have an interest in the subject matter seized may make a motion at any time, which may be heard ex parte, to encrypt any material seized or to be seized under this paragraph that is stored on a storage medium. The motion shall include, when possible, the desired encryption method.

(3) **Remedies.** In a civil action brought under this subsection with respect to the misappropriation of a trade secret, a court may—

(A) grant an injunction—

(i) to prevent any actual or threatened misappropriation described in paragraph (1) on such terms as the court deems reasonable, provided the order does not—

(I) prevent a person from entering into an employment relationship, and that conditions placed on such employment shall be based on evidence of threatened misappropriation and not merely on the information the person knows; or

(II) otherwise conflict with an applicable State law prohibiting restraints on the practice of a lawful profession, trade, or business;

(ii) if determined appropriate by the court, requiring affirmative actions to be taken to protect the trade secret; and

(iii) in exceptional circumstances that render an injunction inequitable, that conditions future use of the trade secret upon payment of a reasonable royalty for no longer than the period of time for which such use could have been prohibited;

(B) award—

(i)

(I) damages for actual loss caused by the misappropriation of the trade secret; and

(II) damages for any unjust enrichment caused by the misappropriation of the trade secret that is not addressed in computing damages for actual loss; or

(ii) in lieu of damages measured by any other methods, the damages caused by the misappropriation measured by imposition of liability for a reasonable royalty for the misappropriator's unauthorized disclosure or use of the trade secret;

(C) if the trade secret is willfully and maliciously misappropriated, award exemplary damages in an amount not more than 2 times the amount of the damages awarded under subparagraph (B); and

(D) if a claim of the misappropriation is made in bad faith, which may be established by circumstantial evidence, a motion to terminate an injunction is made or opposed in bad faith, or the trade secret was willfully and maliciously misappropriated, award reasonable attorney's fees to the prevailing party.

(c) **Jurisdiction.** The district courts of the United States shall have original jurisdiction of civil actions brought under this section.

(d) **Period of limitations.** A civil action under subsection (b) may not be commenced later than 3 years after the date on which the misappropriation with respect to which the action would relate is discovered or by the exercise of reasonable diligence should have been discovered. For purposes of this subsection, a continuing misappropriation constitutes a single claim of misappropriation.

18 U.S.C. § 1837: Applicability to conduct outside of the United States

This chapter also applies to conduct occurring outside the United States if—

(1) the offender is a natural person who is a citizen or permanent resident alien of the United States, or an organization organized under the laws of the United States or a State or political subdivision thereof; or

(2) an act in furtherance of the offense was committed in the United States.

18 U.S.C. § 1838: Construction with other laws

Except as provided in section 1833(b), this chapter shall not be construed to preempt or displace any other remedies, whether civil or criminal, provided by United States Federal, State, commonwealth, possession, or territory law for the misappropriation of a trade secret, or to affect the otherwise lawful disclosure of information by any Government employee under section 552 of title 5 (commonly known as the Freedom of Information Act).

18 U.S.C. § 1839: Definitions

As used in this chapter—

(1) the term "foreign instrumentality" means any agency, bureau, ministry, component, institution, association, or any legal, commercial, or business organization, corporation, firm, or entity that is substantially owned, controlled, sponsored, commanded, managed, or dominated by a foreign government;

(2) the term "foreign agent" means any officer, employee, proxy, servant, delegate, or representative of a foreign government;

(3) the term "trade secret" means all forms and types of financial, business, scientific, technical, economic, or engineering information, including patterns, plans, compilations, program devices, formulas, designs, prototypes, methods, techniques, processes, procedures, programs, or codes, whether tangible or intangible, and whether or how stored, compiled, or memorialized physically, electronically, graphically, photographically, or in writing if—

(A) the owner thereof has taken reasonable measures to keep such information secret; and

(B) the information derives independent economic value, actual or potential, from not being generally known to, and not being readily ascertainable through proper means by, another person who can obtain economic value from the disclosure or use of the information;

(4) the term "owner", with respect to a trade secret, means the person or entity in whom or in which rightful legal or equitable title to, or license in, the trade secret is reposed;

(5) the term "misappropriation" means—

(A) acquisition of a trade secret of another by a person who knows or has reason to know that the trade secret was acquired by improper means; or

(B) disclosure or use of a trade secret of another without express or implied consent by a person who—

(i) used improper means to acquire knowledge of the trade secret;

(ii) at the time of disclosure or use, knew or had reason to know that the knowledge of the trade secret was—

(I) derived from or through a person who had used improper means to acquire the trade secret;

(II) acquired under circumstances giving rise to a duty to maintain the secrecy of the trade secret or limit the use of the trade secret; or

(III) derived from or through a person who owed a duty to the person seeking relief to maintain the secrecy of the trade secret or limit the use of the trade secret; or

(iii) before a material change of the position of the person, knew or had reason to know that—

(I) the trade secret was a trade secret; and

(II) knowledge of the trade secret had been acquired by accident or mistake;

(6) the term "improper means"—

(A) includes theft, bribery, misrepresentation, breach or inducement of a breach of a duty to maintain secrecy, or espionage through electronic or other means; and

(B) does not include reverse engineering, independent derivation, or any other lawful means of acquisition; and

(7) the term "Trademark Act of 1946" means the Act entitled "An Act to provide for the registration and protection of trademarks used in commerce, to carry out the provisions of certain international conventions, and for other purposes, approved July 5, 1946 (15 U.S.C. 1051 et seq.) (commonly referred to as the 'Trademark Act of 1946' or the 'Lanham Act')".

Index